INTERPRETING THE SERMON ON THE MOUNT IN THE LIGHT OF JEWISH TRADITION AS EVIDENCED IN THE PALESTINIAN TARGUMS OF THE PENTATEUCH

Selected Themes

INTERPRETING THE SERMON ON THE MOUNT IN THE LIGHT OF JEWISH TRADITION AS EVIDENCED IN THE PALESTINIAN TARGUMS OF THE PENTATEUCH

Selected Themes

Isabel Ann Massey

Studies in the Bible and Early Christianity
Volume 25

The Edwin Mellen Press
Lewiston/Queenston/Lampeter

Library of Congress Cataloging-in-Publication Data

Massey, Isabel Ann.
  Interpreting the Sermon on the mount in the light of Jewish
tradition as evidenced in the Palestinian Targums of the Pentateuch
: selected themes / Isabel Ann Massey.
    p. cm. -- (Studies in the Bible and early Christianity ; v.
25)
    Includes bibliographical references and index.
    ISBN 0-88946-784-6
    1. Sermon on the mount. 2. Rabbinical literature--Relation to the
New Testament. I. Title. II. Series.
BT380.2.M348 1991
226.9'066--dc20   90-21427
                                                                       CIP

> This is volume 25 in the continuing series
> Studies in Bible and Early Christianity
> Volume 25 ISBN 0-88946-784-6
> SBEC Series ISBN 0-88946-913-X

A CIP catalog record for this book
is available from the British Library.

The Edwin Mellen Press   The Edwin Mellen Press
Box 450   Box 67
Lewiston, New York   Queenston, Ontario
USA 14092   CANADA L0S 1L0
                    The Edwin Mellen Press, Ltd.
                    Lampeter, Dyfed, Wales
                    UNITED KINGDOM SA48 7DY

Printed in the United States of America

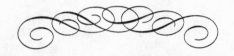

TABLE OF CONTENTS

INTRODUCTION
The Targums and New Testament Study Today

The question of the Semitic sub-stratum of the New Testament is quite complicated. During the past century there have been a variety of studies motivated by the question, "what language did Jesus speak?"[1] There have also been studies which tried to grapple with the relationship of the NT to the OT; and the difficulties involved have led to debates on theories about "testimonies," lost written collections of sayings and favorite passages.[2] However, neither of these lines of research began by utilizing the Palestinian targums of the Pentateuch;[3] the value of these targums had not been understood properly, to a great extent because of the influence of the opinion of Gustaf Dalman who deemed them "late."[4]

That the Palestinian targums were not given serious consideration is the fact underlying their neglect in the following:

Emil Schürer, Geschichte des jüdischen Volkes in Zeitalter Jesu Christi (Leipzig: Hinrich, 1898-1901) 3 vols.

J. Bonsirven, Le Judaïsme palestinien au temps de Jésus-Christ (Paris: Gabriel Beauchesne et ses fils, 1934) 2 vols.

George Foot Moore, Judaism in the First Centuries of the Christian Era: The Age of the Tannaim (Cambridge, Mass.: Harvard University Press, 1927-1930) 3 vols.

Hermann Lebrecht Strack und Paul Billerbeck, Kommentar zum Neuen Testament aus Talmud und Midrasch (München: O. Beck, 1922-1928).

Gerhard Kittel, Theologisches Wörterbuch zum Neuen Testament (Stuttgart: Verlag von W. Kohlmanner, 1933 and 1953).

Dalman himself felt he could find in the Palestinian targums "no sound proofs of great antiquity";[6] however he was aware that there were those who held that the "Jerusalem targums of the Pentateuch include(d) sections from a very ancient and possibly pre-Christian period. . . "[7]

Targum studies took a new turn in 1930 with the publication of a book which included a collection of texts from Palestinian targums from the Cairo Geniza: Paul Kahle, Masoreten des Westens II (Stuttgart, 1930; reprint: Hildesheim: Georg Olms, 1967). In one of the fragments which Kahle presented he noted that the halakah of Exod 22:4 was contrary to that in the Mishnah.[8] The deduced principle that what is contrary to the Mishnah is prior to the Mishnah has since been gaining favour among Kahle's widening circle of disciples, and the "old" ideas of Dalman with respect to the Palestinian targums have been gradually set aside. We have seen widening acceptance of Kahle's "new" ideas on the antiquity of these targums and the necessity of using them to understand ancient Jewish exegesis and the language of Palestine at the time of Christ; this acceptance was fostered by another publication: Paul Kahle, The Cairo Geniza (London: Oxford University Press, 1947).

Then in 1956, Ms. Neofiti I of the Vatican Library was brought to light by A. Díez Macho of Barcelona (who had been a student of Kahle). This manuscript bore a text of a complete targum to the Pentateuch rather closely allied to the known fragment targum texts.[9] The discovery was well received by the scholarly world, and enthusiastically by Kahle[10] and by Matthew Black[11] (who also had been a student of Kahle). Under the editorship of Díez Macho, the Consejo Superior de Investigaciones Científicas has published it in six volumes over a period of eleven years, 1968-1979.

Even though the convictions of Zunz,[12] Geiger,[13] Kahle, Black
and Díez Macho with respect to the dating of the traditions found
in the Palestinain targums is now finding wider and wider acceptance, this old nagging question of the dating still consumes
scholarly effort. In 1970, Joseph Fitzmyer, while acknowledging
that there were written targums in first century Palestine,[14] was
of the opinion that the extant Palestinian targums generally
should be dated after A.D. 200 - this on the basis of "orthographic, lexical, and grammatical considerations."[15] In 1972,
Díez Macho took up the question[16] and wrote: "The study of the
Aramaic of these targumim. . . is to be established on a broad
platform: on orthography, phonetics, morphology, syntax, and
semantics besides. Semantics. . . is of decisive importance."[17]
He then set forth sufficient examples of orthographic, phonetic,
morphological and syntactical inconsistencies in the extant material to illustrate the weaknesses of these criteria. And he concluded thus: ". . . the synchronic and diachronic comparison of
Aramaic texts runs risks, so that after exhausting all the possibilities of orthography, phonetics, morphology and syntax, and
those which paleography and lexicography offer, it is advisable
to lay under contribution the resources, still almost novel, of
semantics."[18] It is on the basis of semantics that Díez Macho
rests his argument for a pre-Tannaitic date of the origin of the
targum handed on to us in Ms. Neofiti I;[19] the situation of this
text is that it is of the rabbinic period but containing pre-
rabbinic materials (as semantic study shows).[20] This is not so
surprising for a targum; for it is the nature of a targum to
preserve tradition and present that tradition to audiences whose
language changes, evolves and is modernized in the course of
time.[21]

Presuppositions and Objectives of the Present Work

Leopold Zunz, who held the targumic material to be pre-
Christian, has been acknowledged as the "father of the modern
science of Judaism."[22] The opening sentence of his fifth chapter,
"Targumim," is this: "There certainly already were written Aramaic translations of most of the biblical books under the Hasmona-
eans."[23] For Renée Bloch (1924-55) the 1892 edition of Zunz' work
was an "ouvrage classique."[24] What was valuable here, and what
R. Bloch herself sought to elucidate, was the dynamic of the Jewish history of exegesis in the midrashic process that had been
born within Scripture itself and proceeded throughout the targums
and midrashim.[25] In the process, we see the actualization of the
ancient ideas, their accommodation in new settings. In the targums the theology of the translators is to be seen; they interpreted the text within the milieu of the oral tradition extant in
their day. The midrashic procedures current at the time are naturally to be found in the New Testament; however, R. Bloch could
write in her article "Midrash," which was published in 1957, that
this was a "domaine encore à peu près complètement inexploré."[26]
Renée Bloch made a proposal for a method of study, the full ramifications of which are still to be worked out. She suggested
that texts bearing on a tradition should be examined together, and
they would be elucidated by using both internal and external criteria in the process of comparison.[27] That is to say, comparisons
of the literary traditions in the targums with those in Philo,
Josephus, Pseudo-Philo, the Pseudepigrapha, the tannaitic midrashim, and the Qumran materials, as well as with the New Testament books and the writings of the Apostolic Fathers should aid
in discerning the development of those traditions.[28] By the use
of the general criteria on the development of literary traditions
together with our knowledge of the (approximate) dates of some of
these materials, the relative dating of the other materials is
facilitated. One of the results would be the progressively better
establishment of the antiquity of those targumic traditions which

are pre-Christian (Tg. Ps.-J., for example, carries some obviously
later insertions.); and thus the better establishment of the
usefulness of these texts for further study of New Testament
passages.

Geza Vermes drew his inspiration from Renée Bloch. Since, as
he says, "her tragic death in 1955 prevented her from doing much
more than grapple with the preliminaries" he goes on to "carry the
test a stage further" in his Scripture and Tradition in Judaism.
building upon her "preliminary synthesis. . . suggested method. . .
working hypothesis."[29]

The methodological work of R. Bloch was presupposed by
Bruce J. Malina in his dissertation, The Palestinian Manna
Tradition: the Manna Tradition in the Palestinian Targums and Its
Relationship to the New Testament Writings.[30] He also presupposed the orientation of G. Vermes, R. LeDéaut and A. Díez Macho.[31]
As a matter of fact, B. Malina's "methodological presuppositions"
listed in his preface[32] have points in common with the "several
laws of general importance concerning the development of traditions" which Vermes had formulated at the conclusion of his
study on the transmission-history of the story of Balaam."[33] We
may then accept that the basic methodological principles have been
established, but must be further refined with each new study.[34]

In the present work, we propose to use the methodology which
is now emerging for handling the development of traditions as
found in the Hebrew Bible, targums and New Testament. When using
early Jewish materials, it would have been impossible to be exhaustive in the confines of the present study. Therefore limit-
ations had to be established. Since the midrash-form was the
earliest halakic form,[35] we have accepted the earliest extant
full compilations in that form, Mekilta, Sipra and Sipre, and also
utilized a few other sources to varying degrees such as Philo and
Josephus, ᵓAbot and ᵓAbot de Rabbi Nathan, the Qumran literature,
the pseudepigrapha and other scattered pieces of Jewish tradition.[36] A sense of right orientation among the sources, rather

than random use, is absolutely necessary. Therefore the earliest
rabbinic materials are to be valued more than materials peripheral
to the general Jewish religion of the first century.[37] Jacob Z.
Lauterbach has reminded us that "the dicta of the Halakah had
their source in Midrash Torah, i.e. an inquiry into the full meaning of the written law from which alone the earliest Halakah derived its authority."[38] Lauterbach's thesis is that midrash-form
is earlier than Mishnah-form, one of the main criteria being its
degree of adherence to written Torah; with the same logic, pride
of place could be accorded the targums.

It is most unlikely that all the targumic traditions come
from one single locality; they show both divergence and similarity. Because of the complexity of the literary influence among
the extant targumic sources, one must proceed with caution. The
basic data on the targums with respect to their character have
been ably presented by Martin McNamara in the introductory part of
his dissertation, The New Testament and the Palestinian Targum to
the Pentateuch, 38-68.[39] Without repeating this, we shall make
only a few further comments. With respect to the fragment targum
tradition: MSS V and N (and L which lacks a great many verses)
are to be considered one source; ed. B, MSS M and S are derived
most probably from MS N.[40] MSS P and Br. each exhibit another
strand of the fragment targum tradition.[41] It is impossible to
say precisely when and how the fragment targum tradition was
formed. Tg. Ps.-J., a complete targum of the Pentateuch, is in
many ways unique; yet it presents many of the same traditions, in
its own words, as the fragment targum tradition - as well as showing some influence from Tg. Onq. Tg. Neof. has affinity to the
fragment targum tradition, yet shows some influences from Tg.
Ps.-J. and Tg. Onq. The Cairo Geniza sources show agreement with
various readings in the other targums, especially the fragment
targum tradition and Tg. Neof.; and there is observable variation
among the Geniza fragments themselves, for example, CTg E and CTg
D for Gen 38:25-26. There is special value in the few cases in

in which Tg. Onq. - usually so literal - shows some evidence of a
haggadic tradition to which other targums witness more fully. The
targums and the early midrashim have a character which shows that
they were formed in a milieu in which the Hebrew Bible - especially the Torah - was accepted as it stood, without any historical
and literary criticism such as that to which the modern scholar is
accustomed.

When a tradition is witnessed in the targumic source(s) as
well as in other sources it is valuable for our purposes; this is
especially so when it is evidenced in Philo or the Qumran literature for which we have accepted dates. Thus, when considering
multiple attestation (or cumulative witness) as an indication of
the antiquity of a tradition, each of our five chapters should be
viewed as a whole. With this in mind, we have presented the evidence from the sources, one after the other, and only drawn conclusions at the end of each chapter. Thus the evidence from the
various sources taken together contributes to our understanding of
the material under discussion in Matthew 5-7.

Our specific objective will be the elucidation of several key
concepts found in Matthew's Sermon on the Mount, "Father," "be ye
perfect," "measure for measure," "word(s)," "vacuous," and the
"fruit" metaphor. Thus our work shall have both the presuppositions and the modest objectives proper to a study in the area of
targum and New Testament at the present stage of scholarship in
that area. It is to be hoped that each study by each scholar
today, in adapting the method to the requirements of the particular theme(s) being discussed, will further refine the method.

Notes

[1]Gustaf Dalman is to be credited with having left no doubt
about the fact that the NT writings do have an Aramaic sub-stratum;
many were convinced by his book:
Die Worte Jesu (Leipzig, 1898; 2nd edn. 1930); trans.:
The Words of Jesus (Edinburgh: T. & T. Clark, 1902).
Then a small article appeared:
C. J. Ball, "Had the Fourth Gospel an Aramaic Archetype?"
Expository Times 21, 1910, 91-93.
This sparked the interest of C. F. Burney, thence his:
The Aramaic Origin of the Fourth Gospel (Oxford:
Clarendon, 1922).
The idea that the Gospels might be outright translations from
Aramaic prototypes was launched. Then there appeared:
C. Ch. Torrey, Our Translated Gospels (N.Y.-London: Harper
& Brothers, 1936).
This was Torrey's presentation of his conjectural translation of
them "back" into Aramaic. The book was actually praised by one
review article:
J. de Zwaan, "John Wrote in Aramaic," JBL 57, 1938, 155-171.
However it was easy to see that Torrey's position was extreme,
and "respectful disagreement" was presented:
David Daube, "Concerning the Reconstruction of 'The
Aramaic Gospels'," BJRL 29, 1945, 69-105.
In 1942-43, a debate took place. It was opened by:
Albert T. Olmstead, "Could an Aramaic Gospel Be Written?"
JNES 1, 1942, 41-75.
Olmstead noted that Leopold Zunz (Die gottesdienstlichen
Vorträge der Juden historisch entwickelt, Frankfurt a. Main,
1892) held that the fragment targum had originated before 70 A.D.;
therefore he said that there was Aramaic literature at that time;
therefore an Aramaic Gospel was conceivable. A reply was im-
mediate:
Edgar J. Goodspeed, "The Possible Aramaic Gospel,"
JNES 1, 1942, 315-340.
Goodspeed thought he had the ascendance over Olmstead whom he
felt had presented "the reverse of the established opinion"
(p. 344). For this "established opinion," Goodspeed referred to
Emil Schürer, History of the Jewish People in the Time of Jesus
Christ, vol. 1, 156 ff. (translation of the work we cite on p. v);
and also Robert Pfeiffer, Introduction to the Old Testament (N.Y.:
Harper, 1941) 77. Goodspeed was countered by:
S. E. Feigin, "The Original Language of the Gospels,"
JNES 2, 1943, 187-197.
Then the whole debate was reviewed by:
C. C. McCown, "Aramaic and Greek Gospels," Anglican
Theological Review 25, 1943, 281-294.
In the course of the debate, reference to actual material in the
Palestinian targums was sparse indeed. Olmstead (p. 60) and
Feigin (p. 196) had cited the text from Tg. Ps.-J. Lev 22:28 as

the obvious parallel to Luke 6:36. The debate seemed to die in 1943.

A wider view than that focusing on the NT texts, that is, the question of the language(s) of first century Palestine, was the basis of related works. There have been the advocates of a form of Hebrew as a predominant language of the time:

Birkeland Harris, The Language of Jesus (Oslo: Avhandlinger utgitt av det Norske Videnskaps-Akademi) 1954.

J. M. Grintz, "Hebrew as the Spoken and Written Language in the Last Days of the Second Temple," JBL 79, 1960, 32-47.

M. H. Segal, A Grammar of Mishnaic Hebrew (Oxford: Clarendon, 1927) 17.

The ideas of these gentlemen have not turned the consensus of opinion. In the discussion of the languages of the first century in Palestine, among those who have accepted the importance of Aramaic, two of the foremost have had a difference of opinion on methods of dating:

Paul Kahle, "Das palästinische Pentateuchtargum und das zur Zeit Jesu gesprochene Aramäisch," ZNW 51, 1960, 46-54.

This article forms a good part of chap. 3 of Kahle's The Cairo Geniza, 1959. Contra:

Eduard Y. Kutscher, "Das zur Zeit Jesu gesprochene Aramäisch," ZNW 51, 1960, 46-54.

Reply:

Paul Kahle, "Erwiderung," ZNW 51, 1960, 55.

The situation was reviewed by two members of the "Kahle school":

A. Díez Macho, "La lengua hablada por Jesucristo," Oriens Antiquus 2, 1962, 95-132. Cf. especially 106-107.

Matthew Black, "Aramaic Studies and the Language of Jesus," BZAW 103: In Memoriam Paul Kahle, 1968, 17-27.

Black summed up his presentation as follows: "Kutscher's attempt to show that the language of the Palestinian Pentateuch Targum was not one of our best representatives of the spoken language of the time of Christ was unconvincing. . . " (22-23). The same debate was to continue at a later date between Joseph Fitzmyer on the one hand, and on the other, Kahle's disciples.

Five articles which sought to present the multi-lingual situation of first century Palestine in a balanced way were:

A. Díez Macho, "La lengua hablada por Jesucristo," cited above.

R. H. Gundry, "The Language Milieu of First-Century Palestine: Its Bearing on the Authenticity of the Gospel Tradition," JBL 83, 1964, 404-408.

H. Ott, "Um die Muttersprache Jesu, Forschungen seit Gustaf Dalman," Novum Testamentum 9, 1967, 1-25.

James Barr, "Which Language did Jesus Speak? - Some Remarks of a Semitist," BJRL 53, 1970-71, 9-29.

Joseph A. Fitzmyer, "The Languages of Palestine in the First Century A.D.," CBQ 32, 1970, 501-531.

It is surprising that as late as 1979 a book should appear in which the author held "Torrey's position valid and convincing,"

and that "the Gospels as a whole were translated from the Aramaic
into Greek." Cf. Frank Zimmermann, The Aramaic Origin of the Four
Gospels (N.Y.: KTAV, 1979) 5. Although Zimmermann knew of Black
he does not utilize R. Bloch, A. Díez Macho, et al; nor does he
mention the manuscripts of the fragment targum tradition, the
Cairo Geniza materials or Targum Neofiti I.

There is a brief, but well documented review of this whole
discussion in the course of a recent article:
George Howard, "The Textual Nature of Shem-Tob's Hebrew
Matthew," JBL 108, 1989, 239-257. Cf. 241-253.

[2]The history of the literature on the testimonia theory has
been carefully reviewed:
Joseph A. Fitzmyer, "'4 Q Testimonia' and the New Testament,"
Theological Studies 18, 1957, 513-537.
This review starts with notice of the suggestions of Edwin Hatch
(Essays in Biblical Greek, Oxford: Clarendon, 1889, esp. p. 203)
and Hans Vollmer (Die alttestamentlichen Citate bei Paulus, text-
kritisch und biblisch-theologisch gewürdigt nebst einem Anhang
über das Verhältnis des Apostels zu Philo, Freiburg & Leipzig,
1895). Of course the contributions of Rendell Harris (Testimonies
I and II, Cambridge, 1916, 192?) and F. C. Burkitt (The Gospel
History and Its Transmission, Edinburgh, 1907) are discussed. Then
follows the "reaction to the hypothesis," the denial of the existence of testimonia collections by O. Michel (Paulus und seine
Bibel, Gütersloh, 1920). There is coolness toward the hypothesis
to be noticed in the work of C. H. Dodd (According to the Scriptures, London: James Nisbett, 1952); and Krister Stendahl's
position is close to that of Dodd (The School of Matthew and Its
Use of the Old Testament, Upsalla, 1954).

Fitzmyer's purpose is to support the testimonia theory in
presenting the evidence that there is, and to situate the document
4Q Testimonia in the context of the theory.

[3]DEFINITIONS AND ABBREVIATIONS. There is nothing special with
respect to our abbreviations; basically they follow the instructions of the Journal of Biblical Literature.
Targum: "A targum is not any translation (of the Hebrew Bible);
it is a translation of the Hebrew Bible into the Aramaic language
for liturgical use of the synagogue." Cf. A. Díez Macho, El Targum,
(Barcelona: Consejo Superior de Investigaciones Científicas, 1972)
p. 6.
(a) Targum Onkelos (Tg. Onq.) is a targum which covers the entire
Pentateuch. It is a rather literal rendition of the Hebrew text,
but with the occasional paraphrase. It transmits traditions which
are basically Palestinian, but it probably was edited in the Jewish academies of Babylonia. (Cf. Bibliography: Sperber, Alexander.)
(b) Targum Pseudo-Jonathan (Tg. Ps.-J.), also known as Targum
Yerušalmi II (Tg. Yer. I), consists of a rendition of the entire
Pentateuch with the exception of a few verses. It is a complex
compilation; the translation is interspersed with paraphrases
and interpolated midrashim which probably originated in various

centuries. (Cf. Bibliography: Clarke, E. G.)
(c) The Fragment(ary) Targum (Frg. Tg.), also known as Targum
Yerušalmi II (Tg. Yer. II), contains periphrastic or midrashic
portions of the targum to sections of all five books of the Penta-
teuch. The Frg. Tg. mss. all contain basically the same text.
They are distinguished as follows: British Museum Or. 10794
(MS Br.); Jewish Theological Seminary (Lukzki) 605 (MS J);
Leipzig I (MS L); Moscow (MS M); Nürnberg, Solger 2.2 (MS N);
Paris 110 (MS P); Sassoon 264 (MS S); Vaticanus 440 (MS V);
with these one often considers the editio princeps of the Frg. Tg.
in the Bomberg Bible of 1517-18 (ed. B). (Cf. Bibliography:
Biblia Rabbinica.) Taylor-Schechter Collection, Cambridge (T.-S.)
     Codex Paris 75 of the Bibliothèque Nationale, Paris (P 75) is
a manuscript of Tg. Onq. with additions from the Frg. Tg. for
Gen 38:25-26 and 44:18.
     (For Frg. Tg. MSS cf. Bibliography, M. L. Klein.)
(d) The Fragments of the Palestinian Targums from the Cairo Geniza.
In text and content these are related to the Frg. Tg. Those
published by Paul Kahle in Masoreten des Westens II are distin-
as follows: CTg A; CTg B; CTg C; CTg D; CTg E; CTg E+; and
CTg F. The same sigla are used by Klein; but he has further
materials to add to the collection. (Cf. Bibliography: M.L. Klein.)
(e) Codex Neofiti I (Tg. Neof.) is a complete text of the Palestinian Targum, except for a few verses omitted through homoiteleu-
ton. In its midrashic sections it is allied to the texts known
from the Cairo Geniza and the fragment targum. (Cf. Bibliography:
A. Díez Macho.)

[4]Dalman was of the opinion that Jesus' speech was "pure"
Aramaic, that the Palestinian targums, Ps.-J. and Frg. Tg. exhibited a hebraized Aramaic and thus were "late," Tg. Ps.-J. no
earlier than the seventh century A.D. Cf. Die Worte Jesu, 1930,
67-72. For comment, cf. Martin McNamara, "Targumic Studies," CBQ
28, 1966, 9.

[5]This list is offered in A. Díez Macho, El Targum, 95. For
discussion on the first three items, cf. McNamara, "Targumic
Studies," 9-11; also his The New Testament and the Palestinian
Targum to the Pentateuch (Rome: Pontifical Biblical Institute,
1966) 20-22. On p. 27 of the same work, McNamara notes that in
the volumes of Strack-Billerbeck, the "targumic material was,
unfortunately, given a very secondary place."

[6]Dalman, Die Worte Jesu,[2] 67.

[7]Ibid.

[8]Paul Kahle, Masoreten des Westens II (Stuttgart, 1930;
reprint: Hildesheim: Georg Olms, 1967, 35 -36): the discussion
introducing the texts. Cf. also Paul Kahle, The Cairo Geniza
1st edn. (London: Oxford University press, 1947) 122-123.

[9]The announcement of the discovery: A. Díez Macho, "Una
copia de todo el targum jerosolimitano en la Vaticana," Estudios

Bíblicos 15, 1956, 446-447. Díez Macho gave a fuller presentation of his judgement of the importance of the discovery: "The Recently Discovered Palestinian Targum: Its Antiquity and Relationship with the Other Targums," V.T. Supp. 7, 1959, 222-245.

[10]Paul Kahle, The Cairo Geniza[2] (Oxford: Basil Blackwell, 1959) 207-208: "We can to-day go further since we now have the oldest Targum itself in its entirety, and not in a later revision. This Targum, as we now have it, can be regarded as being nearly in the same form as when it was in circulation at the time of the beginning of Christianity. We must only bear in mind that it never had a fixed text of the kind to which we are accustomed from Targum Onkelos. . . In the Palestinian Targum of the Pentateuch we have in the main material coming from pre-Christian times which must be studied by everyone who wishes to understand the state of Judaism at the time of the birth of Christianity. And we possess this material in a language of which we can say that it is very similar to that spoken by the earliest Christians. It is material the importance of which can scarcely be exaggerated."

[11]Matthew Black, An Aramaic Approach to the Gospels and Acts[3] (Oxford: Clarendon, 1967) 35: "The most significant new discovery in recent years in the field of Palestinian Aramaic is Codex Neofiti I. . ." Black considered Díez Macho's notice in Estudios Bíblicos to be of such value that he translated it (all but the last clause) and published it in two places: An Aramaic Approach[3] chap. 3, 36-37; also "The Recovery of the Language of Jesus," NTS 3, 1957, 307.

[12]Zunz, Die gottesdienstlichen Vorträge der Juden historisch entwickelt, 65. (Cf. note 1, above.)

[13]Abraham Geiger, Urschrift und Übersetzungen der Bibel in ihrer Abhängigkeit von der innern Entwicklung des Judentums (1867; 2nd edn.: Frankfurt am Main: Verlag Madda, 1928) esp. 451-480.

[14]Attested by 11Qtg Job and 4Qtg Lev.

[15]Joseph A. Fitzmyer, "The Languages of Palestine in the First Century A.D.," CBQ 32, 1970, 501-531. On 525-526: "In my opinion, the evidence from the borrowing of Greek words in the Palestinian targums argues for a date after A.D. 200 - a date that could be supported by a number of orthographic, lexical, and grammatical considerations which are absent from Biblical, Qumrân, and similar Aramaic texts, but that begin to appear in Murabbaʿât and Ḥabra texts and become abundant in the targums, in Syriac, and in dated Aramaic inscriptions from Palestinian synagogues from the third to the sixth centuries, A.D."

[16]Díez Macho, El Targum, 50-73.

[17]Ibid., 50: "El estudio del arameo de estos Targumim. . . ha de asentarse en amplia plataforma: en la ortografía, fonética, morfología, sintaxis y, además, en la semántica. La semántica. . . es de decisiva importancia."

[18]Ibid., 54: "la conparación sincrónica y diacrónica de textos arameos, tiene riesgos, por lo que después de apurar todas las posibilidades de la ortografía, fonética, morfología y sintaxis, y las que ofrecen la paleografía y lexicografía, es aconsejable poner a contribución los recursos, casi inéditos aún, de la semántica."

[19]Díez Macho (El Targum, 54) draws heavily upon the work of M. Ohana in his dissertation "Halaká de Neofiti al Exodo," and he goes on to say that "naturally new investigations in the field of the semanitcs of Neofiti are necessary" (p. 61).

[20]Ibid., 61.

[21]The fact of the variants in orthography etc. among the extant mss. of the fragment targums, while they preserve the same substance, helps us to see how unevenly this "modernization" happened.

[22]Díez Macho, El Targum 96, n. 204: "padre de la ciencia moderna sobre el judaísmo." This was due to Zunz' work Die gottesdienstlichen Vorträge, cited above, n. 1.

[23]Zunz, Die gottesdienstlichen Vorträge, 65: "Geschriebene aramäische Uebersetzungen der meisten biblischen Bücher hat es sicherlich schon unter den Hasmonäern gegeben." Then he goes on to say that the two Talmuds mention the existence of a Job targum in the first century. This information, as well as the new substantiation afforded from the fact of the existence of the Job targum of Qumran, have been carefully set forth by Van der Ploeg, Van der Woude and Jongeling in the Introduction to Le targum de Job de la grotte XI de Qumrân (Leiden: Brill, 1971) 1-9. According to Zunz (65) the book of Job would not logically have been the first book translated, therefore there were, in all probability, Torah targums even earlier.

[24]Renée Bloch, "Note méthodologique pour l'étude de la littérature rabbinique," RSR 43, 1955, 201, n.7.

[25]Renée Bloch, "Écriture et tradition dans le judaïsme," Cahiers Sioniens VIII, 1, 1954, 23 & 25-26. "L'origine du genre midrashique est inséparable de la formation et de la vie des Livres Saints. Les premiers développements du midrash sont à chercher dans la Bible même, et dans la littérature qui s'y rattache: versions, apocryphes, etc. La littérature postérieure de caractère purement midrashique restera en continuité organique avec la Bible et constituera par là un lien organique entre la Bible et la littérature rabbinique, y compris la Loi orale proprement dits. . . (ce genre midrashique) développe, enrichit et transpose le message primitif. Pris dans le mouvement qui, dans l'histoire du people de Dieu, fait mûrir et progresser l'intelligence de la Révélation, souvent les auteurs plus récents ne se rendent même pas compte que le sens qu'ils donnent aux écrits de leurs prédécesseurs est différent du sens originel. Ils

utilisent très librement leurs sources, avec le souci de répondre
aux besoins et aux problèmes de leur temps, et n'hésitent pas à
donner aux vieux textes, par accommodation, un sens nouveau."
[26]"Midrash," Dictionnaire de la Bible Supplément V, 1957,
col. 1279.
[27]Renée Bloch, "Note méthodologique," 194-195.
[28]For frequently cited sources, the following editions have
been used:
Philo, Judaeus, Philo (London: William Heinemann, 1930-1962; Cam-
bridge, Mass.: Harvard University Press, 1970-71) 12 vols.
Flavius Josephus, Josephus (London: William Heinemann, 1950-1963;
Cambridge, Mass.: Harvard University Press, 1969) 9 vols.
Guido Kisch, ed., Pseudo-Philo's Liber Antiquitatum Biblicarum
(Notre Dame, Indiana: The University of Notre Dame, 1949).
J. Z. Lauterbach, ed., Mekilta de Rabbi Ishmael (Philadelphia:
Jewish Publication Society of America, 1933-35, 1949) 3 vols.
J. H. Weiss, ed., Sifra on Leviticus (Vienna, 1862; reprint:
Vienna: J. Scholssberg, 1946).
H. S. Horovitz, ed., Siphre d'be Rab: Fasciculus primus: Siphre
ad Numeros adjecto Siphre Zutta cum variis lectionibus et
adnotationibus (Lipsiae: Gustav Foch, 1917; reprint: Jeru-
salem: Wahrmann Books, 1966).
Louis Finkelstein, ed., Siphre ad Deuteronomium H. S. Horovitzii
schedis usus cum variis lectionibus et adnotationibus
(Berlin: Gesellschaft zur Förderung der Wissenschaft des
Judentums, 1939; republished: N.Y.: Jewish Theological
Seminary of America, 1969).
Eduard Lohse, ed., Die Texte aus Qumran: Hebraïsch und Deutsch
(München: Kösel, 1971).
For sources utilized infrequently, consult bibliography.
The material in the early midrashim is ordinarily accepted as
a compilation, dated according to the persons to whom the various
sayings are attributed. For the Qumran literature, it is accepted
that the final date coincides with the destruction of the Second
Temple. With respect to the Biblical Antiquities of Pseudo-Philo,
"most scholarship dates the work to the first century of the
common era." Cf. Frederick J. Murphy, "Retelling the Bible:
Idolatry in Pseudo-Philo," JBL 107, 1988, 275. Murphy also
suggests that "it is reasonable to assume a single author" and
that the work represents "a general synagogal piety." (Ibid.,
275-287.)
[29]Geza Vermes, Scripture and Tradition in Judaism: Haggadic
Studies (Leiden: Brill, 1961) 7, 10 and 9. J. Neusner elaborates
on this method which he attributes to Vermes in his "The History
of Earlier Rabbinic Judaism: Some New Approaches," History of
Religions 16, 1977, 216-236. An experiment was made with the
method of Neusner: David Goodblatt, "The Beruriah Traditions,"
JJS 26, 1975, 68-85.

[30] Leiden: Brill, 1968. Cf. esp. 42 nn. 3, 4; 86 n. 1; 87 n. 4; 105, n. 2.

[31] Cf. Malina's bibliography, pp. XII, XIII, XV.

[32] P. VII.

[33] Geza Vermes, Scripture and Tradition 176-177.

[34] This does not necessarily mean refinement upon refinement in a linear order; it is possible that in the future we could realize that some refinements apply in one pattern of cases, and others in others.

[35] Jacob Z. Lauterbach, "Midrash and Mishnah: a Study in the Early History of the Halakah," JQR 5, 1915, 503-527; JQR 6, 1915, 23-96; JQR 6, 1915, 303-323. From the first part of articles, 505-507:

"For a long period this Midrash-form was the only form used in teaching the Halakah. This is confirmed by reliable traditions reported to us in Rabbinic literature. One such report is contained in the following passage in the Pal. Talmud (Moed ḳaṭan III, 7, 83b):

איזהו תאמיד חכם? חזקיה אמר כל ששנה הלכות ועוד תורה אמר
ליה ר' יוסי הדא הדת אמר בראשונה אבל עכשיו אפילו הלכות

'Who is to be condidered a scholar? Hezekiah says, One who has studied the Halakot as an addition to and in connexion with the Torah. Said to him R. Jose, What you say was [correct] in former times, but in our day, even [if one has studies merely detached] Halakot, [he is to be regarded as a scholar].' Here it is plainly stated that in earlier times (בראשונה) the only form of teaching Halakot was as an addition to and in connexion with the written Law, that is to say, in the Midrash-form. In those days, therefore, one could not acquire a knowledge of the Halakah, i.e. become a scholar, except by learning the Midrash, for the very good reason that the halakic teachings were not imparted in any other form."

[36] Parts of the Mishnah, Tosepta and scattered Midrash-Baraitot in the Babylonian Talmud should also be recognized (cf. Lauterbach "Midrash and Mishnah," 503) if an exhaustive study were undertaken. The confines of the present work allow only sufficient use of the early midrashim for auxiliary support of the points being made. The main support is from the targums of the Pentateuch.

[37] More detail on this perspective can be obtained from Louis Ginzburg, "Religion of the Jews at the Time of Jesus," HUCA 1, 1924, 307-321.

[38] Lauterbach, "Midrash and Mishnah," 504.

[39] For another description of the same data, cf. John Bowker, The Targums and Rabbinic Literature (Cambridge: The University Press, 1969) 3-28.

[40] Michael L. Klein, "The Extant Sources of the Fragmentary

Targum to the Pentateuch," HUCA 46, 1975, 135.

[41]Ibid., 135. In every case of citation of the witness of the Frg. Tg. to a tradition, we reviewed first the best-attested strand of that tradition (Klein: VNL, BMS) in MSS V and N (which vary a little; for example see p. 76 and nn. 3 and 4 p. 87). We also reviewed ed. B (which follows N; this provides further examples supporting Klein's thesis, ibid., 135). We consistently checked MS P as a variant of the Frg. Tg. tradition. Tgs. Onq., Ps.-J., Neof. and CTg were also consistently checked. Hence it should be understood than whenever one of these sources is not mentioned, this indicates that it does not contain pertinent material. For example, on p. 45 , MS V (N and ed. B), reviewed as indicated, lacked what MS P retained; and Tg. Onq. did not use the verb under discussion, שלם.

CHAPTER I
SPEAKING OF GOD AS "FATHER"

The most prevalent way of thinking of God in the NT is as
"Father." This is most outstanding in the Gospel of John, and
next in Matthew.[1] Of all of the chapters in Matthew, it is the
sixth which carries the preponderant number of references (12 in
this chapter) to God as "Father"; and of all the divisions of
material in Matthew, it is the first great sermon, the Sermon on
the Mount which carries the greatest number (17 in chaps. 5-7).
Matthew uses three expressions, "Father," "Father in Heaven," and
"Heavenly Father"; the second and third of these expressions are
never found in John or most of the NT books, and the third never
in any but Matthew. It is clear then that, in discussing the
Sermon on the Mount, the appellation of "Father" (and the two
variations) for God is one of the features which must draw our
attention.

In order to see the usage in Matthew in as full a light as
we are able, we shall review occurrences of it (1) in the Hebrew
Bible, Apocrypha and Pseudepigrapha; (2) in the traditions
collected in the tannaitic midrashim and targums; (3) in Philo
and Josephus; (4) in the Sermon on the Mount in its NT context.
However, for the sake of seeing the term "Father" in a logically
broader perspective, it is necessary to give attention to the
theological frame of reference at the outset: the theology of

the Name of God. For this purpose, we shall make a preliminary
study entailing particularly outstanding texts from Exodus,
Leviticus and Numbers, and the attention given to these texts in
the targums and tannaitic midrashim. In the course of this work,
as the theology of the Name of God emerges from the material, we
shall, in passing, be able to suggest the high probability of a
very early date for the roots of the theology in question, a date
at least as early as LXX Leviticus and Sirach. Thus, having outlined the theological frame of reference, we can proceed to the
study of the appellation "Father" for God; and finally find our
understanding of that appellation in the NT enriched.

Preliminary: the Theology of the Name of God

When asking about the theology of the Name of God, the
first text about which anyone might ask is Exod 3:14. By the
time of the LXX, the expression ὁ ὤν was known and used twice;
this made for smoother reading than the thrice-repeated אהיה
of the MT:

καὶ εἶπεν ὁ θεὸς πρὸς Μωυσῆν	ויאמר אלהים אל משה
'Εγώ εἰμι ὁ ὤν·	אהיה אשר אהיה
καὶ εἶπεν Οὕτως ἐρεῖς τοῖς	ויאמר כה תאמר לבני ישראל
υἱοῖς Ισραηλ 'Ο ὤν ἀπέσταλκέν	אהיה שלחני אליכם
με πρὸς ὑμᾶς.	

In the texts of Tg. Ps.-J., Tg. Neof. and the Frg. Tgs., MSS V,
P (and ed. B), we observe a ringing of the changes upon the verb
"to be" in a haggadic addition on God's creating the world by the
command that it be.[2] However in Tg. Ps.-J. at this verse, and
repeated at Deut 32:39, we find variations upon the verb "to be"
predicated of God. At Tg. Ps.-J. Deut 32:39:[3]

Behold now, that	חמון כדון ארום
I am He who am and was,	אנא הוא דהוויי והוית
and I am He	ואנא הוא
who will be hereafter.	דעתיד למהוי

In <u>Mekilta</u>, there is an expanded version of this tradition (given anonymously);   it is in the commentary upon the אנכי יהוה of Exod 20:2:[4]

I am He who was in the past;	אני לשעבר
I am He who will be in the future.	אני לעתיד לבא
I am He who am in this world;	אני בעולם הזה
I am He who will be in the world to come.	אני לעולם הבא

These texts bring our attention to the Name, but we note that the Hebrew word אהיה is not copied as it was in some of the targums. Actually, when the targum texts for Exod 3:14 are taken together, we find an ambivalence about including the Hebrew spelling of the Name, אהיה.[5]   From the LXX and targumic treatments of Exod 3:14, and from allied expressions of the traditions in question, we can say that there was an established tradition of care and thought-fulness with respect to the Name יהוה.[6]

It is generally accepted that from the third century B.C. to the third century A.D. there was a prohibition against the spoken use of the Tetragrammaton which was observed among a notable part of the Jewish population. It is held that this prohibition was accepted in the diaspora as early as the LXX interpretation of Leviticus;   for Lev 24:16 reads as follows:

He who blasphemes the Name of	ונקב שם יהוה
the Lord shall be put to death.	מות יומת
All the congregation shall stone	דגום ירגמו בו
him, the sojourner as well as	כל העדה
the native; when he blasphemes	בגר כאזרח
the Name he shall be put to death.	בנקבו שם יומת

He who names	ὀνομάζων δὲ
the Name of the Lord	τὸ ὄνομα κυρίου
shall be put to death.	θανάτῳ θανατούσθω·
All the congregation	λίθοις λιθοβολείτω αὐτὸν
of Israel shall stone him,	πᾶσα συναγωγὴ Ισραηλ·
the proselyte	ἐάν τε προσήλυτος
as well as the native,	ἐάν τε αὐτόχθων,
when he names	ἐν τῷ ὀνομάσαι αὐτὸν
the Name of the Lord	τὸ ὄνομα κυρίου
he shall be put to death	τελευτάτω.

The view of the LXX translator was also known to the targumists.
In Tg. Ps.-J. and Tg. Onq. this is highlighted by setting a certain contrast between vv 15 and 16 in order to make v 16 all the
more forceful:[7]

Tg. Ps.-J.

A young man or an old man	גבר טלי או גבר סיב
who enrages and blasphemes	דירגז ויחרף
the substitute Name of God,	שום כינוי אלהיה
he shall bear his sin.	ויקבל חוביה
But he who pronounces and	ברם מאן דמפרש
blasphemes the Name of the Lord	ומחרף שמא דה'
shall surely be put to death.	אתקטלא יתקטל
All the congregation shall stone	אטלא יאטלון יתיה אבנין
him, sojourners as well as	כל כנשתא כגיורא כיציבא
natives; when he blasphemes	בזמן דיחרף
the Name that is Alone,	שמא דיחרף
he shall be put to death.	יתקטל

Tg. Onq.

Whoever blasphemes before his	גבר גבר ארי ירגיז
God shall bear his sin.	קדם אלהיה ויקביל חוביה
Whoever pronounces the Name of God	ודיפריש שמא דיוי
shall surely be put to death.	אתקטלא יתקטיל
All the congregation shall stone	מרגם ירגמון ביה כל
him, sojourners as well as natives	כנשתא גיורא כיציבא
when he pronounces the Name,	בפרשותיה שמא
he shall be put to death.	יתקטיל

It is noteworthy that this tradition is transmitted by Tg. Onq.,
a targum in which there is so much evidence of "correction" for
alignment with the MT. Aquila is in accord: καὶ ἐπονομάξων ὄνομα
κυρίου, θανάτῳ θανατούσθω, "and he who names the Name of the Lord
shall be put to death."[8] However one might simply say that Aquila
is in line with the Greek tradition which we see in the LXX.

On the same part of Leviticus, the tradition in Sipra 104c
is quite specific:[9]

And a son of an Israelite woman	ויקוב בן האשה הישראלית
cursed the Name	את השם
which is the unpronounceable Name	זה שם המפורש
which he heard from Sinai. . .	ששמע מסיני
It is taught that they do not	מלמד שאינן
put to death (one who curses	הורגים בכינוי
by a substitute (designation	
for the Tetragrammaton).	

Together with the specific case of the blasphemer, we find a
succinct saying of general application; it is located in the
haggadah at Deut 32:3 in Tgs. Ps.-J., Neof., MSS P, V (N and
ed. B):[10]

> Woe to the wicked who make   ווי להון לרשיעייא
> memorial of the Holy Name   דמדכרין שצא קדישא
> with blasphemies.   בגידופין

The multiple attestation and the consistency of the attestation
speak strongly for the antiquity of the saying. Similarly, the
case of the blasphemer is widely attested, known as "one of the
four cases" which Moses tried. The first attestation of the four
cases is at Lev 24:1-12 in MSS P, V (N, ed. B) and Tgs. Ps.-J.
and Neof.; it is repeated quite fully in Tgs. Ps.-J. and Neof.
at Num 9:8, 15:34 and 27:5, and mentioned at these three places
in Numbers in MSS V (N and ed. B). The point is this: the case
of the blasphemer (as one of the four cases) and the allied
saying at Deut 32:3 show unusually wide attestation; therefore
these would have contributed strongly to the maintenance of a
heightened reverence for the Tetragrammaton, in all probability
from a time close to the roots of the haggadic traditions found
in the targums,[11] and certainly prior to Philo.

Philo knew the tradition of the four cases (Mos. ii.192-220)
and expounded upon the material, in the course of which we read,
ὅς δ' ἄν ὀνομάσῃ τὸ ὄνομα κυρίου, θνησκέτω, "whoever names the
Name of the Lord, let him die." A few lines further on: εἰ δε
τις. . . τολμήσειεν ἀκαίρως αὐτοῦ φθέγξασθαι τοὖνομα, θάνατον
ὑπομαινάτω τὴν δίκην, "if anyone. . . ventures to utter His Name
unseasonably, let him suffer the penalty of death."[12]

When considering questions about the pronunciation of the
Tetragrammaton, it is natural to ask about the renditions of
Num 6:27. The several targums which contain the verse show some
difference from the MT. The MT reads:

> And they shall put   ושמו
> my Name upon the people   את שמי על בני
> of Israel, and I   ישראל ואני
> will bless them.   אברכם

Compare Num 6:27 Tg. Ps.-J.:[13]

And they shall put the blessing	וישוון ית בירכת
of my Name upon the people	שמי על בני
of Israel, and I, in my Word	ישראל ואנא במימרי
will bless them.	אברכינון

The slightness of the alterations suggests hesitation to alter a
well known text very significantly (and it would be well known,
coming immediately after the blessing which ordinarily remained
in Hebrew, untranslated). However the type of hesitant modification is that of reserve when confronted with the idea that the
Tetragrammaton was implied, reserve that sought to hold the
Tetragrammaton at a distance and use other designations (the
blessing, the Word) as more proximate to man. In Sipre Num 43
(in an anonymous tradition) it was understood that there was an
implicit reference to the Tetragrammaton in this verse:[14]

It is taught: they shall place	ת"ל
my Name (upon the sons of Israel)	ושמו את שמי
in the sanctuary with the	במקדש בשם המפורש
unpronounceable Name, and in the	ובמדינה בכינוי
country with a substitute (designation).	

That substitute designations were to be used in speech – including prayers recited – with full knowledge that they were substitute designations is also to be seen quite clearly in Sipra 80d;
the passage happens to be about an atonement prayer, taking as
the starting point the word וכפר, "and he shall make atonement,"
in Lev 16:6:[15]

In what manner is confession?	כיצד היה מתודה
"Oh, Ha-Shem, I am guilty,	אנא השם עויתי
unfaithful, I have sinned	פשעתי חטאתי
before Thy face – I and my house.	לפניך אני ובתי
Oh, Ha-Shem, pray pardon	אנא השם כפר מא
the guilt, the infidelities,	לעונות ולחטאים
and the sins of which I have	ולחטאים
been guilty, in which	שעויתי
I have been unfaithful,	ושפשעתי
in which I have sinned	ושחטאתי
before Thy face,	לפניך
I and my house,	אני וביתי
as it is written in the Torah	ככהוב בתרות
of Moses thy servant."	משה עבדך

For on that day that one	לאמר כי ביום הזה
makes expiation for you to	יכפר עליכם לטהר אתכם
purify you from all your sins	מכל חטאתיכם
before YHWH you shall be pure.	לפני ה' תטהרו

"Ha-Shem" stands in the material to be recited, "YHWH" in the literary commentary; the point is inescapable.

Evidence of a developed reverence involved in the very concept of substitute designations is found amply in Tg. Ps.-J.; for example, allusion is made to the Tetragrammaton a number of times by the use of an eloquent phrase, שמא רבא ויקירא, "the Great and Glorious Name."[16] Similarly in Tg. Neof., MSS P, V (N and ed. B) we find the term שמא מפרשה, "the unpronounceable Name";[17] this is also found in the Mekilta, as we shall see.

Turning to the Mekilta of R. Ishmael, we find the ordinary attitude with respect to the Tetragrammaton in this work presented in this passage (given anonymously):[18]

The Tetragrammaton (the "Unpronounceable	שם המפורש
Name") is not to be pronounced	אסור
outside the sanctuary (lit.: is	להאמר
restricted from the saying in the	בגבולין
country).	

Qumran was in the country; there the rule was strict. In I QS 6: 27-7:2 we find:[19]

If any man has uttered the	וא[ש]ר יזכיר דבר
[Most] Venerable Name even	בשם הנכבד על כול ה[
though frivolously, or as	ואם קלל או להבעת מצוה
a result of shock or for any	או לכול דבר אשר לו
other reason whatever, while	הואה קורה בספר
reading the Book or praying,	או מברך והבדילהו
he shall be dismissed and	ולוא ישוב עוד
shall return to the Council	על עצת היחד
of the Community no more.	

In CD 15:1-5[20] we have the strict view of its authors on oath-taking. One was not to swear by אל or אד or by the Torah either; that is, neither by alternates to the Tetragrammaton (which implied It) nor by the Torah which contained the Tetragrammaton. The reason was that if the person swearing should transgress, he would not be liable for the death penalty but only for the guilt-offering.

However, there was no uniform opinion as to whether the
Tetragrammaton should or should not be used in oaths. <u>Mekilta</u>
offers an anonymous passage on the <u>use</u> of the Tetragrammaton
in oaths:[21]

> An oath by the Tetragrammaton (ה"א). From this you can
> draw a conclusion with regard to all the oaths prescribed
> in the Torah. Since all the oaths prescribed in the
> Torah are not explicit as to how they are to be taken
> and the Torah explicitly states in the case of one of
> them that it must be taken only by the Tetragrammaton
> (ה"א), it has thus made it explicit with regard to all
> the oaths prescribed in the Torah that they must be taken
> only by the Tetragrammaton.

This passage offers a certain logical sophistication written in
commentary upon the opening words of Exod 22:10, שבעת יהוה, "an
oath by the Lord." Although the targums do not expatiate on the
manner of oaths at this point in their renditions of the Hebrew,
the concept of swearing by the Name is evident in other places.
At the outset it must be said that the root of the concept is in
the Hebrew text. Only three times in the Torah, in the later
strata at Lev 19:12 (the Holiness Code of P) and at Deut 6:13 and
10:12 do we find the phrase "by My/His Name" modifying the verb
"swear." The evidence for this manner of speaking is greater in
Tg. Ps.-J.: it is most significant that in the presentation of
the commandment of the decalogue at Exod 20:7 and Deut 5:11, Tg.
Ps.-J. has "you shall not <u>swear</u> (לא ישתבע) by the Name of the Word
of the Lord your God in vain. . . " rather than the weaker "you
shall not <u>take</u> (לא תשא). . . "[22] Thus, whereas this stronger usage
was found only in the presentation of the commandments at Lev 19:
12 in the MT, in Tg. Ps.-J. it is found at Lev 19:12, Exod 20:7
and Deut 5:11. (The manner of speaking in question is also present in Tg. Ps.-J. at Lev 16:21 and Deut 9:19.) It could be suggested that it was during a period when the Name was very seldom
"taken" or pronounced at all that the Commandment could be interpreted with reference to the forensic situation, in prohibition
of false oaths.

Philo expatiates on the situation of one who involves the

Name in a false oath:[23]

Such a one may be assured	ἀνίερος δ' ὁ τοιοῦτος
that he is unholy and profane,	ὢν καὶ βέβηλος ἴστω,
since he pollutes the good	μιαίνων τὸ ἀμίαντον
Name which is by nature	φύσει ἀγαθὸν καὶ θεῖον
unpolluted, the Name of God.	ὄνομα.

Thus for Philo, the false oath was heinous in the extreme because of its profanation of the Name. Philo can be counted among those who accepted the use of the Tetragrammaton in oaths.

The early date of the tradition of texts reflecting profound practical respect for the Tetragrammaton is highlighted when we consider how this was spelled out by the author of Sirach (between 190 and 175 B.C.):[24]

Sir 23:9, 10, 12:

. . . do not habitually utter the Name of the Holy One.	... ὀνομασίᾳ τοῦ ἁγίου μὴ συνεθισθῇς'
. . . the man who always swears and utters the Name will not be cleansed from sin. . . There is an utterance which is comparable to death; may it never be found in the inheritance of Jacob.	... ὁ ὀμνύων καὶ ὀνομάζων διὰ παντὸς ἀπὸ ἁμαρτίας οὐ μὴ καθαρισθῇ... "Εστιν λέξις ἀντιπαραβεβλημένη θανάτῳ, μὴ εὑρεθήτω ἐν κληρονομίᾳ Ιακωβ.

Cautious not to draw too great a conclusion from the evidence, we might simply say that prior to the end of the second century A.D. a marked reverence for the Tetragrammaton had been growing, and the length of time that it had been growing might well have been considerable - at least from the time of Sirach, a work of which we have some estimation of the date, and from the time of the LXX translation of Leviticus.

During the time of the profound respect for the Tetragrammaton, popular piety and Pharisaic teaching mutually conditioned one another in the acceptance of and use of substitute designations. On this subject, Lauterbach has written a fairly simplified exposition, but careful and sufficient for giving an orientation:[25]

That the Pharisees conceived God as the One whom no
human being could fully comprehend is especially
evident from the manner in which they would refer
to Him. Whether and to what extent they were res-
ponsible for the prohibition against the pronounci-
ation of the Tetragrammaton is hard to decide. But
this we do know, that, except in prayer and in the
reading of the Scriptures, they avoided using even
any of the other Biblical names of God. They
apparently felt that no one could designate His
essence or describe the totality of His being.
While they interpreted even these Biblical names
as merely describing His attributes, as for example,
when they interpreted "Elohim" to mean the "midat
ha-din", the Attribute of Justice, they nevertheless
feared that the constant use of these names might
lead to their being misunderstood and taken for the
actual proper names of God. They, therefore, referred
to Him merely by using some of His attributes. They
employed such designations of Him as describe His
activity or His relation to the world and to man.
Thus, when they had in mind His relation to the world,
they would speak of Him as "the Possessor," or "the
Creator of the world," "the Master of all works,"
"the Ruler of the Universe," "He by whose word the
world came into being." To indicate His omnipotence,
they would speak of Him as גבורה, "Might", the
Almighty. To emphasize His Omnipresence, they would
speak of Him as המקום, "The Place." For, He is the
place of the world but not limited to it. The world
finds a place and exists only in Him. But the world
does not contain Him, for He is in the world and yet
beyond it, He is immanent and transcendent. To
emphasize that God is eternal, they would call Him
הי עולמים, "the One who lives for ever" or הי וקים,
"the Everlasting One". To express His relation to man,
they would call Him, the Father, the Father in Heaven,
the Father of all that come into the world, the Lord
of Mercy, or shorter, raḥamana, the Merciful One.
To refer to His revealing Himself to man, or mani-
festing His presence in the world, they would speak
of Him as the Shekinah, שכינה, "Divine Presence", and
ruaḥ haḳodesh, רוח הקדש, "Spirit of Holiness."

It is in this context that we can attempt to study the expanded
popularity of speaking of God as "Father" - a title amongst the
others in usage, but a pre-eminent title, for it does have its
root in the Hebrew Bible, and what is more, in the Torah.

The Appellation "Father" in the Hebrew Bible
Apocrypha and Pseudepigrapha

Only once in the Pentateuch is God given the appellation of
"Father," at Deut 32:6:

. . . is not He thy Father   הלוה הוא אביך קנך
who created thee and made   הוא עשך ויכננך:
thee and established thee?

However there are allusions to the fatherhood of God through
terming Israel "son," for example, Exod 4:22: "Israel is my first-
born son"(J); also through the expression of God's having "begot-
ten" Israel, for example, Deut 32:18: ". . . the Rock that begot
you. . . the God who gave you birth." Thus the concept of the
fatherhood of God is found in Israel's foundational writings, the
Torah.

The use of the word "Father" for God is echoed in Pss 68:6
and 89:27; Isaiah (63:15f. twice, 64:8); Jeremiah (3:4, 19 and
31:9); Malachi (1:6, 2:10); and the Chronicler (I Chr 29:10).
(An observation: in the Deuteronomy text, the "Father"-concept
is associated with the creator-concept; the same association of
ideas is found again in Isa 64:7 and Mal 2:10.) What we really
need to note is both the presence and the rarity of the usage in
the Hebrew Bible.

In the Apocrypha we find a few more examples of God specifically called "Father": Wis 2:16, 14:3;[26] Sir 23:1, 4, 51:10;[27]
and in the poetry of Tobit's prayer, Tob 13:4.

Outside the Bible we find a few scattered examples of the
usage. These have been reviewed thoroughly by J. Carmignac.[28]
We note the following from the pre-Christian era:[29]

> Jub. 1:24: I (God) will be their Father and they
> (Israel) will be my sons. They will all be called
> sons of the living God; every angel and every spirit
> will know that they are my sons, that I am their
> Father in power and in justice and that I love them...
> They all will know that I am the God of Israel, the
> Father of all the sons of Jacob, and the King of
> Mount Sion for all eternity.

There are five occurrences in the earlier part of the Sibylline Oracles, III: 278, 296, 550, 604, 726.[30]   In the Qumran materials there is only one relevant locus, I QH 9:35-36:[31]

. . . for Thou (art) a Father	כי אתה אב לכול
for all Thy faithful sons, Thou	[בני] אמתכה
hast rejoiced over them as a	ותגל עליהם
mother over her babe, and as	כמרחמת על עולה
one who holds on his lap, Thou	וכאומן בחיק תכלכל
sustainest all Thy works.	לכול מעש[י]כה

We see that the term "Father" for God is even rarer in the Pseude-pigrapha than in the Hebrew Bible and the Apocrypha. So we are left with a question as to which circles popularized the use of the term.

The Appellation "Father" in Early Jewish
Tradition including the Targums

In the Amidah, we see that the petitions vary in a number of ways, including the form of address for God. Taking the varia-tions into account, the history of the development of the prayer has been studied,[32] and it has been deduced that at a certain stage, the word Abinu replaced the Tetragrammaton; this has been shown by utilizing a text of section 5, the prayer for repentance, from the Cairo Genizeh.[33] Now, the word Abinu occurs in sections 4, 5 and 6, the prayers for wisdom, repentance and forgiveness. It would appear that 4 and 5, with their seven-word formula, would seem to ante-date the other two.[34]

At this point in our treatment of the custom of calling God "Father" we are conscious of a change. The attestations in the Hebrew Bible, the Pseudepigrapha, and the Amidah are of God termed "Father," never "Father in Heaven." The appellation "Father in Heaven" is fairly common in other material. One reasonable conjecture is that, since the Patriarchs had come to be spoken of as "our father Abraham" and the like, at some point speakers saying "our father. . . " would feel the need to specify for clarity's sake, hence "our Father in Heaven."

The reference to God as "thy Father" in Deut 32:6 was given
some attention in the tradition from which the targums came.
Generally, the pronominal suffix was changed to the plural,[35] but
what is more, the additional specification דבשמיא prevailed in the
fragment targum tradition, hence אבוכון דבשמיא, "your Father who
is in Heaven" in MSS P, V (N and ed. B). (An observation: the
linking of the Father-concept with the creator-concept is highlighted in MS P and Tg. Neof. The verb שכלל, "finish/decorate"
appears at Deut 32:6 in Tgs. Ps.-J., Neof., MS N (and ed. B);
Tg. Neof. and MS P show its addition in Gen 1:1, thus acknowledging a link between the two verses. The Hebrew עשה is usually
translated as עבד in the targums; but at Deut 32:6 in Tg. Ps.-J.
MSS V (N and ed. B) and Tg. Neof., it is rendered ברא - another
link between Deut 32:6 and Gen 1:1 and 2:3.)

Num 20:21 acquired an explanatory addition as the targumists
handed it on; Israel's action was justified thus: דהוון מפקדין מן
אבוהון דבשמיא, "because they had been commanded by their Father in
Heaven." This is observed in MSS V (N and ed. B) and Tg. Neof.
Another passage in which we see targumic activity introducing
material additional to the text is to be seen in the free interpretation of the poetic passage at Num 23:23: מה שגר טב מתקן לכון
גבי אבוכון דבשמיא לעלמא דאתי, "What a good reward is prepared for
you beside your Father in Heaven in the world to come." This is
observed in MSS V (N and ed. B).

One text of Tg. Ps.-J. Lev 22:28 carries a haggadic portion
including the saying, "My people, children of Israel, as your
Father (אבונן) is merciful in heaven, so shall you be merciful on
earth."[36] In Tg. Neof. Deut 33:24, the blessing of Asher reads in
part: בריך צן בניא יהוי מרעיה בשבטיה בין אחוי לבין אביהון
דבשמייא, "Blessed above the sons may be be; welcomed in the
tribes between his brothers and their Father who is in Heaven."[37]
Because each of these occurrences of "Father" for God is in one
extant source only, we must reserve judgement accordingly.

In Tgs. Neof., Ps.-J., MSS P and V (and ed. B) in the

midwives' report to Pharaoh, Exod 1:19, the midwives are presented
as having included in their excuse that the Hebrew women pray
קדם אבוהון דבשמיא, "before their Father in Heaven." Further on in
Exodus, at 15:2, the words in the mouths of the babes with reference to the Lord is דין הוא אבונן, "this is our Father"; thus MSS
V (N and ed. B).

There are further passages in the fragment targum tradition
in which the Father in Heaven is the One toward whom prayer is
directed. At Num 21:9, we note the targumists' concern that there
not be even a tiny hint of idolatry; for when the text speaks of
man's looking upon Moses' brazen serpent, the targumic addition
comes immediately: בצלו גב אבוי דבשמיא, "in prayer unto his Father
in Heaven"; then it can be concluded that the man lived. This is
observed in MSS P, V (N and ed. B).

The next passage in which the "Father in Heaven" is the One
toward whom prayer is directed should be carefully considered in
its context. Abraham is the host at his garden in Beersheba; he
gives passers-by food, drink and instruction until they are converted. His instruction to pray is presented as if a direct quotation: צלון קודם אבוכון דבשמיא, "pray before your Father who is
in heaven. . . " This is observed at Gen 21:33 of MSS V, P (N and
ed. B), and Tg. Neof. m.

At Exod 17:11, the fragment targum tradition takes special
interest in Moses' prayer over the battle with Amalek; however,
as an explanation of the word בצלו, "in prayer," only MS P adds
these words: לות אבוי דבשביא, "to his Father in Heaven." Since
this additional phrase stands in only one extant source, we must
reserve judgement accordingly.

Finally, we notice that Tg. Ps.-J. presents an addition to
Deut 28:32 in which we find the expression בצלו קדם אבוכון דבשמיא,
"in prayer before your Father who is in Heaven."

In a context which recalls the Temple in fantastic terms,
and is most probably from a time well after its fall, the writer
in ʾAbot R. Nat. 35 recalls the people's going to the temple thus:

. . . בזמן שישראל עולין להשתחוות לאביהן שבשמים "at the time when
Israel went up to worship their Father in Heaven. . . ."[38] The connection of "Father in Heaven" with the Second Temple period seems
to have survived.

The Mekilta specifically designates God as "Father in Heaven"
six times; twice as handed on anonymously; once in a saying attributed to R. Nathan, tanna of the second century; once each to
the contemporaries R. Joshua (a student of R. Yoḥanan b. Zakkai)
and R. Eleazar of Modi'im (colleague of R. Gamaliel II); and once
as the teaching of R. Yoḥanan b. Zakkai who flourished in Jerusalem
before 70 and afterward at Yavneh:[40]

. . . they lift up their eyes to their Father in Heaven.	מגביהים את עיניהם לאביהם שבשמים
The Israelites were beseeching their Father in Heaven, humbling themselves before Him, just as a son beseeches his father and a pupil humbles himself before his teacher. . .	היו ישראל מתחננין ומתגדרין לפני אביהן שבשמים כבן שהוא מתחנן לפמי אביו וכתלמיד שהוא מתגדר לפני רבו
. . . These wounds caused me to be beloved of my Father in Heaven.	אלו גרמו לי ליאהב לאבי שבשמיא
Rabbi Joshua says: When Amalek came to harm Israel, (removing) them from under the wings of their Father in Heaven. . . R. Eleazar of Modi'im says: When Amalek came to harm Israel, (removing) them from under the wings of their Father in Heaven. . .	רבי יהושע אומר כשבא עמלק להזיק את ישראל מתחת כנפי אביהם שבשמים. . . רבי אלעזר המודעי אומר כשבא עמלק להזיק לישראל מתחת כנפי אביהם שבשמים. . .
R. Yoḥanan b. Zakkai said... They who establish peace are stones. Here is the reasoning kal vahomer with respect to the stones of the altar which are no more:	רבן יוחמן בן זכאי אומר... אבנים שמטילות שלום והרי דברים קל וחומר ומה אם אבני המזבח שאינן

They do not see nor hear,	לא רואות ולא שומעות
nor speak, yet they serve	ולא מדברות
to establish peace between	על שהן מטילות שלום
Israel and their	בין ישראל
Father in Heaven –	לאביהם שבשמים
the Holy One, blessed be He,	אמר הקב"ה
said: 'Thou shalt lift up no	לא תניף עליהם ברזל
iron (tool) against them';	
he who established peace	המטיל שלום
between man and man,	בין איש לאיש
between husband and wife,	בין איש לאשתו
between city and city,	בין עיר לעיר
between nation and nation,	בין אומה לאומה
between family and family,	בין משפחה למשפחה
between government and gov't,	בין ממשלה לממשלה
how much more (should be	על אחת כמה וכמה
be protected) that harm	שלא תבואהו פורענות[45]
would not come to him.	

It is this last citation which is most significant. The tradition
found in it is also found in a parallel presentation in the
<u>Mekilta</u> <u>of</u> <u>R</u>. <u>Simeon</u> <u>b</u>. <u>Yohai</u>, thus it is found in both the trad-
itions of Ishmael and Aqiba.[46] In both, the core phrase, "be-
cause they serve to establish peace between Israel and their
Father in Heaven. . . " is to be found. We note the presence of
"the Holy One, blessed be He" coming immediately after "Father
in Heaven," a sign that two layers of tradition are involved.
(The passage is also recorded in <u>Sipra</u> 92d,[47] without the
second appellation.) It is reasonable to say that "the story is
certainly part of the corpus of Yoḥanan-sayings edited by the
time of Yavneh."[48] There is reason to suggest that the first
part of the pericope might not have been original with Yoḥanan
b. Zakkai, but an older saying he was using; that is, the first
member of the <u>kal</u> <u>vahomer</u>. Now, it is in the first member of
his argument that the old appellation, "Father in Heaven," occurs.
What is more significant for our purposes is the presence of the
appellation "Father in Heaven" in all three of the editions, thus
the likelihood of the currency of that appellation in Jerusalem
in the last days of the Second Temple.[49]

Later in the Yavneh period, R. Aqiba (student of Joshua
b. Hananiah, student of Yoḥanan b. Zakkai) worked. He is well

remembered for his use of the appellation "Father" for God.

"Father in Heaven" and penitence are linked in the following
Aqiba tradition:[50]

R. Aqiba said: Happy are   אמר רבי עקיבא אשריכם
ye, Israel, before whom ye   ישראל לפני מי אתם מיטהרים
cleanse yourselves; and   ומי מטהר אתכם
who cleanses you? Your   אביכם שבשמים
Father in Heaven.

Turning to Bar. Ta'anith 25b, we find a prayer for rain attributed
to R. Aqiba:[51]

'Our Father, Our King,   אבינו מלכנו
we have no King but Thee;   אין לנו מלך אלא אתה
Our Father, Our King,   אבינו מלכנו
for Thy sake have mercy   למענך.רחם עלינו
on us.' And rain fell.   וירדו גשמים

This is especially significant in that it could be said to confirm

the roots of the penitential liturgy Abinu Malkenu as very old;

R. Aqiba's works probably transmit a tradition which in his day

was specifically used to defy earthly rulers.[52] Here the address

"King" is set beside that of "Father"; this usage may stem from

periods of national stress such as the years 40-70 A.D.;[53] and

quite understandably, it would be popular again in the stress of

Aqiba's days, 77-135 A.D. (With the specification "Our King"

of course, the specification "in Heaven" was not required.)

In Sipra there are further instances of the appellation
"Father in Heaven," as examples:[54]

And Moses was (found) worthy to   זכה משה ליעשות שחיח
act as agent between Israel   בין ישראל
and their Father in Heaven.   ליעשות שליח

The man who does Torah and   אדם שעושה את התורה
does the will of his Father   ועושה רצון אביו שבשמים
who is in Heaven - the Place   . . . לא חס עליהן
will not exterminate him   המקום מלהעבירן
from the world. . .   . . . מן העולם.

the man who does not do   אדם שאינו עושה את התורה
Torah and does not do the   ואינו עושה רצון
will of his Father in Heaven   אביו שבשמיא
. . . it is written   .הכתוב מלהעבירו . . .
(He) will exterminate him   מן העולם
from the world.

The parallel of "doing Torah" with "doing the will of the Father in Heaven" is repeated in Sipre Deut 306:[55]

If a man does Torah and does the will of his Father in Heaven, behold he is like mankind on high. . . (if) he does not do Torah and does not the will of his Father in Heaven, behold, he is like mankind below.	אם עשה אדם תורא ועשה רצון אביו שבשמים הרי הוא כבריות של מעלה... לא עשה תורה ולא עשה רצון אביו שבשמים הרי הוא כבריות של מטה

Thus, both Sipra and Sipre Deuteronomy contain juxtaposition of "doing Torah" with "doing the will of the Father in Heaven"; this juxtaposition could be presumed to stem from traditions preceding Sipra and Sipre Deuteronomy.

The general impression we glean from Mekilta, Sipra and Sipre is that the appellation of God as "Father in Heaven" proceeds from a strand of tradition quite some time before their formal codification, and certainly long before their final redaction. The evidence seems to point fairly squarely toward the days before the fall of the Second Temple.

Thus the practice of calling God "Father" had originated in the Hebrew Bible, developed in the circles of traditional teaching that produced the Apocrypha and later the Amidah, as well as the targums and early midrashim. In the latter texts there is a marked preference for the more precise appellation "Father in Heaven."

The Appellation "Father" in Philo and Josephus

Quite frequently throughout his works, Philo simply uses the word πατήρ[56] for God. However, more frequently he uses the word πατήρ paired with the word ποιητής;[57] and this paired expression very often governs τῶν ὅλων,[58] or τῶν συμπάντων[59] or τοῦ παντός,[60] or πάντων,[61] or του κόσμου.[62] The word πατήρ is also paired with ἡγεμών, the paired expression governing πάντων[63] or συμπάντων[64] or τοῦ παντός[65] or τοῦ κόσμου[66] or τῶν ὅλων.[67] When we add to these examples the other occurrences of the name of πατήρ for God as it is found in further assorted name-pairs or phrases, the total come to over 190 instances. Thus terming God "Father" was not at all accidental for Philo, and he did develop some theology in which this term was integral.

In De Abrahamo 121-125, we have the clearest presentation of the meaning of the title "Father":

The Father of the Universe is central,	πατὴρ μὲν τῶν ὅλων ὁ μέσος,
Who in Sacred Scriptures (is) named Lord is called He Who is.	ὅς ἐν ταῖς ἱεραῖς γραφαῖς κυρίῳ ὀνόματι καλεῖται ὁ ὤν.

Here πατήρ is used for designating precisely what is designated by ὁ ὤν; and it is absolutely clear that the Tetragrammaton is to be called to mind. Elsewhere Philo shows his theological awareness of the matter in quoting LXX Exod 3:14: Ἐγώ εἰμι ὁ ὤν.[68] Philo goes on to say that the powers of this Existent One nearest Him are His creative and kingly powers, which are respectively desig- nated θεός and κύριος.[69] In this there is a three-ness about the One God, but logical priority is accorded ὁ ὤν, The Existent, πατήρ, Father, and ὁ εἷς, the One.[70] The designation θεός implies the aspects of making-power and the power of good works: ἡ ποιητικὴ δύναμις[71] and ἡ εὐεργετικὴ (δύναμις).[72] That the Three are One is expressed in De Vita Mosis ii, 100:

For, as He alone really IS, He is undoubtedly also the Maker, since He brought into being what was not, and He is in the nature of things King, since none could more justly govern what has been made than the Maker.	μόνος γὰρ πρὸς ἀλήθειαν ὢν καὶ ποιητής ἐστιν ἀψευδῶς ἐπειδὴ τὰ μὴ ὄντα ἤγαγεν εἰς τὸ εἶναι, καὶ βασιλεὺς φύσει, διότι τῶν γεγονότων οὐδεὶς ἂν ἄρχοι δικαιότερον τοῦ πεποιηκότος.

What is remarkable is that the logical locus of the appellation πατήρ is with ὁ ὤν and ὁ εἷς, and that it is a manner of desig- nating what is designated in Hebrew by the Tetragrammaton.

We observe Josephus' use of the term "Father" for God seven times in his works. He uses the term quite naturally, never stopping to explain its significance, in the way one would employ a commonplace expression. We must bear in mind the non-Jewish readership for whom Josephus was writing. He presents God as

πάντων πατήρ, "Father of all,"[74] or more fully, God who is the

Father of all the race of men: πατὴρ τοῦ παντὸς ἀνθρώπων γένους.[75]

Then God is termed πατὴρ καὶ δεσπότης, "Father and Ruler of all,[76]

but also specifically of the Hebrew race.[77] This universality and

particularity of God is brought together and elaborated in one

passage in Antiquities:[78]

. . . God. . .	... τὸν θεὸν...πατέρα τε
Father and Source of the	καὶ γένεσιν τῶν ὅλων. . .
universe. . . and Creator	καὶ δημιουργὸν ἀνθρωπίνων
of things human and divine	κὰι θείων... καὶ κηδεμόνα
. . . and Guardian of the	γένους τῶν ʹΕβραίων...
Hebrew race.	

The term πατήρ is one among the many terms for God in Josephus'

language; but being more the historian and apologist than the

theologian, his theology is not extensively worked out. The main

theological fact in Josephus' presentation is that there is but

one God,[79] ὁ ὤν, Whom the Jews had worshipped ἀπʹ ἀρχῆς, "from

the beginning."[80] It would be fair just to say that Josephus was

of the same theological mind as Philo; there is evidence for this

in a very similar range of epithets for God and in his short theo-

logical passage in Contra Apionem ii. 166-167.[81] There is reason

to believe that Josephus actually was acquainted with at least

Philo's De opificio mundi.[82] In conclusion, we can say that

Josephus presents us with less theology than does Philo, but not

contradictory to Philo; his references to God as Father are fewer

than Philo's, but all this is to be expected due to the genre of

his works.

Conclusion: the Appellation "Father" in the Sermon on the Mount in its NT Context

It is a fact, whether or not it is fortuitous, that Matthew

does not speak of God as "Father" in the first four chapters; he

begins to do so only in the Sermon on the Mount, at 5:16: οὕτως

λαμψάτω τὸ φῶς ὑμῶν ἔμπροσθεν τῶν ἀνθρώπων, ὅπως ἴδωσιν ὑμῶν τὰ

καλὰ ἔργα καὶ δοξάσωσιν τὸν πατέρα ὑμῶν τὸν ἐν τοῖς οὐρανοῖς, "Let your light so shine before men that they may see your good works and give glory to your Father who is in Heaven." The words τὸν πατέρα ὑμῶν τὸν ἐν τοῖς οὐρανοῖς, being the last words in the sentence, seem to carry the emphasis, and perhaps the emphasis for the passage, Matt 5:13-16.

When we ask what the pattern of recurrence of this phraseology might be in the various NT books, the results are thus: 13 times in Matthew of which 6 are in the Sermon on the Mount,[83] once in Mark,[84] and never elsewhere. The concept is so recurrent in the Sermon on the Mount that several times Matthew has used a stylistic variation for it: ὁ πατὴρ ὑμῶν ὁ οὐράνοις, "Heavenly Father."[85] When the phraseology of Matt 5:16 and this variation are taken together, the total is 20 times in the Gospel of Matthew, of which 10 are in the Sermon on the Mount.

Why is Matthew so markedly different from the other NT writers in this respect? One can only offer conjecture. We have seen some reference to God as "Father" in the Hebrew Bible, LXX, and Pseudepigrapha; and observed that apparently the phrase "Father in Heaven" had also gained popularity and had come into vogue in the circles which produced the targums and the early midrashim (especially Mekilta) in the few decades before the fall of the Second Temple. From this one might suggest that among NT writers, it was Matthew who knew this manner of speaking of God, and who chose to use this phraseology. Matthew's presentation of Jesus as using the term "Father in Heaven" so often in the Sermon on the Mount would then be tantamount to his saying that Jesus was a preacher conversant with the current expressions used for God the Father.

We must take note of the fact that, while Matthew uses "Father in Heaven" 6 times, and "Heavenly Father" 4 times in the Sermon on the Mount, he also uses the simpler "Father" 7 times.[86] This he does in common with other NT writers.[87] In our discussion of the theology of the Name of God, we were able to give some indication why the use of the term "Father" (amongst other terms for God) had grown in popularity during the period of heightened reverence for the Tetragrammaton. Since the relative fewness of the occurrences of the term "Father" for God in the Hebrew Bible and its notable prevalence in the NT are immediately observable,[88] the logical question is to ask what caused the great shift of emphasis. That "Father" is found in so many of the NT books leads us to be sure that its use belonged to the Christian tradition prior to the existence of these books.[89] And that Christian tradition had arisen from concurrent Jewish tradition.

We have observed that in haggadic additions in various targums at Gen 21:33, Exod 1:19, 17:11, Num 21:9 and Deut 28:32, the title "Father in Heaven" is used for the One toward whom prayer is directed. This has some significance; but the significance is heightened especially when we consider the passage located at Gen 21:33 (MSS P, V (N, ed. B) and Tg. Neof. m.) Abraham is the master and host; Abraham is the instructor who leads passers-by to conversion; Abraham instructs that prayer is to be addressed to the "Father in Heaven." The name of Abraham lends a real tone of authority to the instruction. In Matthew it is the name of Jesus which gives authority to the material in the Sermon on the Mount and gives authority to the form of prayer prescribed which begins Πάτερ ἡμῶν ὁ ἐν τοῖς οὐρανοῖς, "Our Father who art in Heaven."

The first word given by Matthew and Luke in Jesus' instruction on words for prayer is Πάτερ.[90] The expectation that a master would be precise in prayer formulation was part of the religious climate of the day; for we have reason to believe that, at the time, the Amidah was receiving some of its precisions due to the influence of the famous pupils of Hillel.[91] Also, we could refer to the formula for confession of sins in Sipra 80d (above p. 6) in which "ha-Shem" is in the prayer to be recited, but "YHWH" in the literary explanation. Further, we can presume that it was the prevailing reverence for the Tetragrammaton which caused several of the petitions of the Amidah to have "Father"

substituted for "YHWH."[92] We observe the precise way that Matthew
introduces his prayer formula with the imperative: οὕτως οὖν
προσεύχεσθε. . . Πάτερ (6:9); and Luke: λέγετε, Πάτερ(11:2). Thus
Πάτερ is the form of address intentionally intended for use. The
title "Father" was one standard substitute for YHWH before the fall
of the Second Temple, and Philo had specifically pointed out that
"Father" had reference to ὁ ὤν/YHWH. Hence we would be led to
suggest that Matthew and Luke knew quite well what appellation of
God they presented Jesus as specifying, and why the specification
was made, a currently normal form of reverence for the name of
YHWH.

Notes

[1]In the "sermon" chapters (5-7, 10, 13, 18, 23-25) of Matthew the name "Father" for God is used 29 times, 17 of which occur in chaps. 5-7. In the "narrative" chapters (11-12, 15, 16, 20, 26) the name is used only 14 times, and then only in words of Jesus. The title "Father" for God occurs for the final time in Matthew in the final verses, the Great Commission (28:18-20). These final verses have been seen as the key to the whole Gospel. Thus the importance of the term "Father" for God in Matthew may be quickly observed from its being used only in the words of Jesus; preponderantly in the weightier material, the sermons; and finally in the last verses, the recaptiulation of the whole book.

[2]The haggadic addition to Exod 3:14 in MSS V and P (and ed.B) דון דאמר לעלמא (MS P only) הוי והוי (מן שוריא) הוי והוי ועתיד למעמר ליה והוי. What we find in Tg. Neof. is similar to that in MS V; the text in Tg. Ps.-J. is: דחן דאמר הוא עלמא אמר והוה כולא.

[3]Tg. Ps.-J. Exod 3:14: אנא הוא דהויתי והוינא ועתיד לניהוי

[4]Jacob Z. Lauterbach, ed. Mekilta de-Rabbi Ishmael, vol. II (Philadelphia: Jewish Publication Society, 1933) 231. Cf. also ibid., 31.

[5]Tg. Ps.-J. and MS P do not include it; MS V (and ed. B) has it only at its third instance in the last clause; Tg. Neof. appears as if it had been under several influences, reading הוא as do Tg. Ps.-J. and MS P in the last clause but copying the אהיה אשר אהיה of the Hebrew text as does Tg. Onq.

[6]A. Marmorstein, The Old Rabbinic Doctrine of God. I. The Names & Attributes of God (London: Oxford University Press, 1927) 19. Marmorstein gives us a fair idea of what scholarship can discern about the history of the use and prohibition of the pronunciation of the Tetragrammaton, pp. 17-40. He summarizes the stages of that history (p. 27) as follows: "(1) After the death of Simon the use of the Name was discontinued; (2) in the time of the early Hasidim the old custom was re-estabilshed in the Temple and extended to ordinary greetings in order to counteract Hellenistic influence; (3) with the establishment of the synagogues a line was drawn between the service in the Temple and outside; and (4) the greetings and the pronunciation in the Temple by the Name were done בהבלעת, and not distinctly."

Consequent upon the care and thoughtfulness with respect to the Tetragrammaton, references to "the Name" multiplied, and would accent its importance. As examples, among the Cairo Genizeh manuscripts, note the following: In MS T-S. B8 (on Exod 6:3) and MS Heb. e 43 (on Exod 20:4), "my Name" becomes "my holy Name." In MS Heb. e 43 (Exod 20:24 and 20:25) "Me" becomes "my Name."

There is an interesting example in MS T-S. NS 189.2 at Exod 15:3 (to which the passage in MS 608 (E.N.A. 565) is similar): The Lord is a man of war;   יהוה איש מלחמה Exod 15:3 The Lord is His Name.   יהוה שמו

MS T-S. NS 189.2

The Lord is the Mighty One	יי ד י ברא
It is He who conducts your	הוא דעבד לכון
victorious battles for you.	בדרי נצחני גרביכון
The Lord is His Name;	יי שמיה
as His Name is (His) might -	כשמיה כן גבורת יה י הא
May His Name be blessed	שמיה מברך לעלמע עלמין
forever and ever.	

The final line is a more evolved expression, probably a later
stratum in the text. Another such exclamatory phrase is observed
in MS Heb. e 43.

Finally, there is mention of the "Name" in Or. 1080 and in
MS 605 (E.N.A. 2587) at Exod 17:15; in MS Or. 1074 at Deut 1:1;
and in MS Heb. e 43 at Exod 20:2.

[7]This degree of contrast is not preserved in Tg. Neof. where
we find v 15 to have been under the influence of v 16, having taken
from v 16 the root פרש "pronounce (distinctly)"; thus vv 15 and 16
become somewhat parallel in meaning in Tg. Neof.:

15. ... Any man who pronounces	גב ר גבר ארום
the Name of God in blasphemy	יפריש שמה דאלה
will receive (the punishment	בגדפין
of) his sins.	יקבל חובוי
16. And whoever pronounces	ומן די יפרש
the Name of the Lord in blas-	שמיה דייי בגדפין
phemy shall surely be put to	מתקטלה יתקטל
death; all the people of the	מרגם ירגמון יתיה
assembly will stone him.	כל עם כנשתה
Sojourners as well as natives,	כגיורייה כיציבייה
when one pronounces the Name	בפרשותיה שמה דאלהה
of God in blasphemy he shall	בגידופין
be killed.	יתקטל

[8]Fredericus Field, Origenis Hexaplorum, vol. I (Oxonii: Clarendoniano, 1891) 120.

[9]J. H. Weiss, ed. Sifra on Leviticus (1892; reprint: Vienna:
J. Schlossborg, 1946).

There is a passage in Mekilta (Lauterbach, Mekilta, vol. III,
48) which makes the same specific point: "And one that curseth his
father and his mother. With the tetragrammaton (בשם המפורש). You
interpret it to mean cursing by using the tetragrammaton (השם
מפורש). Perhaps it is not so, but it means cursing even by using
a substitute designation (בכיני). Scripture says: 'When he blasphemeth the Name (שם), he shall be put to death' (Lev 24:16).
There would be no purpose in saying 'When he blasphemeth the Name'
except to include the case of one cursing his father and mother who
is likewise not to be guilty unless he curses them with the tetragrammaton (בשם המפורש). - These are the words of R. Ahai the son
of Josiah."

[10]Thus Tg. Ps.-J. There are a few minor orthographical variations of the type one normally experiences among the sources in

26

question. Further, Tg. Neof. places לרשיעיה before היי להון; and
MS P omits the final word. The prepositional phrase בגידופין is
also found in Tg. Neof. at Lev 24:16, as opposed to the construction in Tg. Ps.-J. and Tg. Onq. at Lev 24:16. Questions of the
one passage having influenced the other could be debated.

[11]There are two texts (given anonymously) which reveal an un-
equivocal rabbinic attritude in ʾAbot R. Nat.12 and 39 (Solomon
Schechter, Aboth de Rabbi Nathan, corrected edn. [N.Y.: Philipp
Feldheim, 1967] 56 and 116):

And he who puts the crown (i.e.	ודאשתמש בתגא אדם
the Torah) to his own use shall	ואזיל ליה כיצד
utterly perish: What is that:	שכל המשתמש
whoever makes use of the Unpro-	בשם המפורש
nounceable Name has no share	אין לו חלק
in the world to come.	לעולם הבא
Five shall obtain no for-	המשה אין להם סליחה. . .
giveness. . . and whoever has	וכל מי שיש בידו
on his hands (the sin of)	חלול השם
profaning the Name.	

The wording of the texts cannot be dated; but no authority quoted
in ʾAbot de Rabbi Nathan is later than the Tannaitic period, and we
can suppose that these anonymous texts transmit traditions which do
not belong to the latest strata of ʾAbot de Rabbi Nathan. The
point is made with adamance and theological finesse: in the tradition of chap. 12, the penalty is not only death, but "no share in
the world to come"; in chap. 39, "no forgiveness" has a similar
impact. All in all, the tannaitic witness to the tradition of
strict malediction for use of the Tetragrammaton in sophisticated
forms corroborates confirmation of pre-tannaitic roots for this
tradition in its simpler forms.

[12]Mos. ii. 204 and 206.

[13]
                                            Tg. Onq.
וישוון ית ברכת שמי על בני ישראל ואנא אבריכינון
                                            Tg. Neof.
וישוך ית שמי ית ממרי על בני ישראל ואנה במ(י)מרי אברך יתהון
When the several targumic witnesses to the verse are taken together,
one is tempted to make suggestions. (1) What we find in Tg. Ps.-J.
on the one hand and Tg. Neof. and MS P on the other hand were
parallel traditions - diverging in the first clause but having
במימר of the second in common. (2) Tg. Onq., under the constraint
of the fact that the verse was well known, is worded like Ps.-J. in
the first clause, but ventured a lesser modification eliminating
the במימר in the second clause in the spirit peculiar to Tg. Onq.
of word-by-word conformity to the Hebrew as much as possible.

[14]H. S. Horovitz, ed. Siphre d'be Rab, Vol. I (Corpus Tannaiticum Sectio Tertia; Lipsiae: Gustav Fock, 1917; reprint:
Jerusalem: Wahrmann Books, 1966) 48.

[15]J. H. Weiss, Sipra, 80d.

[16] In haggadic additions at Gen 4:15; Exod 2:20, 4:20, 14:21; 32:25; Lev 16:21, 24:11; Deut 9:19. There are some variations on this adjective pair, examples (1) with the introduction of the adjective דחילא, "fearful" at Deut 28:58 and 9:19; (2) with the introduction of the adjective קדישא, "holy" at Exod 33:4 and Num 31:8.

In response to the שמע in the targums at Deut 6:4, we find an acclamation which employs יקריה, "glorious" in Tg. Ps.-J., but MS N (and ed. B) employs רבא, "great":

Blessed be His Glorious	Tg. Ps.-J.
Name for ever and ever.	בריך שום יקריה לעלמי עלמין

Blessed be His Great	MS N (and ed. B.)
Name for ever.	יהא שמיה רבא מברך לעלם

See note 6 (above) for comment on such exclamatory phrases.

Note also רב שמך, "Your Name is Great," MS Antonin Ebr. III B at Exod 15:11; and שמי בייקרא, "Glorious Name," MS Heb e 43 at Lev 22:32.

[17] Tg. Neof. Exod 32:25 and 33:6.

[18] Lauterbach, Mekilta, vol II, 287.

[19] Eduard Lohse, Die Texte aus Qumran (München: Kösel, 1971) 24; the translation is that of G. Vermes, The Dead Sea Scrolls in English (Harmondsworth: Penguin, 1968) 83.

[20] Die Texte aus Qumran, 96.

[21] Lauterbach, Mekilta, vol. III, 122-123. Cf. also vol. III, 123: "Just as here the oath is by the Tetragrammaton (ה"יא), so also there the oath must be by the Tetragrammaton (ה"יא)."

[22] MT: תשא; Tg. Neof. יסב. MS 605 (E.N.A. 2587) on Exod 20:2 reads לא תשתבע, like Tg. Ps.-J.

[23] Spec. Leg. iv. 40.

[24] Martin Hengel, Judaism and Hellenism: Studies in their Encounter in Palestine during the Early Hellenistic Period, vol. I (Philadelphia: Fortress, 1974) 131.

[25] Jacob Z. Lauterbach, The Pharisees and Their Teachings (N.Y. Bloch, 1930) 49-50. Here Lauterbach acknowledges his dependence upon Marmorstein, The Old Rabbinic Doctrine of God. I, The Names and Attributes of God. Lauterbach gives "midat ha-din" as the interpretation of "Elohim," the prevailing view of the later rabbis. There is some evidence that "midat ha-din" had been associated with "YHWH" earlier. Cf. especially Philo. This is discussed in A. Marmorstein, The Old Rabbinic Doctrine of God, 48-49.

[26] There is also a comparison of God with a father at Wis 11:10.

[27] According to the Hebrew; otherwise according to the LXX. Joachim Jeremias ("Abba" in Abba: Studien zur neutestamentlichen

Theologie und Zeitgeschichte, Gottingen, 1966, p. 27, n. 51)
thinks that the Hebrew might show some dependence on Ps 89:27,
and the Greek might have been influenced by Ps 110:1.

[28]Jean Carmignac, Recherches sur le "Notre Père" (Paris:
Editions Letouzey & Ané, 1969) 58-60.

[29]Jubilees dates from the second century B.C. Cf. James H.
Charlesworth, The Pseudepigrapha and Modern Research (Missoula,
Montana: Scholars Press, 1976) 143. The translation we have
given takes into account that of Jean Carmignac, Recherches, 59.

[30]Of the Sibylline Oracles, Book III is the oldest, a com-
posite drawn from various sources. There is general agreement
"that the corpus of the book dates from the middle of the second
century B.C." Cf. Charlesworth, The Pseudepigrapha, 185.
     God is termed "Father" also in 3 Macc 3:21; 5:7; 6:3 and 8.
One can only posit a range of dating for this work: "there is
wide agreement today that 3 Maccabees was composed in the first
century B.C. or A.D. in Egypt, probably in Alexandria, in Greek."
Cf. Charlesworth, The Pseudepigrapha, 149. We are reminded of the
florid Greek style of the work, hence the possibility that πατήρ
could be Greek rhetoric as well as Jewish piety. Thus George Foot
Moore, Judaism in the First Centuries of the Christian Era; The
Age of the Tannaim. Vol. II (Cambridge, Mass.: Harvard University
Press, 1927) 202, n.7.
     The use of the word "Father" for God appears in T. Levi 18:6-8
and T. Juda 24:2-3; however these passages would appear to be
Christian additions made under the influence of the literary tradition of Jesus' baptism. Cf. James H. Charlesworth, "Christian
and Jewish Self-Definition in Light of the Christian Additions to
the Apocryphal Writings,"(Unpub. paper, 1979) 17-18. Of the same
opinion, Joachim Jeremias, "Abba," p. 19, n.5.

[31]Lohse, Die Texte aus Qumran, 148.

[32]The origin of the prayer seems to have been with the men of
the Great Synagogue in the second century B.C.; the final redaction
under Gamaliel II, in the mid-second century A.D. Cf. Louis
Finkelstein, "The Development of the Amidah," JQR n.s. 16, 1925/26,
2 (reprinted in Pharisaism in the Making: Selected Essays, N.Y.:
KTAV, 1972, 246). Among the criteria which Finkelstein has used in
fixing the relative dates of the paragraphs of the Amidah are the
uses of the Tetragrammaton, and of substitute designations. In this
context, his conclusion as to the use of the word Abinu is as follows: "Since we know that the earlier paragraphs use as the term of
address the words אלהינו ה' and the later ones omit it entirely, it
seems reasonable to assume that those in which the word Abinu, "our
Father," is used represent a transitional stage. They date from a
time when objection to the use of the Tetragrammaton had developed,
but people still felt the need of some word to take its place." Cf.
ibid., 11; in Pharisaism in the Making, 255.

[33]Ibid., 10; in Pharisaism in the Making, 254.

[34]Bonsirven, acknowledging dependence on Dalman, presents his "original" reconstructed Palestinian Amidah; it has Abinu only in section 6. Evidently he held the replacement to have taken place only in sections 4 and 5. Cf. Joseph Bonsirven, Textes Rabbiniques des deux premiers siècles chrétiens pour servir à l'intelligence du Nouveau Testament (Roma: Pontificio Istituto Biblico, 1955) 2.

[35]The form אבוכון in Tg. Ps.-J., MSS V, p (N and ed. B); however Tg. Onq. and Tg. Neof. show alignment with the MT, אבוך, the latter probably due to the influence of the former.

[36]For discussion of the text, cf. Martin McNamara, The New Testament and the Palestinian Targum to the Pentateuch (Rome: Pontifical Biblical Institute, 1966) 133-138.

[37]The translation is that of Martin McNamara, Targum and Testament: Aramaic Paraphrases of the Hebrew Bible: A Light on the New Testament (Grand Rapids, Mich.: Eerdmans, 1972) 119.

[38]Schechter, Aboth de Rabbi Nathan, 106.

[39]In the Mekilta, God is termed "Father" and Israel "son"; cf. Lauterbach, Mekilta, vol. I, 8-9.

[40]Jacob Neusner, Development of a Legend: Studies on the Traditions Concerning Yoḥanan ben Zakkai (Leiden: Brill, 1970)1-11.

[41]Lauterbach, Mekilta, vol. I, 18-19.

[42]Ibid., vol. II, 93.

[43]Ibid., vol. II, 247. This is attributed to R. Nathan, c. 160 A.D.

[44]Ibid., vol. II, 158.

[45]Ibid., vol. II, 290.

[46]Neusner, Development, 24.

[47]Weiss, Sifra 92d.
(The stones of the altar)   שמטילות שלום
which introduce peace between   בין ישראל
Israel and their Father in   לאביהן שבשמים
Heaven.

[48]Neusner, Development, 28.

[49]It seems to have been held that the expression "Father in Heaven" was characteristic of Yoḥanan b. Zakkai; this is borne out in two sources of the Merkavah tradition. In t. Hag. 2:1-2 and y. Hag. 2:1 (i.e. two of the four sources of the tradition) the words "Father (who is) in heaven" are presented in the mouth of Yoḥanan b. Zakkai in his blessing of his disciple R. Eleazar b. ʾArakh. Cf. Jacob Neusner, "The Development of the Merkavah Tradition," JSJ 2, 1971, 149-160.

[50]Yoma 8:9. Philip Blackman, ed. Mishnayoth Vol III: Order

Moed, 2nd edn. (New York: Judaica Press, 1963) 312. Cf. A.
Büchler, Studies in Sin and Atonement in the Rabbinic Literature
of the First Century (London: Oxford University Press, 1928) 352-
353.

[51]Bar. Ta'anith 25b; cf. also ibid. 32b. For discussion, cf.
A. Büchler, Studies in Sin and Atonement, 43.

[52]Kaufmann Kohler, "Abinu Malkenu," The Jewish Encyclopedia
Vol. I (New York-London: Funk & Wagnalls, 1901) 85.

[53]Finkelstein, "The Development of the Amidah," 16; in
Pharisaism in the Making, 260.

[54]J. H. Weiss, Sipra 112c and 92d, passages given anonymously.
For further examples see 89c and 93d ("my Father").

[55]Louis Finkelstien, ed. Siphre ad Deuteronomium (Corpus
Tannaiticum Sectio Tertia; Berlin: Jüdischer Kulturbund, 1939;
reprint: N.Y.: Jewish Theological Seminary of America, 1969) 341.
The teaching is given under the name of R. Simai who dates
probably at the end of the second century A.D. The same expression
"the will of thy Father in Heaven" is found in a saying in ꞌAbot
5:20, attributed to R. Yuda b. Tema, also at the end of the second
century A.D.

[56]This is used in many of Philo's works. (In the following
notes we shall use the abbreviations for Philo's works which are
given in Philo, The Loeb Classical Library, Vol. I, xxiii-xxiv.)
Op. 46, 56, 89; L.A. ii. 67; Cher. 23, 106; Sac. 42; Post. 136,
142; Gig. 12; Deus 31, 47; Plant. 9; Conf. 41, 63 (three times)
103; Mig. 31, 194; Her. 119; Fug. 62, 114; Mut. 29, 129; Som.
i. 141, 181, 190; Abr. 207; Mos. ii. 192, 210, 262, 288; Spec. i.
57; ii. 59, iii. 189; Praem. 166 (twice); Cont. 68; De Providentia 6. Found alone or in combination with other appellations of
God: Questions and Answers on Genesis, over 50 times; Questions
and Answers on Exodus, over 15 times.

[57]Op. 7, 10, 12, 77; Her. 198; Mos. ii. 256; Spec. iii. 189
199; iv. 180; once we find the three appellations of God together
πατήρ and ποιητής and ἡγεμών, Spec. i, 34.

[58]Conf. 144; Her. 236; Fug. 84, 177; Abr. 9; Jos. 158;
Decal. 64, 105; Spec. ii. 256, iii. 178; Virt. 34, 65; Praem.
24; Cont. 90; Aet. 15.

[59]Abr. 58; Spec. ii. 165; Praem. 32.

[60]Post. 175; Decal. 51.

[61]Virt. 77.

[62]Mos. ii. 48; De Legatione ad Gaium 115. In this latter
work, 1. 3, the word πατήρ is paired with βασιλεύς; the combination is also found in Op. 144, and God is simply termed "King" in
Op. 71, 88.

[63]Op. 135.

[64]Deus 19; Som. i. 73; Spec. i. 32.

[65]Ebr. 131; Mos. ii. 88.

[66]Decal. 90.

[67]Spec. ii. 6. Other completing genitive phrases after the πατήρ-ἡγεμών combination: Her. 205; Mut. 45.

[68]Mos. i. 75.

[69]See also Som. i. 163 where the gracious and powerful in God is denoted θεός, and the kingly is denoted κύριος.

[70]That which the term ὁ εἷς designates is the same as that which the term ὁ ὢν designates, cf. Abr. 125.

[71]Cf. also Mos. ii. 99.

[72]Abr. 124 and 125.

[73]Cf. also Mos. ii. 99.

[74]In the following notes we shall use the abbreviations for Josephus' works which are given in Josephus, The Loeb Classical Library, Vol. I, xx.
A. II. 152: ὑπὸ τοῦ θεοῦ τοῦ πάντων πατρός.
A. I. 230: . . . θεῷ τῷ πάντων πατρί
B. III. 375: ὁ δὲ τούτον πατηρ θεός. . .
        (i.e. God, the Father of both the good and evil people)

[75]A. IV. 262: καὶ αὐτὸς πατὴρ τοῦ παντὸς ἀνθρώπων γένους ἐστί.

[76]A. I. 20: πάντων πατήρ τε καὶ δεσπότης ὁ θεός.

[77]A. V. 93: ὁ θεός, πατὴρ καὶ δεσπότης τοῦ Ἑβραίων γένους.

[78]A. VII. 380.

[79]A. V. 112; also A. I. 155: θεὸν . . . δημιουργὸν τῶν ὅλων ἕνα. The oneness is urged as reflected in the one Hebrew race and the one temple: A. IV. 201: θεὸς γὰρ εἷς καὶ τὸ Ἑβραίων γένος ἕν, and Ap. II. 193: Εἷς ναὸς ἑνὸς θεοῦ, φίλον γὰρ ἀεὶ παντὶ τὸ ὅμοιον κοινὸς ἁπάντων κοινοῦ θεοῦ ἁπάντων.

[80]A. VIII. 350.

[81]In Ap. II. 166-167, God is viewed as ἕνα, "One," ἀγένητον, "Uncreated/Unbegotten," πρὸς τὸν ἀίδον χρόνον ἀναλλοίωτον, "Immutable to all eternaity," πάσης ἰδέας θνητῆς κάλλει διαφέροντα, "in beauty surpassing all mortal thought," and δυνάμει μέν ἡμῖν γνώριμον, "made known to us by His power," although δὲ κατ' οὐσίαν ἐστὶν ἄγνωστον, "in essence is unknowable."

[82]H. St. J. Thackeray's footnote "b", p. 11 to Antiquities Book I (Josephus, The Loeb Classical Library, Vol. IV); also ibid. footnotes "a", p. 12 and "d", p. 15.)

[83]Matt 5:16, 45; 6:1,9; 7:11, 21; also in Matt at 10:32, 33; 12:50; 16:17; 18:10; 14:19.

[84]Mark 11:25.

[85]Matt 5:48; 6:14, 26, 32; also Matt 15:13; 18:35; 23:9. The adjective οὐράνιος modifies other words once in Luke and once in Acts. Never outside Matthew does it modify any term for the Divinity.

[86]Matt 6:4, 6 twice, 8, 15, 18 twice. In the rest of Matthew: 10:20, 29; 11:25, 26, 27 three times; 13:43; 16:27; 20:23; 24:36; 25:34, 41; 26:29, 39, 42, 53; 28:19.

[87]It is found in every book of the NT except III John.

[88]Hebrew Bible and Apocrypha, less than twenty times; New Testament, two hundred and thirty eight times.

[89]This is analogous to the working hypothesis of C. H. Dodd in his According to the Scriptures: the Substructure of New Testament Theology (London: Collins, 1952) 30.

[90]Matt 6:9 in the course of the teachings of the Sermon on the Mount; par. Luke 11:2 when the disciples specifically solicited such instruction.

[91]That is, beginning about 10-20 A.D. Cf. Louis Finkelstein, "The Development of the Amidah," 13.

[92]Above, p. 12, also note 32.

CHAPTER II
THE IMITATIO DEI AND THE THEME OF PERFECTION

For the first century man of Palestine who learned his Scriptures in the climate of the exegetical methods of the targums and
developing midrashic traditions, the concept of imitatio Dei was
expressed in a variety of ways. The Pentateuch contains the roots
of the concept; it was developed in the haggadah of the targums
and early midrashim. Philo returned to this again and again
throughout his writings; he handled the imitatio Dei both in the
Greek and Hebrew thought patterns. One of the lesser themes in
the general ambiance of imitatio Dei centres on the word "perfect."
Therefore first we must review the general theme of imitatio Dei
in the Hebrew Pentateuch, the Pentateuch targum traditions and
other early Jewish tradition, then we can turn to the specific
theme of perfection in the same sources.

The text which stands out most is Tg. Neof. Deut 18:13: "My
people, sons of Israel, be ye perfect in good work as the Lord
your God." In the understanding of this text it is logical to
employ Deut 32:4: "the Rock (i.e. God), His work is perfect."
The implications for the exegesis of Matt 5:48 are striking; but
for the sake of a sound understanding, corroboration of further
material from early Jewish tradition and the early Church ought to
be sought. Such material can be found, and sufficient examples
will be presented in the course of this study.

The General Theme of Imitatio Dei

in the Hebrew Pentateuch, Targums of the Pentateuch

and other Early Jewish Tradition

The main Biblical sources for the theology of the imitatio
Dei are Lev 19:2, Lev 26:12, Exod 18:20, Deut 10:12, 11:22 and
26:17. Lev 19:2 is the leading text:

Be ye holy, as I the Lord   קדשים תהיו
your God am holy.   כי קדוש אנא יהוה אלהיכם:

It is a question of being godlike in actions; two very plain
examples: loving the sojourner (Deut 10:18-19) and keeping the
Sabbath rest (Exod 20:10-11).

This idea of God's teaching his people by concrete example was
deduced from several of the Pentateuchal narratives and formed
into a haggadah which has been preserved in the fragment targum
tradition, MSS V, P (N and ed. B) and Tg. Neof. at Gen 35:9, also
in Tg. Ps.-J. at Deut 34:6. Rather than describing this material,
we offer translations of it from MS V and Tg. Ps.-J.:

> MS V. God of the world. May his name be blessed
> forever and ever. You have taught us fitting precepts
> and pleasing statutes.
>   You have taught us the blessing of the bridegroom
> and the bride from Adam and his partner. As it is
> explicitly written; And the Word of the Lord blessed
> them and the Word of the Lord said to them: be
> strong and multiply and fill the earth and subdue it.
> You have taught us to visit the afflicted from our
> father Abraham, the righteous one, when You were
> revealed to him in the Plain of the Vision, and
> commanded him to circumcise his foreskin, and he
> sat in the door of his tent in the heat of the day.
> As it is explicitly written, and it says, And the
> Word of the Lord was revealed to him in the Plain of
> the Vision. And again, You have taught us to bless
> those who mourn, from our father Jacob, the righteous
> one, when You were revealed to him when he was coming
> from Padan Aram when the way of the world (death)
> happened to Deborah, the nurse of Rebekah his mother.
> And Rachel died "to his sorrow" on the journey, and
> Jacob our father sat screaming and wailing and
> lamenting and crying for her. And You, Master of
> all the world, the Lord, in the perfection of Your

good mercy, were revealed to him, and comforted him
and blessed him, and blessed him with the mourners'
blessing on (the death of) his mother. For it is
explicitly written and it says, And the Word of the
Lord was revealed to Jacob a second time on his
coming from Padan Aram and He blessed him.

Tg. Ps.-J. Blessed be the name of the Lord of the
world who has taught us his straight way.
He has taught us to clothe the naked as he clothed
    Adam and Eve.
He has taught us to unite the bride and the groom
    as He united Eve with Adam.
He has taught us to visit the sick as He revealed
    Himself in a vision of the Word to Abraham when
    he was ill from the circumcision.
He has taught us to console mourners, as He revealed
    Himself again to Jacob when he returned from Padan
    the place where his mother died.
He has taught us to feed the poor as He sent the sons
    of Israel bread from heaven.
He has taught us to bury the dead from (what He did
    for) Moses, for He revealed Himself to him in His
    Word and with Him the companies of ministering
    angels. . . and buried him in the valley opposite
    Beth Peor. . .

From style and content, it would appear that MSS V, P (N and ed.
B) and Tg. Neof. on the one hand, and Tg. Ps.-J. on the other
hand, give witness to two polished strands of the same tradition.
We are led to believe that the targums are presenting an interpolated ancient discourse for the following reasons: (1) the
style and content show sufficient similarity and yet variation;
(2) all the sources introduce the material by using an obviously
"introductory" preface to the material, [1] MSS V, P (N and ed. B)
agreeing, but Tgs. Ps.-J. and Neof. showing individuality;
(3) the discourse is not located at the same place in all the
extant targums; (4) we see four of the same works of mercy
juxtaposed in Sir 7:32-35 (which is held to have been composed
sometime between 190 and 175 B.C.[2]). In Sirach, since there is
neither indication of their derivation from the Pentateuchal
narratives nor any explicit indication of their lying within the
theme of imitatio Dei, we might well conclude that this is a

summary of well-known material.[3] Thus we have reasons to hold
that we have an example of the idea of the imitatio Dei in concrete and specific actions spelled out in an ancient and traditional haggadah, a haggadah derived in a clear and simple way
from the narrations in the Pentateuch, yet having received the
polish of time in the targumic texts.

In the course of time, it was inevitable that a popular
haggadah would be rewritten in various circumstances.[4] Soṭah 14a
presents four works: clothing the naked, visiting the sick, comforting the mourners and burying the dead (as in Sirach); it
juxtaposes them with Pentateuchal citations; but it associates
the comforting of mourners with God's blessing of Isaac after
Abraham's death - and in this differs from all the other sources.
Soṭah 14a uses "the Holy One, blessed be He" in naming God; in
this we have another confirmation that the passage was a re-
writing of the haggadah later than the targums in which this
expression is not a characteristic. Soṭah 14a does stress that
the works of mercy in imitation of God are offered for the purpose of exegeting passages on "walking (הלך) after the Lord your
God" (for example, Deut 13:5); but this was no new idea.

Deut 10:12, 11:22, 19:9, 26:17, and Exod 18:20 all speak of
walking (הלך) in the ways of God; Lev 26:12 also features the
verb הלך. In subsequent sources, each of these passages would
carry some comment having a bearing on the topic under
discussion.

The MT for Deut 10:12 and 11:22 has ללכת בכל דרכיו, "to walk
in all His ways" (19:9, 26:17: וללכת בדרכיו). Tgs. Onq., Ps.-J.,
and Neof. interpret 10:12 and 11:22 as: ולמהך בכל אורחן[5]
דתקנן קדמוי, "to walk in all the right/straight ways before Him"
(19:9 and 26:17: ולמהך באורחן דתקמן קדמוי). Tgs. Onq., Ps.-J.,
and Neof. are thus consistent in these four passages (and no
other targumic passages in Deuteronomy carry this phraseology).
Thus these four passages are linked, and show that הלך in this
context requires a particular exegesis.

In Tg. Ps.-J. Exod 18:20 there is a pointer in the direction
of the works of mercy as the exegesis of הלך. For the words of
the MT את הדרך ילכובה, "the way in which they shall walk," Tg.
Ps.-J. substitutes:

. . . the prayers they	ית צלותא דיצלון בבית
should pray in their	כנישתהון וית אורחא דיפקדון
synagogues, the way	למריעין ודיהכון למיקבור מיתייא
of visiting the sick	ולמיגמול בה חיסדא
and how to bury the dead	
and to be charitable therein. . .	

Continuing Exod 18:20, for the words of the MT ואת המעשה אשר
יעשון, "and the things that they shall do," Tg. Ps.-J. has:

and the doing of the line	וית עובדא דשורת דינא
of justice, and that they	ודיעבדון מלגוו
should punish the evildoers.	לשורתא לרשיעין

There is a parallel for this material in Mekilta on Exod 18:20
attributed to rabbis who lived at the end of the first century
A.D. Here one has the impression of a summary of the whole law
and the whole halakah:[6]

And Shalt Show Them the Way,	והודעת להם את הדרך וגו'
etc., meaning the study of	זה תלמוד תורה
Torah; And the Work that	ואת המעשה אשר יעשון
they Must Do, meaning good	זה מעשה הטוב
deeds - these are the words	דברי רבי יהושע
of R. Joshua. R. Eleazar	רבי אלעזר המודעי אומר
of Modi'im says: And Shalt	והודעת להם
Show Them, means show them	הודע להם חייהם
how to live; The Way, refers	את הדרך
to visiting the sick; They	זה בקור חולים
must walk, refers to burying	אשר ילכו
the dead; In, refers to	זו קבורת מתים
bestowal of kindnesses; And	בה זו גמילות חסדים
the Work, meaning along the	ואת המעשה
line of strict justice; That	זו שורת הדין
They Must Do, beyond the line	אשר יעשון
of strict justice.	זה לפנים משורת הדין

In the lines presented in the MT as an oracle of Balaam, Num 23:
19f., God is contrasted with the common people. The opening
words, לא איש אל, "God is not man. . . " apparently needed interpretation; all of the targumic versions[7] have a poetic passage
at Num 23:19 which employs the comparative כ in the first line,

38

Tg. Onq. for example, לא כמלי בני אנשא מימר אלהא, "not as the
words of the sons of man (is) the word of God." In castigating
the contrary wickedness, the passage promotes the morality of
being like (כ) God. The passage as it reads in MS V:

Not as the word of the sons	לא]כ[ממי בני אינשא
of man is the word of the	הות מימרי דאלהא חייא
Living God; nor as the works	ולא כעובדיהון
of the sons of men (are)	דבנא אינש
the works of God.	עובדוי אלהא
The sons of men say	בני אינשא אמרין
but do not do,	ולא עבדין
decree but do not fulfill;	גזרין ולא מקיימין
and they retract and deny	וחזרין וכפרי המיליהון
their words.	ברם אלהא אמר ועבד
But God says and does,	גזר ומקיים
decrees and fulfills,	וגזירתוהי קיימין
and His decrees are	עד. . . לעלם
established for...ever.	

The morality presented here is basic; that the deeds must follow
upon the word is stressed in Deuteronomy chaps. 5 and 6 - the
Commandments must be heard and done (esp. Deut 5:1, 27, 31-33;
6:1, 3, 25). The imitatio Dei is thorough-going, first in the
basic harmony of the deeds with the word, then in the whole
range of good deeds from prayer and Torah-study to the various
works of mercy.

The imitatio Dei, besides being spelled out in specific
actions, is also expressed in exhortations to imitate the
attributes of God.[9] An interpolated haggadah at Tg. Ps.-J. Lev
22:28 reads in part:[10]

My people, children of Israel	עמי בני ישרשל
as I am merciful in heaven	היכמא דאנא רחמן בשמיא
so shall you be merciful	כן תהוון רחמנין בארעא
on earth.	

The root רחם is to be remembered. Two of the texts primary to the
theme of imitatio Dei, Deut 11:22 and 10:12, speak of the duty of
loving (אהב) God; it is to be observed that in both Tg. Ps.-J.
and Tg. Neof.,[11] the verb רחם is used to render אהב at both places;
the love-mercy of God is proposed for imitation.

There is further corroboration of this theme of imitation of

the attributes of God in the Tannaitic midrashim. The Mekilta on
Exod 15:2 presents an apophthegm-like teaching of Abba Saul[12]
which fits but loosely into its context:[13]

Abba Saul says: O be like Him!	אבא שאול אומר
Just as He is gracious and	נא דמה לו
merciful, so be thou	מה הוא חנון ורחום
gracious and merciful.	אף אתה תהא חנון ורחום

Commenting of Deut 11:22, there is an anonymous tannaitic[14]
haggadah in Sipre Deut 49:[15]

'The Lord is a God of mercy and graciousness.'[16]	ה' אל רחום וחנון
As it is said: 'And it shall come to pass that all who are called by the name of the Lord will be saved.' And how is it	ואומר והיה כל אשר יקרא בשם ה' ימלט
possible for a man to be called by the name of the Place? But (i.e. it	וכי היאך איפשר לו לאדם לקרא בשמו של מקום
may be derived that) the Place is called merciful so be thou merciful. The Holy One, blessed be He, is called gracious so be thou gracious - that is to say that the Lord is gracious and merciful, etc... The Place is righteous... so be thou righteous. The Place is called pious... so be thou pious. Wherefore it is said, 'And it shall come to pass that he who is called by the name of the[17] Lord shall be saved...'	אלא נקרא המקום רחום אף אתה היה רחום הקדוש ברוך הוא נקרא חנון אף אתה היה חנון שנאמר חנון ורחום ה'... נקרא המקום צדיק ... אף אתה היה צדיק נקרא המקום חסיד ... אף אתה היה חסיד לכך נאמר והיה כל אשר יקרא בשם ה' ימלט

The citation from Joel is situated almost at the beginning of the
passage and almost at the end (a hint of inclusio); and thus its
content is stressed as a motivation for the imitation of the
attributes of God: to be named as God is named and be saved.
The hortatory character of the haggadah is also underscored.

At this point we can return to the leading text, Lev 19:1-2.
These verses and Lev 20:26 have a certain relationship, the latter
reflecting the former; this has long been recognized and chaps.

19-20 accepted as forming a unit,[18] this we see, for example, in

Sipra 86c-93d which treats them as a unit closing with the words

חסלת פרשת קדושים, "the end of parasa qedosim."[19] Lev 20:26 reads:

You shall be holy to me;	והייתם לי קדשים
for I the Lord am holy,	כי קדוש אני יהוה
and have separated you	ואבדל אתכם מן העמים
from the peoples that	להיות לי:
you should be mine.	

The significance of being separated from the peoples is under-

stood in Sipra 93d as separated from the peoples who do not keep

the statutes and ordinances of the Lord but have other customs;

consequently, separation from transgression:[20]

I have separated you from	ואבדיל אתכם מן העמים
the peoples to be mine. He	להיות לי
(Israel) finds himself	נמצא פורש מן העבירה
separated from transgression	ומקבל עליו מלכות שמים
and he receives upon himself	
(i.e. accepts his duties with	
respect to) the kingdom of	
heaven.	

Lev 20:26 and its exegesis are reflected in the exegesis of Lev

19:1-2, Sipra 86c:[21]

Be ye holy. To be	קדושים תהיו.
understood as "separated"	מלמד שהפרשה...
... Abba Saul said: What	אבא שאול אומר
is the duty of the king's	פמליא למלך
retinue? To follow in the	ומה עליה להיות
footsteps of the king (i.e.	מחקה למלך
to imitate his customs).	

There is no targumic explanation of Lev 19:2[22] but Tg. Neof. does

add a few words to emphasize the verse, כדן אמר ייי אלהכון, "thus

says the Lord your God," a formula implying that the words are

sent from a sovereign.

Thus Lev 19:1-2 is understood to present the exclusive

sovereignty of God and demand the separation necessary to acknow-

ledge that exclusive sovereignty in life according to the Law; and

in no other customs; the King is the exemplar for the people of

his kingdom.

Next, we turn to Lev 26:12 which reads:

And I will walk among you,	והתהלכתע בתוככם
and I will be your God and	והייתי לכם לאלהים
you shall be my people.	ואתם תהיו לי לעם:

The pertinent haggadah in Sipra 111ab uses a slight play on words.
The Hebrew התהלכתי, "I will walk" has been reflected in שיצא
לטייל, "who went out to walk about"; but יצא ב- is also an expression meaning to "be like." This expression occurs further on
in the text. Thus the similarity to God (one of the expressions
in the general ambiance of imitatio Dei) is attached to the
verb הלך:

> A parable is told: to what is the matter likened?
> To a king who went out to walk about (שיצא לטייל)
> with his farmer into a paradise. And the farmer
> hid from him. The king said to the farmer, 'what
> is the matter with you that you hide from me?'
> Behold I am like you (הריני כיוצא בך).' The Holy
> One, blessed be He, said to the righteous ones
> (מדיקים), 'what is the matter with you that you
> tremble before me?' Similarly in the future, the
> Holy One, blessed be He, will walk about with the
> righteous ones in the Garden of Eden in the time
> to come. And the righteous ones will see Him and
> tremble before Him – Behold I am like you
> (הריני כיוצא בכם). 23

In this passage of Sipra, God is likened to man rather than vice-
versa; this feature, a sort of imitatio hominis, though not so
frequent[24] as expressions of imitatio Dei, could be considered its
logical correlative. The allusions to Genesis suggest that by the
time this passage was written, it was taken for granted that the
creation in God's image and likeness was understood as figuring
in the theme of imitatio Dei. In the second part of the passage,
the people addressed are the צדיקים; it is specifically the
צדיקים who are the imitators of God. This also can be assumed to
be an old idea.[25]

The General Theme of Imitatio Dei in Philo

For Philo, the imitation of God has its basis in his interpretation of man's creation; it is in mind and reason (νοῦς καὶ
λόγος) that man was made in the image (εἰκόνα) of God, and is
thus God's copy (μίμημα) and likeness (ἀπεικόνισμα).[26] Similarly,
the virtue of man is only a μίμημα καὶ ἀπεικόνισμα, "copy and
likeness" of the divine virtue.[27] Yet Philo does stress that
only God has virtue in the absolute, θεὸς πιστός, καὶ οὐκ ἔστιν
ἀδικία ἐν αὐτῷ (Deut 32:4); man only has images of the excel-
lences of God which are far below the archetypes due to the
counterforces in man which detract from his godlikeness.[28]
Philo does not make a distinction between ὁμοίωσις, "similarity"
and μίμησις, "imitation"; these words function as synonyms.[29]
Borrowing from Plato (Theaetetus 176), Philo advocates fleeing
from evils to become ὁμοίωσις θεῷ. . . δίκαιον καὶ ὅσιον μετὰ
φρονήσεως, "similar to God. . . righteous and holy in understanding."[30] This is very carefully presented in the following
passage:[31]

But as He is by all means	ἀλλ' ὡς οἷόν τε
the Most Righteous;	δικαιότατος,
indeed nothing exists	καὶ οὐκ ἔστιν
more like Him than who-	αὐτῷ ὁμοιότερον
ever of us, in turn,	οὐδὲν ἢ ὅς ἂν ἡμῶν
becomes as the Most	αὖ γένηται ὅτι
Righteous.	δικαιότατος.

Philo presents God the Creator as Teacher whose perfection
is to be imitated: πρώτη δὲ τῶν εἰσαγομένων ἀρετῆ τὸ διδάσκαλον
ὡς ἔνεστι τέλειον ἀπελεῖς μιμεῖσθαι γλίχεσθαι, "the first virtue
of beginners is that the imperfect ones strive to imitate the
Perfect One as far as possible."[32] The passage from which this
sentence is taken concludes with depicting God as Father to be
imitated: Δεόντως οὖν μιμούμενοι τὴν τοῦ πατρὸς φύσιν οἱ ὁπήκοοι
παῖδες. . . τὰ καλὰ δρῶσιν, ὧν ἔργον ἐστὶ κάλλιστον ἡ ἀνυπέρθετος
θεοῦ τιμή, "necessarily then, the loyal children, imitating the
nature of the Father. . . accomplish good works of which the best

work is unsurpassingly the honour of God."[33] The imitation of
the works of God is taken for granted (in passing, in a genitive
absolute): . . . τοῦ μιμεῖσθαι θεοῦ τὰ ἔργα ὄντος ὁσίου. . .
"to imitate God's works being a holy act. . . "[34] The consonance
of word and work in the imitatio Dei is presented simply and
clearly:[35]

The diligent man does everything, blamelessly keeping the straight path of life, so that the works of the wise man are none other than godly words. . . I said that the words of God were the deeds of the wise man.	οὕτως ὁ σπουδαῖος ἔκαστα δρᾷ τὴν ἀτραπὸν εὐθύνων ἀμέμπτως τοῦ βίου, ὥστε τα ἔργα τοῦ σοφοῦ λόγων ἀδιαφορεῖν θείων. . . ἔφην, τοὺς τοῦ θεοῦ λόγους πράξεις εἶναι τοῦ σοφοῦ.

Philo mentions a few significant instances of imitation of God,
parents in the getting of children,[36] the mediator who imitates
the merciful power of God,[37] and he who shows kindness.[38]
Similarity to God is the ultimate aim of worship and the perfection of happiness.[39] In summary, we must say that Philo's
strongest emphasis is not in abstractions but in the concrete;
imitation of God is accomplished in deeds.

The Theme of Perfection in the Hebrew Pentateuch
Targums of the Pentateuch
and other Early Jewish Tradition

In the Hebrew of the Pentateuch, the occurrences of the
adjective תמים, "perfect," form a pattern in which the two
occurrences in Genesis and the two occurrences in Deuteronomy
stand out.[40] First, a review of Gen 6:8-9 and 17:1. In Gen
6:8-9 we note that three words are associated, הלך, צדיק and
תמים, "walk, righteous, perfect"; attention must be focused on
these words. Gen 6:8-9, in the Hebrew and in Tg. Ps.-J. (which
adds a little targumic clarification), reads:[41]

Gen 6:8-9		Tg. Ps.-J.	
But Noah	ונח	But Noah who was	ונח דהוה
		righteous	צדיקא
found	מצא	found	אשכח
grace	חן	grace	חינא
before	בעיני	before	קדם
the Lord.	יהוה	the Lord.	ייי
These are the	אלה	These are the	אלין
generations	תולדת	genealogies	יחוסין
		of the race	דגניסת
of Noah:	נח	of Noah:	נח
Noah was	נח	Noah was	נח הוה
a righteous man,	איש צדיק	a righteous man;	גבר זכאי
perfect	תמים	perfect	שלים
		in good works	בעובדין טבין
he was;	היה	he was;	הוה
in his generations	בדרתיו	in his generations	בדרוהי
		in the fear	בדחלתא
with God	את האלהים	of the Lord	דייי
Noah walked.	התהלם נח	Noah walked.	הליך נח

In Gen 17:1b the words הלך and תמים are associated:[42]

Gen 17:1b		Tg. Neof.	
Walk before Me,	התהלך לפני	Serve before Me	פלח קדמי
		in truth,	בקשטא
and be perfect.	והיה תמים	and be perfect	והוה שלם
		in good work.	בעבדא טבא

The hithpael verb התהלך, "walk," is not frequent in the Pentateuch;[43] several of its occurrences in Genesis have targumic
renditions. At Gen 5:22 and 24, Tgs. Neof. and Ps.-J. substitute
פלח (Tg. Onq. retains הלך). At Gen 17:1 and 24:40, Tgs. Neof.,
Ps.-J. and Onq. all substitute פלח; at Gen 48:15, Tgs. Ps.-J.,
and Onq. substitute פלח (Tg. Neof. retains הלך); at Gen 6:9,
Tg. Neof. alone substitutes פלח (Tgs. Onq. and Ps.-J. both
retain הלך). Thus at the time of the genesis of the targumic
traditions, "walk" (in appropriate contexts) was often understood
as a theological term, generally taken to mean "worship/serve."

The targums of the Pentatuech made the root שלם more prevalent than it had been in the Hebrew Pentateuch; the Aramaic
root שלם being used to translate several Hebrew roots, including
תם.[44] At first sight, it seems by way of exception to the

general translation practice that the Aramaic שלם is used for כלה,
"finish" at Gen 2:1 and 2:2 in Tgs. Ps.-J. and Neof. (also MS P
at Gen 2:1);[45] but upon closer inspection we see that it is
quite possible that there is an Aramaic cliché involved - שלם
plus עובד[46] - which defied alteration in Tgs. Ps.-J. and Neof.
at Gen 2:1-2 (and MS P at Gen 2:1).[47] The conclusion of the
first creation account in Genesis would, of course, be very well
known. The Aramaic שלם used there was a widely used word with
more than one nuance; God "completed/perfected His work." The
patriarchs Noah (Gen 6:9) and Abraham (Gen 17:1) who walked
before God were termed תמים in the Hebrew text; the Aramaic
is used for the translation, and the targums round out the
attribution, "perfect in good work." The targumic description
"perfect in good work" was attached to the name of Abraham (Tg.
Neof. Gen 17:1), Jacob (Tg. Neof. Gen 25:27 and 33:18), the men
of Jacob (CTg C and Tg. Neof. Gen 34:21), and Noah (Tgs. Neof.
and Ps.-J. Gen 6:9). Here the targumic traditions have taken
one more step in drawing out the theme of imitatio Dei.

Here we should note the targumic haggadah at Lev 22:27
which recalls the patriarchs Abraham, Isaac and Jacob; in this
haggadah, in MS V, CTg F (N and ed. B),[48] the people are exhorted to remember זכוותיה דתמימא, "the righteousness of the
perfect one," that is, Jacob. This is significant especially
because the word תמים (rare in the Torah modifying persons) has
been used in this passage; it points to the targumists' idea of
the singular perfection of Jacob.

Now we must observe the word תמים in Deuteronomy. Deut 18:13,
a verse which has no particular connection with its context, has
the character of an isolated logion:

Be ye perfect/blameless	תמים תהיה
with/before/unto/as	עם
the Lord your God. [49]	יהוה אלהיך

Deut 18:13 is the only locus in the Torah where this adjective
תמים is used as a modifier for the people in general, the people

addressed.   The LXX translates: τέλειος ἔσῃ. . . a special translation according to the understanding of the LXX translator (not
the usual translation of תמים).[50]   The uniqueness of the Hebrew
and of the LXX translation are not the only features of the verse
that must be considered.

The particle עם attracts notice.   There are two usages of
the word (not the most prevalent) which might be suitable here:
(1) a vague "with/toward"[51] and (2) a comparative.[52]   Examples:
first, עם is used as a weak comparative in Ps 28:1: ונמשלתי עם
יורדי בור, "I have become like those who go down into the pit."
Second, when Lev 19:2 and Deut 18:13 are observed together (cf.
below p. 53), one could infer that עם in Deut 18:13 has the same
meaning as כ in Lev 19:2.   Third, in Job 9:26, the particles עם
and כ are used in parallel, both meaning "like."

In the LXX, the עם of Deut 18:13 is translated ἐνάντιον, a
word used to translate the many occurrences of לפני and בעיני in
Deuteronomy, but only once to render עם, in this verse.   This
shows that here the LXX translator was making an interpretation,
specifying a meaning for his audience by avoiding the possibility
of a comparative interpretation;   also pointing out the singul-
arity of the text.

Besides Deut 18:13, there is only one other verse in Deuteronomy in which the word תמים occurs: Deut 32:4: הצור תמים פילו
"the Rock, His work is perfect. . . " The ancient exegete would
have found the phenomenon of only two occurrences significant, an
indication that the meaning of either verse was to be drawn out
with the aid of the other verse.

The Contribution of Tg. Neof. to the Discussion of Deut 18:13. —
Tg. Neof. has drawn attention to the mandate by prefixing the
solemn hortatory phrase עמי בני ישראל, "My people, sons of
Israel";[53]   it has carried over the word עם and added the phrase
ביבדה טבה, "in good work":

My people sons of Israel,   עמי בני ישראל
by ye perfect in good work   שלמין תהוון בעבדה טבה
unto/as the Lord your God.   עם ייי אלהכון

While Tg. Neof. has carried over the particle עם from the Hebrew,
Tgs. Onq. and Ps.-J. have removed the possibility of comparison
with God by replacing עם with the phrase בדחלתא, "in the fear
of. . . "[54] This editing could well have been motivated by theological concerns like those of the LXX translators who also
clearly removed the possibility of comparison. (See above p. 46.)
However, it would seem that Tg. Neof., in retaining עם, retained
the possibility of comparison, but avoided direct comparison with
God, diverting the attention to an imitation of God in good work.
(Furthermore, the vague comparative meaning of the particle
is possible in Aramaic, as is known from Dan 5:21.[55]) If this
meaning is accepted, then the verse in Tg. Neof. would have this
import: "My people, sons of Israel, be ye perfect in good work
as the Lord your God. . . " The second clause has become ellip-
tical, and would logically be completed, ". . . is perfect in
good work." However, due to the rabbinic method of interpreting
one verse with the aid of another, it is reasonable to accept the
phraseology of Deut 32:4 which Tgs. Onq., Ps.-J., MS V (N and ed.
B) all render דשלמין עבדוי, "whose works are perfect."[56]

Finally we note that the adjective שלם, "perfect" is completed by the phrase בעבדה טבא, "in good work," as its normal exegesis at Gen 6:9 in Tgs. Neof. and Ps.-J.; at Gen 17:1, 25:27
and 33:17 in Tg. Neof.; and at Gen 34:21 in Tg. Neof. and CTg C.[57]
It is not surprising to find the cliché at Tg. Neof. Deut 18:13
also. Thus the implied understanding for Tg. Neof. Deut 18:13 is
"My people, sons of Israel, be ye perfect in good work as the
Lord your God (is, whose works are perfect)." Here then, we suggest that the concept from the targumic traditions, שלם בעבדה טבה,
"perfect in good work" should be counted among the attributes of
God to be imitated.

The perfection of God's works and the idea of the perfection
of the people also reappears in Sipre Deut 172 (on Deut 18:13).

However, there is an ambivalence with respect to the word עם; as in the targums and LXX, the interpretation varies.[58]

Among the interpretations of Deut 18:13, in the LXX, targums and early midrashim, עם in a comparative sense was problematic; clarification - exegesis - was apparently required. Tg. Neof. offered one plausible understanding of Deut 18:13: "My people, sons of Israel, be ye perfect in good work as the Lord your God (is, whose works are perfect)."

The Theme of Perfection in Qumran Literature

There is a pervading theme of perfection in the Qumran literature,[59] especially in I QS, the Rule of the Community. The roots of this theme are certainly biblical. Let us review a few biblical texts. II Sam 22:31: האל תמים דרכו, "God, His way is perfect"; Ps 18:33: ויתן תמים דרכי. . .האל, "God. . . He made my way perfect"; Ps 101:6b: הלך בדרך תמים הוא ישרתני, "he who walks in the way of the perfect, he shall serve Me"; Ps 84:12: יהוה לא ימנע טוב להלכים בתמים, "the Lord does not withhold good from those who walk in the way of perfection." Ps. 15:2: הולך תמים ופיל צדק, "he who walks perfectly and does righteousness. . . " Here we see the beginning of word associations: perfect, way, walk, righteousness.

These word associations developed into speech patterns polished by usage in the Qumran literature, for example:[60]

	IQS i.13
. . . according to the perfection of His ways.	בתם דרכיו
	IQS v.24
. . . and the perfection of his (i.e. man's) way.	ותום דרכו
	IQS ii.2
. . . all the men. . . who walk perfectly in all His ways.	כול אנשי...ההולכים תמים בכול דרכיו
	IQSb i.2
. . . and hold fast to His holy covenant, and walk perfectly.	ומחזקי בב⌈רי⌉ת קודשו והולכים תמים

IQS viii.1-2

(three priests) perfect in
all that is revealed by all
the Law and do truth and
righteousness and loving
kindness and humility in .
human relations.

תמימים בכול הנגלה
מכול התרוה לעשות אמת
וצדקה ומשפט ואהבת חסד
והצנע לכת איש אם רעהו

IQS VIII.20-21

And these are the
ordinances in which they
shall walk - the men of
perfect holiness in human
relations. Each who comes
into the Council of Holiness,
those who walk in the perfect
way which (God) has commanded. . .

ואלה המשפטים
אשר ילכו בם
אנשי התמים
קודש איש את רעהו
כול הבא בעצת הקודש
ההולכים בתמים דרך
כאשר צוה. . .

The word associations have been somewhat extended, and the thought
pattern has become quite well defined. Perfection is an attribute
of God's ways, and is also to be an attribute of man's ways, the
ways in which he walks.[61] Perfection in the Law is an over-
arching idea, a heading for the virtue list of IQS viii.1. Living
according to the Law, the Covenant, walking perfectly in the way,
doing truth, righteousness, etc. - all these have become quite
synonymous for practical purposes. Basically, then, perfection
was primarily practical, consisting in obedience to the ordinances of God; this obedience was dependent on knowledge of God's
revelation of the Law and knowledge of the specific ordinances of
Qumran.

The Theme of Perfection in Philo

Before reviewing Philo's theology of perfection, we must make
a few observations on the LXX. At Gen 2:1-2 for the verb כלה the
LXX reads συντελέω.[62] The word τέλειος is used for תמים at Gen
6:9 and Deut 8:13.[63] These two related concepts of "complete/
finish" and "integral/perfect" are closer together in the Greek
than in the Hebrew due to the use of the words of the τελ- root
in both cases. The increased usage of one root in Greek could
possibly be a factor underlying a development of theological
thought centered upon this root; such a development can be

observed in Philo.

First, with the LXX of Gen 2:1-2 in mind, we can see that there was a possibility of viewing creation as God's _perfect_ _work_, a very fine development of thought. Philo apparently assumed this and described this "perfect work" in many ways. He wrote that in creating, the Creator used all four elements ἵνα ἐκ μερῶν τελείων τελειότατον ἀπεργάσηται τὸ πᾶν, "that out of perfect parts He might make the whole most perfect."[64] The idea was highlighted by the use of the superlative and adjective-groups, for example:[65]

The world, the fairest and greatest and most perfect work.	ὁ δὲ κόσμος, τὸ κάλλιστον καὶ μέγιστον καὶ τελεώτατον ἔργον.

Since the cosmos was the perfect work, then by inference, it follows that God is the perfect Creator:[66]

The Lord of all things. . . (is) the most perfect (Master of) the art (of creation).	τὴν τέχνην τελειότατος ὁ τῶν ὅλων ἡγεμών ἐστι. . .

The perfection of man, as of the world, is achieved by God in His creative Word:[67]

Thus you may learn that God prizes the Wise Man as the world, for that same Word, by which He made the universe, is that by which He draws the perfect man from earthly things to Himself.	ἵνα μάθῃς, ὅτι τὸν σοφὸν ἰσότιμον κόσμῳ ὁ θεὸς ἡγεῖται τῷ αὐτῷ λόγῳ καὶ τὸ πᾶν ἐργαζόμενος καὶ τὸν τέλειον ἀπὸ τῶν περιγείων ἀνάγων ὡς ἑαυτόν.

In Philo's explanation of ἐγὼ κύριος, "I am the Lord," he included not only the absolute attributes of God, but also those titles in which God is related to man - not only τὸ τέλειον καὶ ἄφθαρτον καὶ πρὸς ἀλήθειαν ἀγαθόν, "the Perfect, the Imperishable and the truly Good," but also ὁ ἄρχων καὶ ὁ βασιλεὺς καὶ δεσπότης, "the Sovereign and King and Master."[68] So man is perfect in those ways in which he is related to God. For example, Moses, the Perfect One,[69] was described as ἱκέτης καὶ θεραπευτῆς. . . τέλειος θεοῦ, "a perfect suppliant and servant

of God."[70] Besides Moses, other patriarchs were also called
"perfect": Abraham,[71] Aaron,[72] Levi in his life of perfect virtue,[73] and Jacob who was perfected in his change of names.[74]

For Philo, there was no question that man should have
perfection:[75]

I have made up my mind that happiness is the exercise of perfect virtue in a perfect life.	εὐδαιμονίαν δὲ χρῆσιν ἀρετῆς τελαίας ἐν βίῳ τελείῳ νενόηκα.

The tone of this citation is Hellenistic, but Philo could also
express his idea of man's perfection in a decidedly Hebraic
way:[76]

Those who are worthy: (he whose name is) inscribed in the way of life according to the laws is "perfect". . . in matters before God.	ἀξιοῖ γὰρ τὸν ἐγγραφόμενον τῇ κατὰ τοὺς νόμους πολιτείᾳ "τέλειον" εἶναι. . . ἐν τοῖς πρὸς θεόν.

Finally, for Philo ὁ τέλειος, "the perfect man" was the fully
instructed man; to such a man, τελείῳ τῷ κατ' εἰκόνα, "to the
perfect man (formed) according to the (Divine) image," exhortations need not be given.[77] The form of perfection is in the
cosmos due to the impression and εἰκὼν τελείου λόγου, "image of
the perfect Word."[78] And yet, for the human beings τοῖς μήπω
τελειωθεῖσον, "who are not yet perfected"[79] growth is required;
this is one of the main themes of De Plantatione. The growth in
perfection was summed up in the idea of the "path" or "way" to
God.[80]

On the theme of perfection, Philo has used his Hebraic heritage and added considerable Hellenistic colouring; nevertheless
the Hebraic core of his thought remains undamaged. Creation,
creation by the Word, creation completed and perfect, God who is
Perfect and the Perfect Good, the image of God in the cosmos and
in man, man's coming to perfection - these ideas are related and
interwoven in the thought of Philo.

The Saying in Matt 5:48 and its NT Context

Matt 5:48 and Luke 6:36 read as follows:

Be ye perfect even as your Heavenly Father is perfect.	"Εσεσθε οὖν ὑμεῖς τέλειοι ὡς ὁ πατὴρ ὑμῶν ὁ οὐράνιος τέλειός ἐστιν.
Be ye merciful, even as your Father is merciful.	Γίνεσθε οἰκτίρμονες καθὼς ὁ πατὴρ ὑμῶν οἰκτίρμων ἐστίν.

The words τέλειος and οἰκτίρμων are rare indeed in the Synoptics. The former is used only by Matthew (5:48 twice, and 19:21); the latter only in Luke 6:36. Because Matt 5:48 is a sentence of the same construction as that in Luke 6:36, and because each of these is preceded by material bearing on the same theme, it was inevitable that these verses would have been compared and the question of literary "priority" raised. Commentators, having assumed that there was one original logion, are not agreed whether the primitive form of that logion had τέλειοι or οἰκτίρμονες.[81] When one takes into consideration the infrequency of these words in the Synoptics, one might well be wise not to take a stand on "priority." Another reason to refrain from taking such a stand has been offered in the conclusion of E.P. Sanders' The Tendencies of the Synoptic Tradition: "the canons (the characteristics of the tendencies of the literary tradition) are not so certain that one may say that a detail in one of Matthew's pericopes proves it to be later than the parallel in Luke."[82] We conclude that rather than debating the priority of one of these verses to the other, it would be of more value to study them in the light of the tradition wider than the Synoptics.

There are two variations of the traditional theme in I John. It is helpful to observe the four passages together:

Matt 5:48
"Εσεσθε οὖν
ὑμεῖς τέλειοι ὡς   ὁ πατὴρ ὑμῶν ὁ οὐράνιος τέλειός ἐστιν.

Luke 6:36
Γίνεσθε
οἰκτίρμονες   καθὼς ὁ πατὴρ ὑμῶν   οἰκτίρμων ἐστιν.

I John 3:3
καὶ πᾶς
ὁ ἔχων
τὴν ἐλπίδα
ταύτην ἐπ'
αὐτῷ ἀγνίζει
ἑαυτὸν   καθὼς ἐκεῖνος[83]   ἀγνός   ἐστιν.

I John 3:7
ὁ ποιῶν τὴν
δικαιοσύνην
δίκαιός ἐστιν, καθὼς ἐκεῖνος   δίκαιός ἐστιν.

Not only do all four sentences have the same form in the second
clause, but in each case the attribute of God in the second
clause is a word repeating a root in the first clause. In the
first clause this attribute is proposed to men, in Matt 5:48 and
Luke 6:36 in the imperative, in I John 3:3 and 3:7 in the affirm-
ative. Each of the attributes, ἀγνός, "pure," δίκαιος, "righteous," and οἰκτίρμων, "merciful," can be accepted as quite
common concepts in the first century religious milieu.[84]
Especially צדיק, "righteous," and רחום, "merciful," were concepts known in early Jewish traditions concerned with the
imitatio Dei.

At this point we must return to the MT and the LXX for the
purpose of examining the form of the saying in Matt 5:48:

Matt 5:48	Lev 19:2		Deut 18:13	
Ἔσεσθε	קדשים	ἅγιοι	תמים	τέλειος
οὖν ὑμεῖς				
τέλειοι	תהיו	ἔσεσθε	תהיה	ἔση
ὡς	כי	ὅτι	עם	ἐναντίον
ὁ πατὴρ		ἐγὼ		
ὑμῶν ὁ	קדוש	ἅγιος		
οὐράνυος	אני יהוה	κύριος	יהוה	κυρίου
τέλειός	אלהיכם	ὁ θεὸς	אלהיך	τοῦ θεοῦ
ἐστιν.		ὑμῶν.		σου.

Since Matt 5:48 is in the same form as Lev 19:2, the leading
text for the whole theme of imitatio Dei, then it follows
clearly that Matthew has used this form precisely for emphasis
and to underscore its authority. Since Matt 5:48 borrows the
concept "perfect"from Deut 18:13, we must seek to understand the

probability of this editorial activity on the part of Matthew.
The idea of men being "perfect" was probably current: we note
the predilection for the concept in the Qumran literature, also
its acceptance into the thought of Philo. To this, we suggest
adding the exegesis of Tg. Neof. Deut 18:13 outlined above,
understanding this text as "My people, sons of Israel, be ye
perfect in good work as the Lord your God (is, whose works are
perfect)."

Such an understanding of Tg. Neof. Deut 18:13 is useful for
understanding Matt 5:48 as the conclusion of Matt 5:43-48. When
we accept the Aramaic שלם, "perfect," as present in the saying
lying behind Matt 5:48, then we see that this word was appropriate in its context. The previous verse read, "and if you
greet (ἀσπάσησθε) only your brothers. . . "; the normal Aramaic
behind the verb would have been שלם. Thus the sequence of ideas
in Aramaic thought would have been: שלם with one meaning in v 47
and שלם with an alternate meaning in v 48. This word play could
not be expressed in Greek, but Matthew did use a somewhat clum-
sier word play, using two partially similar words: τελῶναι,
"tax collectors" in v 46 and τέλειοι, "perfect" in v 48.

The passage, Matt 5:43-48, has the theme of the impartiality
of God and the exhortation to love not only one's brothers but
also one's enemies. On this subject we might observe that the
same comment is made in the targumic traditions on both Exod 23:5
(on helping the enemy whose ass has fallen under its burden) and
Deut 22:4 (on helping the brother whose ass has fallen). The
comment in MS V Deut 22:4 reads משבק תשבוק ית מה דאית בלבך עלוי,
"You shall forgive what is in your heart against him."[85] It is
obvious that Exod 23:4-5 and Deut 22:1-4 were seen as parallel
passages, even though one read "enemy" and the other "brother."
Sipre Deut 225[86] raises the question as to why the word "brother"
was used, suggesting that it was an aid to overcoming the natural urge (יצר) not to help the enemy.

In the mention of God's giving the sun to both the evil and

the good, and the rain to both the just and the unjust (Matt 5:40)
there is the theme of the universal goodness of God. The blessing
for rain was ברוך הטוב והמטיב, "Blessed is He who is Good and does
good"; this is quoted five times in Genesis Rabbah.[87] This universal goodness of God is to be noted in Mekilta, for example, in
its commentary on Exod 18:12:[88]

. . . the Holy One,	הקב"ה
blessed be He, who gives	שהוא נותן
to everyone his wants,	לבל אחד ואחד צורכו
and to everybody	ולכל גויה וגויה
according to his needs;	כדי מחסורה
and not to good people	ולא לבני אדם כשרים
alone, but also to	בלבך אלא אף
wicked people. . .	לבני אדם רשעים

Josephus also alludes to God the Father of both the good and the
wicked.[89]

In the targumic traditions of Gen 2:1-2, the Creator com-
pleted/perfected (שלם) his work (עובד). The patriarchs Noah
(Gen 6:9) and Abraham (Gen 17:1) were perfect in good work (שלם
בעבדא טבא), and the description was also used of Jacob. Furthermore, Jacob is termed the perfect one (תמימא/שלימא) in the targumic traditions at Lev 22:27. The tradition of thinking of
creation as God's perfect work is stressed by Philo: μέγιστον
καὶ τελεώτατον ἔργον, "greatest and most perfect work"; for
Philo, God is τελειότατον ἀγαθόν, "the Most Perfect Good"; and
men who are not yet perfect are led by Him to knowledge of Himself, the Most Perfect Good. In the Qumran literature also there
is a theme of perfection: God's ways are perfect; man is to
walk in them perfectly. Thus, in the targumic traditions, in
Philo and in the Qumran literature, the theology of perfection
and imitatio Dei are allied.

Throughout Matt 5:43-47 there is a strong suggestion that
the impartiality and goodness of God should be imitated; in
Matt 5:48 this is concluded with the imperative, "Be ye perfect
even as your heavenly Father is Perfect." Both the material of
5:43-47 and 5:48 have their setting in the Jewish traditions

attested in the targums, the Qumran literature, Philo and the
early midrashim.

In the elucidation of Matt 5:48 we can turn to Tg. Neof.
Deut 18:13 understood as "My people, sons of Israel, be ye perfect in good work as the Lord your God (is whose works are perfect)." The works in which God is perfect are primarily those of
creation; the mention of the sun and rain in Matt 5:43-47
subtly evokes the creation theme. Moreover, the appellation of
"Father in Heaven" arose from the traditions of the targums and
early midrashim. The association of the concepts of "Father" and
"Creator" arose from the Hebrew text (Deut 32:6, Isa 64:7 and
Mal 2:10); this association of concepts is evident in the targumic tradition which linked Gen 1:1-2:2 with Deut 32:4-6 even
more than the Hebrew text had done, repeating words from one
passage to the other. The association of "Father" and "Creator"
was also stressed by Philo who repeatedly paired the names Πατήρ
and Ποιητής. Given the development of the association of concepts involved, Matthew's saying in 5:48 is not at all surprising.
In the light of this development and in the light of its context,
Matt 5:43-48, the saying could well be understood as "Be ye
perfect (in good work) as your heavenly Father is perfect (in
good works)." Basically, this would be the imitation of the
universal goodness of the Creator.

Further Evidence in the Tradition of
the NT and Apostolic Fathers

The idea of imitatio Dei recurs in various NT epistles. The
primary example is I Pet 1:15-16:

. . . as He who called	... κατὰ τὸν καλέσαντα
you is holy, be holy	ὑμᾶς ἅγιον καὶ αὐτοὶ
yourselves in all	ἅγιοι ἐν πάσῃ
(your) conduct;	ἀναστροφῇ γενήθητε,
since it is written,	διότι γέγραπται,
'You shall be holy,	"Ἅγιοι ἔσεσθε,
for I am holy.'	ὅτι ἐγὼ ἅγιος.

The behaviour required is quite specific in III John 11, "doing good":

Beloved, do not imitate evil but good. He who does good is of God; he who does evil has not seen God.	Ἀγαπητέ, μὴ μιμοῦ τὸ κακὸν ἀλλὰ τὸ ἀγαθόν. ὁ ἀγαθοποιῶν ἐκ τοῦ θεοῦ ἐστιν᾿ ᾿κακοποιῶν οὐχ ἑώρακεν τὸν θεόν.

Paul also knows the theme and has developed it; that is, the imitation of God, of Christ and of fellow-Christians are shown to be really related in a number of texts,[90] for example, Eph 5:1 and I Thess 1:6:

Therefore be imitators of God as beloved children.	γίνεσθε οὖν μιμηταὶ τοῦ θεοῦ, ὡς τέκνα ἀγαπητά.

... you became imitators of us and of the Lord...	ὑμεῖς μιμηταὶ ἡμῶν ἐγενήθητε καὶ τοῦ κυρίου.

The imitatio Dei is also thematic in the epistles of Clement and Ignatius. In 1 Clem. 33:1, ἀγάπη is placed as a literary parallel for ἀγαθοποιΐας and πᾶν ἔργον ἀγαθόν - love, well-doing and every good deed. Then 33:2-6 recalls Genesis 1, God's creating the heavens and earth, animals and sea-life, and man both male and female; and πάντα τελειώσας, "having finished all these things," He blessed them. Clement then exhorts his audience to imitate the Creator in good works:[91]

For the Creator and Master of the universe Himself rejoices in His works... Let us observe that all the righteous have been adorned with good works, and the Lord Himself adorned Himself with good works and rejoiced. Having therefore this pattern let us follow His will without delay, with all our strength let us work the work of righteousness.	αὐτὸς γὰρ ὁ δημιουργὸς καὶ δεσπότης τῶν ἁπάντων ἐπὶ τοῖς ἔργοις αὐτοῦ ἀγαλλιᾶται... ἴδωμεν, ὅτι ἐν ἔργοις ἀγαθοῖς πάντες ἐκοσμήθησαν οἱ δίκαιοι, καὶ αὐτὸς δὲ ὁ κύριος ἔργοις ἀγαθοῖς ἑαυτὸν κοσμήσας ἐχάρη. ἔχοντες οὖν τοῦτον τον ὑπογραμμὸν ἀόκνως προσ- έλθωμεν τῷ θελήματι αὐτοῦ ἐξ ὅλης τῆς ἰσχύος ἡμῶν ἐργασώμεθα ἔργον δικαιοσύνης.

Ignatius' epistle <u>Trall</u>. 1:2:[92]

I have found you. . .	εὑρών ὑμᾶς. . .
imitators of God.	μιμητάς ὄντας θεοῦ.

This theme finds a decidedly Christian development in Ign.
<u>Phld</u>. 7:2:[93]

Be imitators of Jesus	μιμηταὶ γίνεσθε 'Ιησοῦ
Christ, as was He also	Χριστοῦ, ὡς καὶ αὐτός
of His Father.	τοῦ πατρὸς αὐτοῦ.

The idea of the perfection of God's people by their good
works is quite explicit in James; as examples, 1:4 and 2:22:

. . . and let steadfastness	. . . ἡ δὲ ὑπομονὴ ἔργον
bring about[94] perfect works	τέλειον ἐχέτω, ἵνα ἦτε
that you may be perfect and	τέλειοι καὶ ὁλόκληροι
complete, lacking nothing.	ἐν μηδενὶ λειπόμενοι.

You see that faith was	βλέπεις ὅτι ἡ πίστις
active along with his	συνήργει τοῖς ἔργοις
(Abraham's) works, and	αὐτοῦ καὶ ἐκ τῶν ἔργων
faith was completed by	ἡ πίστος ἐτελειώθη.
works.	

In the letters of Ignatius, τέλειος, "perfect" (and cognates) is
a recurring word. For Ignatius, Jesus Christ was the perfect
man[95] and perfect hope.[96] In Ign. <u>Eph</u>. 1:1, the theme of
<u>imitatio Dei</u> is joined to the idea of works perfectly
accomplished:[97]

You are imitators of God,	μιμηταὶ ὄντες θεοῦ,
and having kindled your	ἀναζωπυρήσαντες ἐν αἵματι
brotherly work by the	θεοῦ τὸ συγγενικὸν
blood of God, you	ἔργον τελείως
completed it perfectly.	ἀπηρτίσατε.

This thought is echoed by Polycarp in <u>Phil</u>. 12:3:[98]

. . . that your fruit[99]	. . . ut fructus vester
may be manifest among	manifestus sit in
all men, that you may	omnibus, ut sitis in
be perfected in Him.	illo perfecti.

In the expectation of perfection, the example of the patriarchs
was to be taken, according to 1 <u>Clem</u>. 9:2:[100]

Let us fix our gaze on	ἀτενίσωμεν εἰς τοὺς
those who have rendered	τελείως λειτουργήσαντας
perfect service to his	τῇ μεγαλοπρεπεῖ δόξῃ
excellent glory. . .	αὐτοῦ. . .
Enoch... Noah...	'Ενώχ... Νῶε...
Abraham...	'Αβραάμ...

These are the three who "walked" with/before God, the latter two being designated "perfect" in Genesis.

Summary

In the targumic traditions, the early midrashic traditions, and in Philo, the main thrust of the imitatio Dei was the doing of good deeds, imitation of God in righteousness. The general theme of imitatio Dei could be made specific in many ways; Gen 6:8-9 (with respect to Noah) and 17:1 (with respect to Abraham) give the primary words associated with "perfect" in this context: to walk with God, to be righteous, and to be perfect. Here was a pattern of concepts which could be made more explicit by early exegesis. In the traditions extant in the targums and early midrashim, exhortations to imitate God's righteousness are generally given greater place than exhortations to imitate other attributes. Exhortations to good works as imitation of God are frequent. When the word "perfect" appears in the targums, it is generally made more explicit: "perfect in good works." The people are exhorted to be perfect in good works as God is (Tg. Neof. Deut 18:13); for God is the Rock whose works are perfect (Deut 32:4).

The LXX used the verb συντελέω and the targums used the verb שלם at Gen 2:1-2 where the Hebrew was כלה. The possibility was opened both in the Aramaic and Greek for the nuance "God completed/perfected His work." The idea of "perfect work" was markedly more frequent in the targums than in the Hebrew text, and it was assumed by Philo and given further explanations and embellishments. The description "perfect in good work" was attached to the names of Abraham (Tg. Neof. Gen 17:1), Jacob (Neof. Gen 25:27 and 33:18), the men of Jacob (Neof. and CTg C Gen 34:21), and Noah (Neof. and Ps.-J. Gen 6:9). Philo also used the epithet "perfect" in connection with revered ancestors, Moses, Abraham, Aaron, Levi and Jacob. It was a targumic trait to attach the current exhortations to the names of the patriarchs

so that the example - as it were - of those revered ancestors
should stand also as an exhortation to proper conduct of life.
Thus in the targums, both directly and indirectly, in the general
context of imitatio Dei, the people are exhorted to be perfect in
good works. In Philo, the theme of imitatio Dei is spelled out
much more fully than in the targums; his words on perfection are
straightforward: "the first virtue of beginners is that the imperfect ones strive to imitate the Perfect One as far as possible
(Sac. 65). God who is Perfect and the Creator of His perfect
work, the world, is the goal of a perfect life.

The imitatio Dei is a theme of various NT writers. It is
presented plainly in Matt 5:48, Luke 6:36, I John 3:3 and 3:7 -
the imitation of God in being perfect, merciful, pure and righteous respectively. Matt 5:48 concludes Matt 5:43-48 in which
there is strong inference that the universal goodness of the
Creator is to be the model of behaviour. Thus Matt 5:48 stands
in harmony with its immediate context and its wider NT context.
It also stands in harmony with the imitatio Dei and the theme of
perfection in the Apostolic Fathers.

We understand Tg. Neof. Deut 18:13 as "My people, sons of
Israel, be ye perfect in good work as the Lord your God (is,
whose works are perfect)." This helps with the understanding of
Matt 5:48 as "Be ye perfect (in good works) even as your heavenly
Father is perfect (in good works)." This "heavenly Father" is
the Creator whose goodness is universal.[101]

Notes

[1] <u>MS</u> V reads:　　　　　　אלהא דעלמא יהי שמיה מבורך להלמי עלמין

<u>Tg</u>. <u>Ps.-J</u>. reads:　　　בריך שמיה דמרי עלמא דאליף לן ארחתיה תקניה

<u>Tg</u>. <u>Neof</u>.: O God of eternity -　　　　אלהא דעלמא יהא שמיה מבורך
may His name be blessed for ever and　　　　　　לעלם ולעלמא עלמין
forever and ever - your meekness and　　　　　ענוות נו תיך וישרותך
your rectitude and your justice and　　　　וצדיקותך ותוקפך והדרך
your strength and your glory will not　　　　　לא פסקין לעלמי עלמין
pass for ever and ever.

Cf. Arthur Marmorstein, <u>Studies in Jewish Theology</u>, 113.

[2] Martin Hengel, <u>Judaism and Hellenism</u>, 131.

[3] The works of feeding the hungry, giving drink to the thirsty and clothing the naked are juxtaposed and attributed to Job in ᵓ<u>Abot</u> <u>R</u>. <u>Nat</u>. פרק ז (Schechter, pp. 33-34), a passage entirely anonymous.

[4] <u>Bereshith Rabba</u> VIII. 13 in בראשית רבה, מדרש רבה, vol. 1 (Tel Aviv, 1956) 58.

[5] In <u>Tg</u>. <u>Neof</u>. Deut 10:12, 11:22 and 26:17: ולמהלכה.

[6] Lauterbach, <u>Mekilta</u>, vol. 2, 182.

[7] <u>Tgs</u>. <u>Onq</u>., <u>Ps.-J</u>., <u>Neof</u>., <u>MSS</u> V, P (N and <u>ed</u>. B).

[8] Similarly <u>MS</u> P (N and <u>ed</u>. B). <u>Tgs</u>. <u>Onq</u>., <u>Ps.-J</u>. and <u>Neof</u>. are similar but show individual variation in accord with the character of those targums.

[9] There is an anonymous passage in <u>Sipre</u> Deut 355 which dwells upon the preposition כ, "like"; it is attached to Deut 32:26, "There is none <u>like</u> God. . ." The text strings together Biblical texts so as to form a dialogue between the Holy Spirit and Israel. One of these texts is Exod 15:2; we find a second attestation to the whole haggadah in <u>Mekilta</u> at the appropriate place (again given anonymously). It is also included in later midrashic works. (For discussion cf. A. Marmorstein, <u>Studies in Jewish Theology</u>, 50-52 and 118-119.) In <u>Sipre</u> Deut 355 (Finkelstein, 422) the passage reads:

Israel said,	ישראל אומרים
there is none like God;	אין כאל
the Holy Spirit said,	רוח הקודש אומרת
the God of Jeshrun.	אל ישרון
Israel said,	ישראל אומרים
Who is like Thee among the gods, O Lord? (Exod 15:11)	מי כמוכה באלים ה'
The Holy Spirit said,	ורוח הקודש אומרת
Happy art thou, O Israel. Who is like thee?(Deut 33:29)	אשריך ישראל מי כמוך
Israel said, Hear O Israel. The Lord is our God.	ישראל אמורים שמע ישראל ה' אלהינו

62

The Lord is One. (Deut 6:4)	ה' אחד
The Holy Spirit said,	ורוח הקודש אומרת
Who is like Thy people Israel,	ומי כעמך ישראל
a unique nation? (I Chr 17:21)	גוי אחד
Israel said,	ישראל אומרים
Like the apple tree among the	כהפוח בעצי היער
trees of the forest. (Cant 2:3)	
The Holy Spirit said,	ורוח הקודש אומרת
Like the lily among thorns.	כשושנה בין החוחים
(Cant 2:2)	
Israel said,	ישראל אומרים
This is my God. I will	זה אלי ואנוהו
exalt Him. (Exod 15:2)	
The Holy Spirit said,	ורוח הקודש אומרת
This people I have created	עם זו יצרתי לי
for myself. (Isa 43:21)	
Israel said,	ישראל אומרים
For Thou art the glory of	כי תפארת עוזמו אתה
His might. (Ps 89:18)	
The Holy Spirit said,	ורוח הקודש אומרת
Israel, through thee I am	ישראל אשר בך אתפאר
glorified. (Isa 49:3)	

[10] Cf. M. McNamara, The New Testament and the Palestinian Targum, 135.

[11] There are no other targumic witnesses to these two verses. Tg. Neof., seemingly for both reverential and theological reasons, adds a few words: "to love the teachings of the law." An explanation for attachment to the Law was the equivalent to God on High; thus explains Sipre Deut on 11:22.

[12] Probably Abba Saul of the Yavneh period, since he is mentioned among two others of that period; cf. A Marmorstein, Studies in Jewish Theology, 111.

[13] Lauterbach, Mekilta, vol. 2, 25.

[14] This haggadah has the tannaitic trait of using ואומר, a terminus technicus, for linking Scriptural passages (the Amoraic usage was זה שאמר הכתרב). Cf. A. Marmorstein, Studies in Jewish Theology, 112.

[15] Finkelstein, Siphre, vol. 2, 114.

[16] These are the first two of the list of attributes of God at Exod 34:6 ff.

[17] Joel 3:5. The Translation of Joel 3:5 which we have offered construes יקרא as nifal. This is a translation of the consonantal text of the verse, and is made necessary by the sense of the whole passage.

[18] If we see a sort of inclusio here for chaps. 19-20, Lev 20:27 would have to be explained as an afterthought, a verse tacked on at the end of the chapter.

[19] J.H. Weiss, Sipra 86c-93d. There is the same note at the conclusion of chap. 20 in Tg. Neof.

[20] J.H. Weiss, Sipra 93d.

[21] J.H. Weiss, Sipra 86c. Sipra 57b repeats the same thoughts in commenting on Lev 11:45: God brought Israel out of Egypt on the condition that the commandments be kept; further, פרוש is equated with קדוש: "as I am separated, be ye separated." Cf. also J.H. Weiss, Sipra 91d.

[22] Tgs. Onq. and Ps.-J. translate the Hebrew literally; the verse is lacking from the mss. of the fragment targum.

[23] J.H. Weiss, Sipra 111ab.

[24] A good example of imitatio hominis is to be seen in Ps 18:26-27. Further, that God would be merciful towards those who practice mercy is expressed in Gen. Rab. XXXIII. 3 - and that He would not be merciful with those who forget to be merciful, Gen. Rab. XXXIII.5.

[25] Cf. as examples, Sipre Deut 49 above; Philo, Fug. 82 and 63 below.

[26] Det. 83; Decal. 134.

[27] Det. 160.

[28] Mut. 183.

[29] Spec. iv. 188; Virt. 168.

[30] Fug. 63.

[31] Fug. 82.

[32] Sac. 65.

[33] Sac. 68.

[34] L.A. i. 48.

[35] Mig. 129-130.

[36] Decal. 111; Spec. ii.2 and ii. 225.

[37] Mut. 129.

[38] Spec. iv. 73.

[39] Decal. 73: εὐχῶν ἀρίστην εἶναι συμβέβηκεν, ὦ γενναῖοι, καὶ τέλος εὐδαιμονίας τὴν πρὸς θεὸν ἐξομοίσιν, "O noblemen, it happened that the best of prayers and the goal of happiness are to be made similar unto God.

[40] Gen 6:9 with reference to Noah; Gen 17:1 with reference to Abraham; Deut 18:13 with reference to the people; and Deut 32:4 with reference to God's works. (The related תם is used once of Jacob at Gen 25:27, and in connection with Sarah at Gen 20:5-6.)

Reviewing the usage in the Hebrew text as a whole: תמים is used for Job twice: 12:4 and 36:4; once in the book of Job it has reference to God at 37:16: מפלאות תמים דעים. It is used with reference to the people seven times in Psalms and three times in Proverbs; also once in the poetry of Ezekiel, at 28:15. However its far most prevalent usage is as a modifier of the type of animal for the sacrifice: this is its exclusive use in Exodus, Leviticus, Numbers, and Ezekiel with the one exception noted.

[41]Gen 6:8 is similarly found in Tg. Neof., MSS V, P (N and ed. B) but with a typical targumic expansion: חן וחסד, "grace and favour" (which expansion is also found in Pseudo-Philo: "gratiam et misericordiam"; cf. Guido Kisch, ed. Pseudo-Philo's Liber Antiquitatum Biblicarum [Notre Dame, Indiana: The University of Notre Dame 1949] 115). Gen 6:9 is also found in Tg. Onq. with the same final clause as in Tg. Ps.-J.; but Tg. Neof. has פלח נח בקושטא, "Noah worshipped/served in truth," a phraseology found also in Tgs. Neof. and Ps.-J. at Gen 5:22 and 5:24 with reference to Enoch (MT: התהלך).

[42]Gen 17:1 is attested only in Tgs. Onq., Ps.-J., and Neof. The presence of פלח קדמי בקשטא in Tg. Neof. (not in Onq. or Ps.-J.) could be attributed to the tendency of Tg. Neof. to internal consistency.

[43]Genesis, 8 times; Exodus, once; Leviticus, once; Deuteronomy, once.

[44]Aramaic שלם is used consistently for the Hebrew שלם, consistently for תם (and תמים), and also sometimes for כלה (see note 45.

[45]In the Pentateuch, כלה occurs 46 times. Only the three qal occurrences (in Tgs. Onq., Ps.-J. and Neof.) and the piel occurrences at Exod 15:13-14 (in Tgs. Onq. and Ps.-J.) and Gen 2:1-2 (Tgs. Ps.-J. and Neof.) are translated with שלם. In Tgs. Onq. and Ps.-J. this is the full extent of the use of שלם for כלה; Tg. Neof. shows peculiarity in a much wider use of שלם for כלה.

[46]In the targums of the Pentateuch, the root עבד is very frequent. The Hebrew substantive מעבד is translated with the עבד root in Tgs. Onq. and Neof. consistently, passim. Also it would seem that there is no particular word in Aramaic which could specifically and consistently be used to translate the Hebrew מלאכה; it has become one of the words rendered in Aramaic by the עבד root. Actually, in the Pentateuch, over 90 per cent of the instances of the Hebrew מלאכה are renedered by the עבד root in Tg. Onq. (the remainder being in special contexts). What is more, the phrase "to do work" in the Hebrew with the verb עשה and the noun מלאכה is found in Tg. Onq. consistently with the עבד root for both the verb and the noun.

[47]At Exod 5:13 (Tgs. Ps.-J. and Neof.) the object of the

verb שלם is עבידכון (translating the Hebrew מעשיכם); at Gen 2:2
(Tgs. Onq., Ps.-J. and Neof.) the object of the verb שלם is
עיבידתה (translating the Hebrew מלאכה). In both cases: "com-
pleting/perfecting work(s)."

[48]The reading quoted is from MS V. CTgF (N and ed. B) show
slight orthographical variations. Tg. Ps.-J. has the more
common Aramaic synonym: זכות שלימא.

[49]Among the various current English translations there is
real variety in the renditions of תמים and עם.

[50]The usual LXX translation of תמים (and cognates) is
ἄμωμος. The translation here is among the unusual translations
of the root. For statistics, cf. Gerhard Delling, "τέλειος,"
TDNT VII, 1972, 72, n. 20.

[51]The passage seems to be read this way by Francis Brown,
S.R. Driver and Charles A. Briggs in A Hebrew and English
Lexicon of the Old Testament (Oxford: Clarendon, 1907-1972) 767,
sect. d. BDB could have been influenced to include it here by
the interpretation known from the LXX.

[52]A category of R.J. Williams in his Hebrew Syntax: An Outline (Toronto: University of Toronto Press, 1967) 60, no. 334.

[53]Usually found before the commandments of the decalogue;
and extended to introduce a number of other mandates as well.

[54]The reading in Tg. Ps.-J. is:
Be ye perfect in the fear of the   שלמין תהוון בדחלתא
Lord your God.   דייי אלהכון
    Similarly, Tg. Onq. The phrase "in the fear of. . . " is
characteristic of those targums.

[55]Cf. Franz Rosenthal, A Grammar of Biblical Aramaic
(Wiesbaden: Harrassovitz, 1968) 36, section 83: "placed with"
means "made like."

[56]The orthography of the words in question varies slightly,
as one might expect. Tg. Neof., at this point, gives only the
attached haggadah without a rendition of the text. MS P gives
the haggadah and then only the first two words reflecting the
text, then cuts its rendition short with ' וגו': וגו' תקיפא דשלמין.
(The LXX has met an unusual situation with an unusual translation: it uses ἀληθινός, which is most often used to translate
אמן/אמת.

[57]In the same manner, the clause "He is righteous and holy"
of Deut 32:4 is appropriately completed by the phrase "in his
judgements" in Tg. Neof. and MS V (בדינא). This addition of
prepositional phrases is a targumic trait for the sake of making
the reading more explicit.

[58]Sipre Deut 173; Finkelstien, Siphre, vol. 2, 220:

Be ye perfect עם the Lord your God   תמים תהיה עם ה' אלהיך
If you do all that is said   אם עשית כל האמור
on this subject, you (will be)   בענין הר'
perfect ל the Lord your God.   אתה תמים לה' אלהים

The "ל", as indicated, can be taken in the same meaning as the Hebrew עם. Cf. M.H. Segal, A Grammar of Mishnaic Hebrew (Oxford: Clarendon, 1927) 141: prepositions are preserved from Biblical Hebrew in their old significance. Also R.J. Williams, Hebrew Syntax: An Outline, 52, no. 274.

Sipre Deut 173 gives two exegeses of Deut 18:13, the one above preserving the anomaly by using a vague preposition; also an interpretation which avoids any comparison of man with God: When you (are) perfect, your inheritance   כאשתה תם חלקך
is with the Lord your God.   עם ה' אלהיך

[59] תמים: IQS i.8; ii.2; iii.3,9; iv.22; viii.9, 10, 18, 20, 21; ix.2, 5, 6, 8, 9, 19; IQSa i.28; IQSb i.2; IQM vii.5; xiv.7; IQH iv.30.
תים: IQS v.24; x.21; xi.2, 11; IQSa i. 17; IQH iv.30.
תם: IQS i.13; viii.25; xi.17; IQH iv.32.

[60] Eduard Lohse, Die Texte aus Qumran, pp. 4, 20, 6, 54, 28, 30.

[61] The idea of perfection is linked to the root דרך: IQS i.13; ii.2; iv.22; v.24; viii.10, 18, 21, 25; ix.2, 5, 9; xi.2, 11, 17; IQSa i.17, 28; IQSb v.22; IQM xiv.7; IQH i.36; iv.30, 32; CDC ii.15. It is linked to the root הלך: IQS i.8; ii.2; iii.9; viii.18, 20, 21; ix.6, 8, 9, 19; IQSb i.2; v.22; CDC i.21; ii.15; vii.5.

[62] The verb כלה is usually translated with συντελέω in the Pentateuch, Judges, Ruth, I and II Sam, I and II Kgs, I and II Chr.

[63] Also at Exod 12:15, and three times outside the Pentateuch. In the LXX, the word τέλειος is used only for the roots תם and שלם (and once for כלה in Ps 139:22).

[64] Det. 154; cf. also Aet. 26 and De Providentia, frag. 1.

[65] Abr. 74; similarly Deus 106: πρῶτον καὶ μέγιστον καὶ τελεώτατον. . . Moreover all the realms, from the height of the heavens to the depth of the waters, were described as τέλεια καὶ πλήρη πάντα διὰ πάντων εἶναι, "being perfect and complete all in all" Plant. 128. (Further texts of Philo referring to the world as God's "perfect work": Cher. 112; Mos. ii, 267; Conf. 97; Spec. ii, 59.

[66] Plant. 2; cf. also Her. 156.

In parallel construction, Philo wrote of the perfection of the world and of God in Aet. 1:
Nothing among sensible things   οὔτε γὰρ ἐν αἰσθητοῖς
is more perfect than the world;   παντελέστερόν τι τοῦ κόσμου
nothing among noetic things   οὔτε ἐν νοητοῖς

is more perfect than God.   θεοῦ τελεώτατον. . .

God is the Perfect Good - Decal. 81 and Conf. 180:
. . . Who is the first   ὅς ἐστι τὸ πρῶτον ἀγαθον
and Most Perfect Good.   καὶ τελεώτατον. . .

He (God) is the most   τὸ πρεσβύτατον τῶν ὄντων
Ancient of Beings and   καὶ τελειότατον ἀγαθον
the Most Perfect Good.   αὐτὸς ἦν.

It follows that perfect goodness is attributed to God - Deus 73:
But God, remembering His   μεμνημένος δὲ τῆς περὶ
perfect and universal   πάντα τελείας ἀγαθότητος
goodness. . .   ἑαυτοῦ ὁ θεός. . .

For Philo, it ia a very plain fact that absolute perfection belongs to God alone - Her. 121 (also Plant. 14 and Post. 143):
For no one reaches perfection   τέλειος γὰρ οὐδεὶς ἐν
in any of his pursuits, but   οὐδενὶ τῶν ἐπιτηδευμάτων
undoubtedly all perfection   ἀλλ' ἀψευδῶς αἱ τελειότητες
and finality belong to   καὶ ἀκρότητες ἑνός εἰσι μόνου.
One alone.
In this passage there is the implication of man's striving for a
certain perfection.

[67] Sac. 8.

[68] Gig. 45.

[69] L.A. ii. 91; cf. also Ebr. 94.

[70] Det. 160. It was God's choice to give particular laws
διὰ τοῦ τελειοτάτου τῶν προφητῶν, "by the most perfect of prophets," Moses (Decal. 175).

[71] Deus 4, Abr. title.

[72] Det. 132.

[73] Sac. 120.

[74] Mig. 214; Ebr. 82; Agr. 42; Som. i, 214.

[75] Det. 60. Cf. also Questions and Answers on Genesis, Book
I, Q 97 on Gen 6:9: "But righteousness and perfection and being
pleasing to God are the greatest virtues."

[76] Spec. i, 63.

[77] L.A. i, 94.

[78] Fug. 12; cf. also Som. ii, 45.

[79] Plant. 94.

[80] Philo wrote that men were called to honour God βουλόμενος
δὲ τὸ γένος τῶν ἀνθρώπων. . . εἰς ὁδον. . ., "because he wishes
to lead the huamn race. . . in the way," the goal being
ἐπιστήμην τοῦ ὄντως ὄντος, ὅς ἐστι τὸ πρῶτον ἀγαθον καὶ τελεώτατον, "knowledge of the Being of Beings, who is the First and

most Perfect Good" (Decal. 81).

[81]Numerically, exegetes have been almost equally divided on
which was "prior," Matt 5:48 or Luke 6:36. A quite full list is
given in Jacques Dupont, Les Béatitudes[2] t. 1. (Bruges-Louvain:
E. Nauwalaerts, 1968) 153, n.2. Three of the influential voices
for the priority of the Lukan wording were:
J. Wellhausen, Das Evangelium Matthaei (Berlin, 1904) 24; Alfred
Loisy, Les Evangiles Synoptiques I (Ceffonds, 1907) 589; M.-J.
Lagrange, Evangile selon Saint Matthew (Paris: Gabalda, 1927) 118
acknowledging Wellhausen.

The argument favouring the priority of Luke runs thus: when
Matt 19:21 (and context) has been set beside Luke 18:22 (and context), it is deduced that Matthew inserted the word τέλειος in
19:21. Thence, as the argument goes, Matthew's τέλειος in 5:48
is an introduction also, hence the sentence in Luke was the
primitive form. The argument is given further support since an
almost exact parallel to Luke 6:36 is found in Tg. Ps.-J. at
Lev 22:28.

Some writers have been cautious. Adolf Harnack (The Sayings
of Jesus: The Second Source of St. Matthew and St. Luke [London:
Withams & Norgate; N.Y.: Putnam's Sons, 1908] 63) wrote that it
was "difficult to decide whether τέλειοι or οἰκτίρμονες is the
original word." Like Harnack, Rudolph Bultmann was cautious in
not giving a decision as to which was prior: "One of the two
has made alterations; either Matthew to use the saying as the
conclusion of what preceded it, or Luke to make it the introduction to what follows" (The History of the Synoptic Tradition
[Oxford: Blackwell, 1963] 96). In 1945, David Daube devoted
seven pages to the verses in question ("Concerning the Reconstruction of the 'Aramaic Gospels'" BJRL 29, 1945, 69-105, cf.
97-104). In the light of his researches, Daube wrote that "the
question of priority need not here be raised at all." In 1959,
Jacques Dupont devoted an article to the verses in question:
("'Soyez parfaits'[Mt. V, 48] 'Soyez miséricordieux' [Lc. VI,
36]" Sacra Pagina II, [Paris: Librarie Lecoffre; Gembloux:
Duculot, 1959] 150-162). Dupont's position was stated: "Je ne
compte pas m'attarder à cette question de priorité; mon but est
plutôt de faire ressortir la difference de mentalité qui se
révèle dans ces deux rédactions"; however Dupont's leaning was
in favour of Lukan priority, and this he had acknowledged as his
stand in Les Béatitudes, t. 1 (1958) 158.

In spite of the painstaking work of those who find it wiser
not to debate the question of priority, there are modern exegetes
still repeating that the one or the other was the more "original."
For Lukan priority: Gerhard Barth (Günther Bornkamm-Gerhard
Barth- Heinz Joachim Held, Tradition and Interpretation in
Matthew [Philadelphia: Westminster, 1963] 97); Werner Georg
Kümmel (The Theology of the New Testament [N.Y.-Nashville:
Abingdon, 1973] 49); and W.D. Davies (The Setting of the Sermon
on the Mount [Cambridge: University Press, 1966] 210). On the

other hand, Matthew Black (An Aramaic Approach to the Gospels and Acts[3] [Oxford: Clarendon, 1967] 181) attributes the "original form of the saying as spoken by Jesus" to Matthew.

[82] E.P. Sanders, The Tendencies of the Synoptic Tradition (Cambridge: The University Press, 1969) 274.
Here is a slightly fuller excerpt from this conclusion: "There are no hard and fast laws of the development of the Synoptic tradition. On all counts the tradition developed in opposite directions. It became both longer and shorter, both more and less detailed, and both more and less Semitic. Even the tendency to use direct discourse for indirect, which was uniform in the post-canonical material which we studied, was not uniform in the Synoptics themselves. For this reason, dogmatic statements that a certain characteristic proves a certain passage to be earlier than another are never justified. . . One may only say that the balance of probability is that material richer in detail and direct speech is later. Further, these criteria should be applied to an entire document, and not to any one pericope. The canons are not so certain that one may say that a detail in one of Matthew's pericopes proves it to be later than the parallel in Luke." (pp. 272 and 274).

[83] Independent ἐκεῖνος, rather than attributive, is a characteristic of John. Cf. A. Blass and A. Debrunner, A Greek Grammar of the New Testament and Other Early Christian Literature (Chicago-London: University of Chicago Press, 1961) no. 291, 152.
John uses ἐκεῖνος as a pronoun with a wide variety of antecedents. In the Gospel of John, a few of the occurrences have clear reference to Jesus (for example, 7:11, 9:12, 28, 37; 19:15) and a few have reference to the Father (for example, 5:19, 37, 38; 6:29; 8:42 and probably 1:33). In I John, the reference is apparently to Jesus at 2:6, 3:16 and 4:17. In 3:1-7 there are no immediate antecedents but "God" and he who "appeared" and who is (or is not) "seen" or "known." This vocabulary (φαίνω-φανερός, ὁράω, γινώσκω) is highly reminiscent of that in John 1:1-34 (cf. especially 1:5, 10, 18, 31, 34).
If, by reference to the wider context of the Johannine writings, the antecedent of ἐκεῖνος is thought to be "Jesus" in I John 3:3 and 3:7, then it ought to be conceded that this would be Jesus specifically in the capacity of the Word revealing God. It might more simply be said that the antecedent in this context is God-revealed. However, a specific word in the context cannot be pinpointed as the antecedent, as is also the case in John 1:33. Here is the question: could John use the emphatic pronoun this way seemingly for God and expect his readership to have no problem with the usage?
The word הוא used as "He" for God is found at Num 23:19: אל . . . ההוא אמר ולא יעשא, "God. . . has He said, and will He not do (it)?" In the context, the "He" is emphatic, in a contrast to the people who do not keep their word. (The haggadah in the fragment targums on the verse does not utilize this הוא;

only Tg. Onq. retains it. The LXX uses αὐτός.)

The last words of the well-known verse, Exod 3:14, have been syntactically "improved" in Tgs. Neof. and Ps.-J. and in MS P. Exod 3:14: אהיה שלחני אליכם, "'I am' has sent me to you."‾‾‾ Tg. Neof.: הוא שלח יתי לוותכון, "'He' has sent me to you." By handing down this translation, the targumic traditions would have fostered an understanding of הוא standing as a name, as it were, for God. (The LXX, by use of the participle, reads more smoothly than does the Hebrew text: Ὁ ὤν ἀπέσταλκέν με πρὸς ὑμᾶς.) The practice was known in Rabbinic tradition. (Amongst others, Hillel and Rabbi Meir used it.) Cf. A. Marmorstein, The Old Rabbinic Doctrine of God, no. 37, p. 84.

[84]When we examine the usage of ἁγνός (and cognates) among the NT writers, we find that James has placed it first in a list of attributes of the "wisdom that is from above" (3:17); it occurs in the virtue lists at Phil 4:8, II Cor 6:6 and Tit 2:5; it is proffered as appropriate behaviour for Christian wives (I Pet 3:2) and for Timothy (I Tim 5:22). The verb ἁγνίζω is used with respect to purification before formal worship (John 11: 55; Acts 21:24, 26, and 24:18). Conceptually, ἁγνός (and cognates) and ἅγιος (and cognates) have a certain relationship; the latter is the usual translation of the root קדש in the LXX, however the much less frequent ἁγνός seldom translates anything but the root קדש. Purity, then, is an aspect of holiness which stresses being fit for worship.

When we examine the usage of δικαιοσύνη (and cognates) among the NT writers, we find it to have a broad but definite meaning. In both Paul and Matthew it stands as the opposite of ἁμαρτία (and cognates: Rom 5:21, 6:12-14, 8:10; Gal 3:21-22, 12:16-18; the opposite of ἀδικία (and cognates): Rom 1:17-18; 3:5, 6:13; Matt 5:45; and the opposite of ἀνομία (and cognates) Rom 6:19; II Cor 6:14; Matt 23:28.

Righteousness - Hebrew צדקה; Aramaic זכותא or זכו - consisted primarily in doing the commandments (Deut 6:25). The word זכו has a very broad meaning ranging form innocent or guiltless to well-deserving, privileged, worthy or meritorious. The root זכי is not only used to translate the Hebrew צדק but also נקי/ה in the Pentateuch targums; the most noteworthy instance of the latter occurs in the commandments, Exod 20:7 and Deut 5:11, ". . . the Lord will not hold him זכי, guiltless, who takes His name in vain." In the targumic haggadah we find a developed theology of זכותיה, "merits." Thus we can observe a broad but well-defined meaning of זכי in the targums.

Righteousness is an attribute of God in the Hebrew Bible and in the targums, especially Tg. Ps.-J. Also, throughout the targumic tradition it is an attribute of the revered ancestors; and it is an attribute of those who keep the commandments of God, the Law. For the righteous who keep the Law in this world, the result is reward in the world to come; for those who do not, the result is the retribution due to the wicked. We can suggest that all this lies behind the conceptual content of δικαιοσύνη (and cognates) in the first century writers of the NT.

When we examine the usage of οἰκτίρμων and cognates) in Paul, we find that it is predicated of God (Rom 9:15, 12:1; II Cor 1:3) and of Christ (Phil 2:1). Thus Luke 6:36 is not at all discordant with Paul's orientation. Jas 5:11 gives a text: "the Lord is compassionate and merciful (οἰκτίρμων)," reflecting an OT combination of concepts (cf. for example, Exod 33:19, Deut 13:16, Pss 103:8 and 111:4).

There was a targumic predilection for the root רחם, "mercy" - often in the plural, רחמין. A few examples: (1) translating the Hebrew אהב at Deut 10:12, 15, 19; 11:13, 22; 13:4; 9:9; 30:6, 20 in Tgs. Onq., Ps.-J. and Neof.: (2) רחם in additions to the text in Tgs. Ps.-J., Neof., MS V (N and ed. B) at Deut 3:24; and at 9:18, 26 also in Ps.-J. and Neof.; further in 9:14 20, 25, 27 in Tg. Neof. The very outstanding addition at Tg. Ps.-J. Lev 22:28 contains a parallel for Luke 6:36 (above p. 38).

[85] Occurrences: Tg. Neof., MS V (N and ed. B) at Deut 22:4; Tgs. Ps.-J. and Neof. at Exod 23:5.

[86] Finkelstein, Siphre, vol. 2, 257.

[87] Gen. Rab. 13:15 three times and 57:2 twice. Cf. מדרש רבה בראשית רבה vol. 1, 100; vol. 2, 278-280.

[88] Lauterbach, Mekilta, vol. 2, 178. Further examples:

Vol. 2, 23-24:

Thou art a helper and a	ערזר וסומך אתה
supporter of all who come	לכל באי העולם
into the world but of me	אבל לי ביותר
especially. . .	
Thou art the song of all	זמרה אתה
who come into the world,	לכל באי העולם
but of me especially. . .	אבל לי ביותר
Thou art the salvation of	ישועה אתה
all who come into the world	לכל באי העולם
but of me especially.	אבל לי ביותר

Vol. 2, 32-24:

The Lord is His name,	יי שמו
in that He is merciful with	שהוא מרחם
respect to His creatures. . .	על בריותיו
The Lord is His name,	יי שמו
in that He sustains and	שהוא זן ומפרנס
provides for all His creatures. . .	כל בריותיו

Vol. 2, 110:

If God thus (provided manna)	אם כן זימן
for those who provoked Him,	המקום למכעיסיו
how much more will He in the	על אחת כמה וכמה
future pay a good reward to	ישלם שכר טוב
the righteous.	למדיקים לעתיד לבא

72

[89]Josephus, B. III. 375. Cf. above Chap. I, n. 74, p. 31.

[90]Besides the two texts offered, note: I Cor 4:16, 11:1;
I Thess 2:14; II Thess 3:7, 3:9. Cf. also Heb 6:12 and 3:7.

[91]1 Clem. 33:2, 7, 8. The Apostolic Fathers I, 62 and 64.

[92]The Apostolic Fathers I, 212. The imitation of God is the
theme of a passage in the Epistle to Diognetus (normally counted
among the Apostolic Fathers but of uncertain authorship and date).
Man is in the image of God (10:1); the conclusion is that man
imitates God in His goodness. Cf. The Apostolic Fathers II, 370-
372. One outstanding line (10:4) is:
And do not wonder that it is   καὶ μὴ θαυμάσῃς εἰ δύναται
possible for man to be the   μιμητὴς ἄνθρωπος γενέσθαι
imitator of God.   θεοῦ.

[93]The Apostolic Fathers I, 246.

[94]Cf. William F. Arndt and F. Wilbur Gingrich, A Greek-
English Lexicon of the New Testament and Other Early Christian
Literature (Chicago: University of Chicago Press; London:
Cambridge University Press, 1957) 333, sect. I. 4.

[95]Ign. Smyrn. 4:2, The Apostolic Fathers I, 256:
. . . and the perfect man   . . . αὐτοῦ με ἐνδυναμοῦντος
himself gives me strength.   τοῦ τελείου ἀνθρώπου.

[96]Ign. Smyrn. 10:2, The Apostolic Fathers I, 262:
And he who is perfect hope,   ἡ τελεία ἐλπίς,
Jesus Christ. . .   Ἰησοῦς Χριστός.

[97]The Apostolic Fathers I, 172.

[98]The Apostolic Fathers I, 298.

[99]"Fruit" used in the same way as in Matt 7:20.

[100]The Apostolic Fathers I, 22. Bearing on the same theme:
1 Clem. 53:5, ibid. 100:
(Speaking of Moses) O great love!   ὦ μεγάλης ἀγάπης,
O unsurpassable perfection!   ὦ τελειότητος ἀνυπερβλήτου.
Clement connects love and perfection in 49:5, ibid. 92:
In love were all the elect   ἐν τῇ ἀγάπῃ ἐτελειώθησαν
of God made perfect.   πάντες οἱ ἐκλεκτοὶ τοῦ θεοῦ. . .
Also in 50:3, ibid. 94:
but those who were perfected   ἀλλ' οἱ ἐν ἀγάπῃ
in love. . .   τελειωθέντες. . .

[101]Older commentaries often suggest moral perfection. More
recent commentaries, taking Matt 5:48 only in its NT context,
suggest a complete, overabundant righteousness. Cf. for example:
Daniel Patte, The Gospel According to Matthew: A Structural
Commentary on Matthew's Faith (Philadelphia: Fortress, 1987) 76.
Pierre Bonnard has a yet more comprehensive view; cf. his
L'Evangile selon saint Matthieu (Genève: Delachaux et Niestle,

1970 and 1982) 75-76: "Le thème de la perfection, dans les
écrits bibliques, n'exprime pas tant l'idée de pureté morale
que celle d'engagement total. . . " Bonnard's resources range
from Lev 19:2 to the most pertinent NT comparisons. Hence both
the OT and NT form the context from which he has made his
deduction.

It is by our use of broader resources that we can suggest
that the focus in "perfection" lies in creative good works, the
pinacle of the "engagement total."

CHAPTER III
MEASURE FOR MEASURE

Matt 7:2b: καὶ ἐν ᾧ μέτρῳ μετρεῖτε μετρηθήσεται ὑμῖν,
"and with what measure you measure, it shall be measured to you."
In Matt 7:2b, Luke 6:38b and Mark 4:24b, we have a saying with
the character of an old proverb. The contexts in Matthew and
Luke vary from that in Mark; the saying in Luke varies slightly
in form from that in Matthew and Mark. It is difficult to say
much more without turning to the saying as we find it in other
sources, notably the Palestinian targums of the Pentateuch.

We shall review occurrences of the idea of due measure,
then the specific occurrences of the "measure for measure" maxim
in the Pentateuch targums of Gen 38:25 and Lev 26:43. These
latter texts show how "measure for measure" was a principle of
exegesis and also a popular saying which could be invoked at
appropriate times. In early Jewish literature, we find the
"measure for measure" saying, also the development that in the
eschatological context the measure of good reward would be
greater than the measure of evil. When the contexts of the
saying in the targums and early midrashim, the Gospels and the
Apostolic Fathers are observed together, we can come to a
better appreciation of the place of the saying in the ongoing
Palestinian tradition.

"Measure for Measure" in the Hebrew Bible and Targums

The concept of "measure" is infrequent in the Pentateuch[1]
where its normal meaning is that of physical measure, the ac-
curacy of which is stressed as just, for example, Lev 19:35:
"You shall do no wrong in judgement, in measure (מדה) of weight
or quantity." The word מסת occurs only once in the entire Hebrew
Bible at Deut 16:10b:

> . . . the measure of the   מסת נדבת ידך
> freewill offering of your   אשר תתן כאשר
> hand which you shall give   יברכך יהוה אלהיך
> as the Lord your God
> blesses you.

The word מסת apparently drew the attention of the targumists.
Not only was it retained in Deut 16:10 (Tgs. Neof., Ps.-J. and
Onq.) but also used elsewhere. As examples: (1) Deut 25:1-3 in
Tgs. Neof., Ps.-J., Onq. (N and ed. B), "According to the
measure of (כמיסת) his offense"; (2) Deut 18:4 Tg. Ps.-J. has an
additional phrase: "according to the measure of (כמסת) a girdle";
(3) Tg. Ps.-J. Num 6:21: "according to the measure of (כמיסת) his
vow"; (4) Tgs. Ps.-J. and Neof. Num 7:5 and 7:7: "according to
the measure of (כמיבת) his/their service"; (5) Tgs. Ps.-J. and
Neof. Deut 16:17: "every man according to the measure of (כמיסת)
the gift of his hands, as (כ) the blessing of the Lord God who
gave to you" (however Tg. Onq. retained the parallel כ and כ of
the Hebrew text. This meant reciprocating to God.

Gen 38:25, Lev 26:43 and the contribution of the targums to the
discussion of these texts. - The reciprocal idea took yet another turn in the targumic traditions - that as a man did, so
would events redound upon him. This is illustrated by the
following material.

The location of chap. 38 in Genesis has often drawn comment;
it has been viewed as an interruption of the Joseph story.[2] Perhaps one reason for its present position is that there is a
small sytlistic parallel between Gen 37:32-33 and Gen 38:25-26:

Gen 37: 32-33: And they sent (וישליו) the long robe
with sleeves and brought it to their father and said
(ויאמרו) "This we have found; see now (הכר נא) whether
it is your son's robe or not." And he recognized it
and said (ויכירה ויאמר), "it is my son's robe. . ."

Gen 38:25-26: . . . she sent (והיא שליה) to her father-
in-law. . . And she said, see now (ותאמר הכר נא) whose
these are, the signet and the cord and the staff." Then
Judah recognized them and said (ויכר יהודה ויאמר), "She
is more righteous than I. . ."

This stylistic parallel did not go unnoticed by the targumists.

The words הכר נא in Genesis 37 were taken as spoken by Judah who

was causing grief to his father; and in Genesis 38 as spoken to

Judah and causing grief to him. In their explanation, the tar-

gumists invoked the saying, "the measure according to the meas-

ure" in a longer and in a shorter form - twice - in the course of

their haggadic midrash upon the verse. According to MS V:

In the measure in which	במכלה דאנש
a man measures, it shall	מכיל ביה
be measured to him, whether	מתכיל ליה
it be a good measure or	בין מכלה טבה
a bad measure. . .	ובין מכלה בישא. . .
the measure to which	מכלה לו
corresponds the measure	קביל מכלה
and orders to which	וסדרין לו
correspond orders.	קבל סדרין

Thus MSS V (N and ed. B) - and Tg. Neof. which has the first form
of the saying only.[3] There is some variation in MS P and P 75:[4]

In the measure in which	במכילתא דאיניש
a man measures on earth	מכייל בארעא בה
it shall be measured	מכיילין ליה
to him in heaven, whether	בשמיא
it be a good measure or	בין מיכלא טבא
a bad measure. . .	ובין מיכלא בישא. . .
measure for measure,	מיכלא לקביל מיכלא
order of judgement	וס]ד[ר דין
for order of judgement.	לקבל ס]ד[ר דין

CTg D is akin to the former citation in the first form of the

saying; and to the latter in the second form of the saying.

The variation of MS P and the P 75 tosephta brings out an

eschatological note in the contrasted words: בארעא and בשמיא; in

these manuscripts and CTg D the word association of measure-

judgement is clear (but might be taken as implied by the context
in the other manuscripts).

A caution must be enunciated: because both the longer form
and the shorter form of the saying stand in MSS V (N and ed. B)
MS P and the P 75 tosephta, and CTg D, there is no way (either
logically or chronologically) of conjecturing priority of one to
the other; this should not be done. Neither can we say when the
shorter saying was coupled with its parallel: "the order of
judgement according to the order of judgement."

We find in the "blessings and curses" chapter of Leviticus
(chap. 26), a discussion of divine retribution. For our purposes, the most significant line is v 43b:

. . . and they shall make	והם ירצו את עונם
amends for their iniquity	
because they spurned my	יען וביען
ordinances, and their soul	במשפטי מאסו
abhorred my statutes.	ואת חקתי געלה נפשם

The wording יען וביען with its element of redundancy provoked
interpretive commentary by the targumist-exegetes. This is
evidenced in the material in the targums which replaces the
words יען וביען:

Tg. Ps.-J.

Measure for measure   מיכלא כל קביל מיכלא היא

MS P

Measure for measure,	מיכלא חולף מיכלא
order of judgement	וסדר דין
for order of judgement.	חולף סדר דין

MS V

Measure for measure,	מכלא חלף מכלא
orders for orders.	וסדרין חלף סדרין

It is clear from the context that the targumists have in mind the
divine recompense. In MS P there is the word-association:
measure-judgement - consistent with the same manuscript for
Gen 38:26.

The widely attested haggadah on Gen 38:26 would have contributed to the "measure for measure" maxim being widely known.
The exegetes were commenting upon the turn of events in Judah's
life, but the eschatological dimension did enter into the hag-

gadah. Because the passive voice had become a usage for signifying the Divinity, it is not surprising that it would acquire
this signification in the second clause: ". . . it shall be
measured." The divine recompense is implied in the targumic
treatment of Lev 26:43, "measure for measure." The "measure for
measure" principle in the targums stands as part of the evidence
for its popularity; this is corroborated by its repeated attestation in other early Jewish literature.

"Measure for Measure" in other Early Jewish Literature

In the midrashic works compiled in the tannaitic period, we
find the saying incorporated into the commentary on a variety of
texts. We offer a few examples. The clause of Gen 1:31, "it was
very (מאד) good" was elaborated in Gen. Rab. 9:11 with the
"measure for measure" idea because of the similarity of the word
מדה (measure) to the word מאד (very):[5]

R. Simon said	אמר ר' סימון
in R. Simeon b. Abba's name:	בשם ר' שמעון בר אבא:
All measures have ceased,	כל המדות בטלו
yet the rule of measure	מדה כנגד מדה
for measure has not ceased.	לא בטלה.
R. Huna said in R. Jose's name:	ר' הונה בשם ר' יוסי:
from the very beginning	מתחלת בריתו
of the world's creation,	של עולם
the Holy One, blessed be He,	צפה הקדוש ברוך הוא
foresaw that with the measure	שבמדה אשדם מודד
a man measures, with it they	בה מודדין לו.
will measure to him.	
Therefore Scripture said	לפיכך אמרו חכמים:
And behold it was very good,	והנה טוב מאד--
meaning, behold, there is	הנה טוב מדה.
a good measure.	

The Mekilta has an extended passage on Exod 13:19a[6] which
offered the comment that Moses took the bones of Joseph with him.
Several thoughts are gathered together by the compilers of the
Mekilta: as Joseph was concerned to bury his father, Moses was
concerned over the bones of Joseph, and God Himself buried Moses.
In the midst of these ideas we find the old maxim:[7]

(This is) to teach you that	ללמדך שבמדה
with the measure with which	שאדם נודד
a man measures, the (i.e. God)	בה מודדין לו
measure to him.	

Almost immediately, commenting on Exod 13:21a,[8] the same maxim is evoked in exactly the same words and presented as the principle upon which God responded to the needs of the people in the wilderness: as Abraham had acted hospitably toward God - Abraham had accompanied his guests - so God accompanied the people; Abaraham had fetched water, so God gave a well in the desert, and so forth. In this manner, the "measure for measure" maxim has become an exegetical principle in the Mekilta.[9]

In Sipre on Num 12:13, we read that it was just that the desert encampment had to wait because of Miraim's leprosy; it was just, for at one time she had had to wait for Moses; so the saying is invoked:[10]

. . . according to the measure	שבמדה
with which a man measures,	שאדם מודד בה
they (i.e. God) measure to him.	מודדים לו

In Sipre Deut 32:5 and 32:15, the saying is given not with the passive voice in the second clause, but with the first person, with God presented as the speaker. Sipre on Deut 32:15:[11]

The Holy One, blessed be	אמר להם
He, said to them, 'with the	הקדוש ברוך הוא
measure that you measure, with	במדה שמדדתם
it I will measure to you.'	כי מדדתי לכם

An eschatological overtone is sounded in the discussion of the measures or reward and punishment in Mekilta on Exod 12:12; it appears twice on the one page there (with variety only to suit the two contexts); here is one of them:[12]

Behold the words kal vahomer:	והרי הדברים קל וחמר
and if with respect to the measure	ומה אם מידת
of retribution (which is) less,	הפורענות מעוטה
the Holy One, blessed be He,	אמר הקב"ה לעשות
says (He will) act and acts,	ועשה מידת
(how much more with respect to)	הטובה שמרובה
the measure of good which (is)	
greater.	

This appears almost verbatim in ʾAbot R. Nat. 30,[13] three times (with variety only to suit the three contexts); here is one of them:[14]

Now then, which is the	וכי איזה מדה מרובה
greater measure, the measure	מדה טובה
of good or the measure of	או מדת פורענות
retribution? Surely the	
measure of good!	הוי אומר מדה טובה
Behold the words <u>kal vahomer</u>:	והרי דברים
If (it is a matter of)	קל וחומר
the measure of retribution	אם מדת פורענות
(which is) less, (if one is)	מעוטה
in doubt (whether) he	העובר עבורה בספק
committed a transgression,	מעלה עליו
the guilt is upon him.	הכתוב כאלו
How much more with respect	עשאה בודאי
to the measure of good	קל וחומר
(which is) greater.	למדת הטוב מרובה:

The strict "measure for measure," then, was modified by the idea of the abundance of the blessing of God.[15] Apparently, this teaching has been fairly standardized in its wording. The main idea spelled out here seems to have been taken for granted by the commentator in <u>Sipra</u> in the discourse on Lev 5:18:[16]

R. José said:	ר' יוסי אומר
if you wish to know	אם נפשך לידע
what the given wages	מתן שכרן
of the just are in the	של צדיקים
future to come, go and	לעתיד לבוא
learn from the first man.	צא ולמד מאדם הקהמזני
There was only one	שלא נצטוה אלא
negative precept	מצוה אחת
imposed on him; he	בלא תעשה
violated it.	ועבר עליה
See how many of the	ראה רמה
dead were punished:	מיתות נקנסו
him and his generations,	לו ולדורותיו
generations of generations	ולדורות דורותיו
to the end of his generations.	עד טוף דורותיו
Well, the greater measure	וכי אי זו מידה מרובה
is the measure of good	מידת הטובה
(greater) than the measure	או מידת פורענות
of retribution.	

The midrashim, as we have seen, introduce the "measure for measure" idea as the principle upon which explanations can be built, or as a kind of justification for events or ideas discussed. It is introduced either in a shorter or a longer form as the case required. Since this is so, we have reason to believe that the maxim was an old one by the time of these writings.[17]

Already in Jub. 4:31 (probably dating from the second century B.C.[18]), the "measure for measure" principle had been used in elaborating on Gen 9:6a, a verse which lent itself very well to such treatment: ". . . for his (Cain's) house fell upon him and he died in the midst of his house, and he was killed by its stones; for with a stone he had killed Abel, and by a stone was he killed in righteous judgement."[19] After this, the writer of Jubilees recalled the law of talion in the "heavenly tablets," probably an allusion to Exod 21:23-25 or Lev 24:19-20. Gen 9:6a had evoked a few extra words in CTg E and Tg. Neof.: ". . . by hand of a son of man (על ידי בר נש) shall his blood be shed." Tgs. Onq. and Ps.-J. show a rather forensic expansion on the verse. Philo briefly comments on the verse,[20] and in his writings uses the idea of measure for measure,[21] but does not cite the saying in the manner of the Mekilta. Finally, Bib. Ant. 44 (probably dating from about 100 A.D.[22]) ends with the idea in an eschatological context:[23]

And when the soul parts	Et cum discernitur
from the body, then they	anima a corpore tunc
shall say, 'Let us not	dicent: Non contrist-
mourn for the things	amur in his que passi
we have suffered, but	sumus, sed quia
because what we have	quecumque adinvenimus
devised, that shall	hec et recepimus.
we also receive.	

The early Jewish literature we have reviewed is sufficient for seeing the manner in which the idea of "measure for measure" was used, whether or not the explicit saying was cited. It was used as a well-known principle, which apparently developed from an everyday understanding of talion to an exegetical principle; then God could be viewed as the source of the recompense, and the saying could be used in eschatological contexts. This helps us to understand that the actual beginnings of both the idea,

and the explicit "measure for measure" saying were in all probability ancient and prior to the era of the available literature.[24]

"Measure for Measure" in Matt 7:2 and Luke 6:38

Among the NT writers, μέτρον/μετρέω, "measure," is used with
both concrete[25] and metaphorical[26] senses. However, it is only
in the Synoptics that we find a "measure for measure" saying as
such. The passive voice in the second part of the saying may
indicate God as agent. The profound character of the retribution - perhaps subtly eschatological - can be deduced only from
the use of the future tense and the broad context. Both Matthew
and Luke conclude the same kind of material with the "measure for
measure" saying as a justifying principle:

Matt 7:1-2

Judge not that you be	Μὴ κρίνετε, ἵνα μὴ
not judged. For with the	κριθῆτε° ἐν ᾧ γὰρ
judgement you judge you	κρίματι κρίνετε
will be judged, and with	κριθήσεσθε, καὶ ἐν
the measure you measure	ᾧ μέτρῳ μετρεῖτε
it will be measured to you.	μετρηθήσεται ὑμιν.

Luke 6:37-38

Judge not that you be not	Καὶ μὴ κρίνετε, καὶ
judged; condemn not and	οὐ μὴ κριθῆτε καὶ μὴ
you will not be condemned;	καταδικάζετε, καὶ οὐ
	μὴ καταδικασθῆτε
forgive and you will be	ἀπολύετε, καὶ
forgiven; give and	ἀπολυθήσεσθε δίδοτε,
it will be given to you,	καὶ δοθήσεται ὑμῖν°
good measure, pressed down,	μέτρον καλὸν πεπιεσμένον
shaken together, running	σεσαλευμένον ὑπερ-
over will be put into your	εκχυννόμενον δώσουσιν
lap. With the measure you	εἰς τὸν κόλπον ὑμῶν
measure it will be	ᾧ γὰρ μέτρῳ μετρεῖτε
measured to you (again).	ἀντιμετρηθήσεται ὑμῖν.

While both Matthew and Luke present the saying in a context implying the Judgement, Mark presents it in the context of the man-
ifestation of hidden things, similarly an eschatological theme.
In Mark 4:24b the reading is: ἐν ᾧ μέτρῳ μετρεῖτε μετρηθήσεται
ὑμῖν καὶ προστεθήσεται ὑμιν, "With the measure you measure it
shall be measured to you, and more will be given you."[27] We

have already seen the juxtaposition of "measure for measure" with "judgement for judgement" in the fragment targum tradition; the recurrence of this juxtaposition in Matthew and Luke is not surprising. In Mark we observe the added abundance of the return measure; in Luke the abundance of the returned gift immediately preceded the "measure for measure" saying. It is quite possible that the implication is the same as what is spelled out in the Mekilta on Exod 12:12, ʾAbot R. Nat. 30 and Sipra on Lev 5:18.

This added dimension of the abundant blessing is present in Mark and Luke, as in the more developed passages of the early midrashim; however this dimension is absent from Matthew and from the targums of the Pentateuch. The observation can be made, but a deduction as to why Matthew preferred the simpler idea would only be conjecture. One exact form of the saying should not be promoted as preferable; the precise wording and content would best be accepted as fluid.

Further Evidence in the Tradition of the Early Church

Both 1 Clem. 13:1-2 and Pol. Phil. 2:3 use the "measure for measure" saying in the same way as do Matthew and Luke. It concludes a series of maxims similarly expressed, as the concluding justifying principle for them all:[28]

I Clem 13:1-2

| Especially remembering the words of the Lord Jesus... for he spoke thus: 'Be merciful, that ye may obtain mercy. Forgive, that ye may be forgiven. As ye do, so shall it be done unto you. As ye give, so shall it be given unto you. As ye judge, so shall ye be judged. As ye are kind, so shall kindness be shown you. With what measure ye measure, it shall be measured to you. | μάλιστα μεμνημένοι τῶν λόγων τοῦ κυρίου Ἰησοῦ. . . οὕτως γὰρ εἶπεν° Ἐλεᾶτε ἵνα ἐλεηθῆτε° ἀφίετε, ἵνα ἀφεθῇ ὑμῖν° ὡς ποιεῖτε οὕτω ποιηθήσεται ὑμῖν° ὡς δίδοτε, οὕτως δοθήσεται ὑμῖν° ὡς κρίνετε, οὕτως κριθήσεσθε° ὡς χρηστεύεσθε οὕτως χρηστευθήσεται ὑμῖν° ᾧ μέτρῳ μετρεῖτε ἐν αὐτῷ μετρηθήσεται ὑμῖν. |

Pol. Phil. 2:3

... but remembering what
the Lord taught when he
said, 'Judge not that ye
be not judged, forgive
and it shall be forgiven
you; be merciful that
ye may obtain mercy;
with what measure ye
measure, it shall be
measured to you (again).

μνημονεύοντες δὲ ὧν
εἶπεν ὁ κύριος
διδάσκων° Μὴ κρίνετε,
ἵνα μὴ κριθῆτε°
ἀφίετε, καὶ ἀφεθήσεται
ὑμῖν° ἐλεᾶτε, ἵνα
ἐλεηθῆτε°
ᾧ μέτρῳ μετρεῖτε,
ἀντιμετρηθήσεται
ὑμῖν. . .

These two passages are introduced by words indicating that the
writers intended to present the sequence of instructions as
teachings of the Lord, that is, these amplified sequences have
been presented as material incorporated from the earliest Christian tradition. Both 1 Clem. 13:2 and Pol. Phil. 2:3 have
mandates with reciprocal clauses on judging and on mercy.
Matthew's "mercy for mercy" is placed not in such a list, but
among the Beatitudes, Matt 5:7; and it is reflected in Matt
18:33. In the parable of the unforgiving servant, Matt 18:23-25,
we find reflections of both "mercy for mercy" and "forgiveness
for forgiveness." The ideas of κρίσις, "judgement" and ἔλεος,
"mercy" were the first two of Matthew's "weightier matters of
the law" (23:23), and were also considered together by other
early Jewish and Christian writers.[29] Both 1 Clem. 13:2 and
Pol. Phil. 2:3 have mandates with reciprocal clauses on forgiveness. This is one of the features of the Our Father (Matt 6:12,
Luke 11:4, Did. 8:2[30]) and the Matthean embolism to that prayer
(Matt 6:14-15); it also was well known in Jewish tradition.[31]
Thus it can easily be seen how 1 Clem. 13:2 and Pol. Phil. 2:3
reflect the traditions extant in their milieu.

Summary and Concluding Remarks

The targums of the Pentateuch fostered the idea of the reciprocal measure in using כמסת, "according to the measure" in contexts of service of God or of offerings to God. The idea was taken up to explain the causes of events - as a man did, so it would befall him. This is evident in the haggadah on Gen 38:25-26 in the fragment targum tradition where the "measure for measure" saying was presented in both a longer and a shorter form, with or without eschatological overtones:

In the measure in which	במכלה דאנש מכיל (בארעא)
a man measures (on earth)	ביה נתכיל ליה (בשמיא)
it shall be measured to	
him (in heaven). . .	
measure for measure. . .	מיכלא לקביל מיכלא

The shorter form occurs in Tg. Ps.-J. and MSS P and V also at Lev 26:43b. Both in these sources of Lev 26:43b and in the fragment targums on Gen 38:25-26, the "measure for measure" saying is parallel to a "judgement for judgement" saying:

Order of judgement	סד⌈⌉ר דין לקבל סד⌈ד⌉ר דין
for order of judgement.	

In the Mekilta the "measure for measure" maxim has become an exegetical principle, a way of understanding good deeds and their reward in the events of the narratives of the Torah. Here, as well as in Sipra and Sipre, God is the agent in the second clause; and in some passages it is accepted that the measure of good - God's blessings - would be greater than the measure of retribution. Sometimes the saying was cited, and sometimes it was not, when the exegetical principle of "measure for measure" was employed. From the wide usage and from the contexts of the principle, we gain the impression that it was no new idea at the time of the tannaim. This accords with the manner in which the "measure for measure" saying is used in the targums - a saying at hand to be employed where the Biblical material provided an opening for it: in Gen 38:25-26 in explaining Judah's acceptance of his grief at his trial, and in Lev 26:43b when the translator was provoked simply by a turn of phrase in the Hebrew.

The added dimension of the abundant blessing is present in
Mark and Luke, as in the more developed passages of the early
midrashim; however this dimension is absent from Matthew and
from the targums of the Pentateuch. In Luke, other material is
inserted between "judgement for judgement" and the "measure for
measure" saying; but in Matthew, nothing intervenes - in Matt
7:1-2 there are only the two maxims. Thus among the Synoptics,
it is Matthew which preserves the simple pair that we saw in the
targums. The "measure for measure" maxim serves to underscore
"judge not that ye be not judged." Judgement is God's and not
man's; in this, the imitation of God is prohibited. The simple
form of Matt 7:1-2 stresses this single idea.

The texts we have offered from 1 Clement and Polycarp are
both longer and more detailed than those from Matthew or Luke
(or Mark). The Matthew text is longer and more specific than
the simple targumic comment at Lev 26:43b, but it comes very
close to the parallels in the targumic texts of Gen 38:26. Since
the natural tendency of literary tradition is such that texts
become longer and more detailed in the course of time,[32] we can
make a suggestion that the chronological order of the texts is
quite probably (1) those in the targums, (2) those in the
Synoptics, (3) those in 1 Clement and Polycarp. The sophistication in the early midrashim and the amplified sequences in
1 Clement and Polycarp are more akin to Luke than to Matthew.
The possibilities of such presentations as both Matthew's and
Luke's were probably present in the Jewish and early Christian
milieu; the question of priority should not be forced. Each
Evangelist made his choice.

87

Notes

[1] מדה at Lev 19:35 and Num 13:32; this word is found more frequently in the later books, especially Ezekiel. (מדד once in each of Exodus, Numbers, Deuteronomy; infrequently in the later books, but 35 times in Ezekiel.) In the LXX, μέτρον occurs nine times in the Pentateuch translating מדד, איפה and סאה.

[2] Cf. Judah Goldin, "The Youngest Son or Where Does Genesis 38 Belong?" JBL 96, 1977, 27-44.

[3] Among the sources there is slight orthographical variation. In the second part, MS N reads:

מכילא לקביל מכילא וסדדין לקבֿיל סדדין

[4] Thus MS P. Again, among the sources there is slight orthographical variation. For the first part, cf. also a tosephta of Biblia Hebraica, Ixar, 1490 and Biblia Hebraica, Lisbon, 1491, quoted in Alexander Sperber, The Bible in Aramaic based on Old Manuscripts and Printed Texts, Vol. 1 (Leiden: Brill, 1959) 354. Tg. Ps.-J. offers only דמיכלא קבל מיכלא. CTg D uses כלקבל in both stichs of the second part.

[5] מדרש רבה, בראשית רבה vol. 1, 63.

[6] Lauterbach, Mekilta, vol. 1, 176-179.

[7] Ibid., 177. Oxford Bodleian Heb c 75 (Klein, Genizeh Manuscripts, 91) and the tosephta T-S NS 182.2 (ibid., 93) have a short form similar to the Mekilta - above.

[8] Ibid., 183.

[9] At Exod 14:25, that the chariots of the Egyptians were caused to drive heavily (כבד), the "measure for measure" idea became an exegetical principle; Exod 5:9 comes to mind, the heavy (כבד) work laid upon the people in Egypt by the Egyptians. The result is as follows (Lauterbach, Mekilta, vol. 1, 241-242):

R. Judah says: With what	רבי יהודה אומר
measure they measure, with	במדה שמדדו
it Thou measurest unto them.	בה מדדת להם
They had said: 'Let the work	הם אמרו תכבד העבודה
be laid heavily' and Thou,	ואף אתה מדדת להם
likewise didst measure to	באותה המדה
them with the same measure.	
Therefore, it is said:	לכך נאמר
	וינהגהו בכבדות

'And made them to drive heavily.'
(Cf. also ibid., 244-245 where the same principle is implicit.) The mention of Pharaoh's chariots and his host in Exod 15:3-4 again reminded the compilers of the Mekilta of the same maxim:

With what measure a man measures,	במדה שאדם מודד בה
it is measured (they measure -	מודדין לו
God measures) to him.	

Here again, God is the One who provides "the same measure" when the Egyptians were cast into the sea who had formerly done the

same to the Hebrew babies (ibid., vol. 2, 36). Similarly, three
other rather forced examples (ibid., vol. 2, 36 twice and 39) –
in all these examples the "measure for measure" saying is explicitly cited. Just as with Pharaoh, so also with Amalek, and
"likewise every nation or kingdom that comes to harm Israel God
always judges according to this rule," and the maxim is again
cited exactly as above (ibid., vol. 2, 148).

[10] Horovitz, Siphre, vol. 1, 105. Cf. also Lauterbach,
Mekilta, vol. 1, 177-178.

[11] Sipre Deut 318, Finkelstein, Siphre, 363.
Sipre Deut 308, ibid., 348:

Moses told Israel another word	דבר אחר אמר להם
(of God), 'with the measure	משה לישראל
that you measure, with it I	במדה שמדדתם
will measure to you.'	בה מדדתי לכם

[12] Lauterbach, Mekilta, vol. 1, 55; cf. also vol. 2, 113,
246, 277.

[13] ʾAbot de Rabbi Nathan is a compilation. No authority
quoted in it is later than the tannaitic period; and "almost
everything about it, its language and substance, belongs to the
Tannaitic period" (John Bowker, The Targums and Rabbinic Literature [Cambridge: The University Press, 1969] 88). So it would
appear that the composition cannot be later than the third or
fourth century. The compilation, then, is of elements of varying
dates, some probably as early as the first century.

[14] Schechter, Aboth de Rabbi Nathan, 89. Each of the three
repetitions begins with וכי איזו, "thus then. . ."; each follows
a discussion under the name of one of the teachers: R. Meʾir,
R. Nathan ben Joseph, R. Aqiba. Hence our material appears as the
validating principle evoked for what is being taught. It would
appear to be interpolated and older than the final text for this
reason.

[15] Cf. Sipre on Num 10:36; Horovitz, Siphre, 83.

[16] J. H. Weiss, Sipra, 27a.

[17] For example, in the Mekilta (Lauterbach, vol. 2, 148) the
maxim is introduced simply by אמרו, "they say," which could be
taken to indicate a saying that has been handed down for an indefinite length of time - anonymity probably indicating antiquity.

[18] Charlesworth, The Pseudepigrapha, 143.

[19] R.H. Charles, The Apocrypha and Pseudepigrapha of the Old
Testament, vol. 2 (Oxford: Clarendon, 1913) 19.

[20] Questions and Answers on Genesis 61.

[21] Cher. 75, Mos. i. 44; cf. also Sac. 76, Som. ii. 193.

[22] Charlesworth, The Pseudepigrapha, 170.

[23] Guido Kisch, ed. Pseudo-Philo's Liber Antiquitatum Biblicarum (Notre Dame, Indiana: The University of Notre Dame, 1949) 232.

[24] For the very numerous parallels in later rabbinic literature, for the saying in both the longer and shorter forms, cf. Hermann L. Strack and Paul Billerbeck, Kommentar zum Neuen Testament, vol. 1, 444-446; H. P. Rüger, "Mit welchem Mass ihr messt, wird euch gemessen werden," ZNW 60, 1969, 174-182.

[25] Rev 11:1-2; 21:15, 16, 17.

[26] II Cor 10:12, 13; Rom 12:3; Eph 4:7, 13, 16; cf. also John 3:34 and Matt 23:32.

[27] If one sees only the idea of physical measure in the saying, then the comment of Boismard applies: "Mc 4:24b semble un élément aberrant. . . En Mc. le logion perd son sens initial, et il est difficile de lui en trouver un satisfaisant!" Cf. P. Benoit & M.-E. Boismard, Synopse des quatre évangiles en français, t. 2 (Paris: Cerf, 1972) 189.

[28] The Apostolic Fathers I, 30 and 284.

[29] As examples: Lauterbach, Mekilta, vol. 2, 28:

With me He dealt according	עמי נהג במדת רחמים
to the rule of mercy, but with	ועם אבותי נהג
my fathers He dealt according	במדת הדין
to the rule of justice. . .	. . . אלי
"My God" is but (signifies)	אלא מדת רחמים
the rule of mercy.	

Sipra 85c: J. H. Weiss, Sipra 85c; Rom 2:1-11, 9:14-15; Jas 2:13, 5:7-12, 1 Clem. 28:1.

[30] The Apostolic Fathers I, 320.

[31] Further, cf. J. Massingberd Ford, "The Forgiveness Clause in the Matthean Form of the Our Father," ZNTW 59, 1968, 127-131; Raymond E. Brown, New Testament Essays (N.Y.: Doubleday, 1965) 308-314.

[32] See n. 82, p. 69. Pace T. W. Manson, The Sayings of Jesus (Grand Rapids: Eerdmans, 1957) 55, who, amongst many others, felt compelled to suggest one version as "probably original"; for him it was Luke's version.

CHAPTER IV
THE ΛΟΓΟΙ AND THE ΜΩΡΟΣ

In Matt 7:24-27, the criterion of the behaviour upon which
the destiny of man is poised is "words": "he who hears My words
(μου τους λόγους) and. . . " In a reading of the obvious sense
of the passage, we see that the destinies consequent upon the
hearing and doing are severe. So the term λόγος, "word" must be
of a decisively serious nature. Therefore our first task is to
explore the conceptual content of the term "word(s)." Our second
task is to explore the conceptual content of the word μωρός,
"vacuous/vitiated" and the cognate verb μωραίνω; for the adjective
figures in Matt 7:24-27, and the verb in Matt 5:13. Since the
verb has as its subject in 5:13 the noun ἅλας, "salt," we also
have to observe contexts in which "salt" is used figuratively.
Having investigated the conceptual content and context of these
key terms, we can discuss Matt 7:24-27 and 5:13, the opening and
concluding passages of the Sermon on the Mount.

The aim in this section of our work is a better understanding of Matt 7:24-27 and 5:13. Our materials are arranged so
as to converge towards and culminate in discussion of these
passages. We begin with the more remote (in time) yet absolutely necessary material from the Hebrew of the Pentateuch, then
review pertinent passages from the Apocrypha and Pseudepigrapha,
the Qumran documents, the targums and early midrashim, with the

greatest attention given to the targums. The highlights of the
Christian tradition on the topic under discussion are briefly
reviewed (available when two or more NT writers, other than two
Synoptics, present the same idea). This is followed by a short
discussion of the mind of Matthew on the topic (or aspects of
the topic). Finally we reach each desired focal point: first,
Matt 7:24-27 can be appreciated in the light of the materials
previously presented; second, Matt 5:13 can be appreciated
similarly. Then a conclusion is added in which Matt 7:24-27
and 5:13 are discussed together as the opening and concluding
passages of the Sermon on the Mount.

A Discussion of Terminology: the "Words,"

the "Commandments," and the "Law" in the

Hebrew Bible, Apocrypha and Pseudepigrapha

The term "words"[1] for what God has commanded comes from the
earliest traditions in Exodus. Written upon the tables of stone
were "words"; reference to the "words" upon the stone tables was
made at the beginning and at the end of Exod 34:1-28, the presentation of the Sinai covenant by the Yahwist:

> The Lord (יהוה) said to Moses, 'Cut two tables of
> stone like the first; and I will write upon the
> tables the words (הדברים) that were on the first
> tables which you broke. . . And he wrote upon the
> tables the words of the covenant, the Ten Words
> (דברי הברית ישרת הדברים). (vv 1 and 28b)

The ceremonial of the covenant ratification in Exod 24:3-8
features the same vocabulary:

> Moses came and told the people all the words of the
> Lord (דברי יהוה) and the ordinances; and all the
> people answered with one voice and said, 'All the
> words (הדברים) which the Lord has spoken we will do
> (נעשה).' And Moses wrote all the words of the Lord
> (דברי יהוה). . . . Then he took the book of the
> covenant and read it in the hearing of the people;
> and they said, 'All that the Lord has spoken we
> will do and we will hear (נעשה ונשמע).' And Moses
> took the blood and threw it upon the people, and
> said, 'Behold the blood of the covenant which the

Lord has made with you in accordance with all these
words (הדברים).' (vv 3, 4a, 7, 8)

When the Elohist presented the Ten Words, his introduction was
thus: "And Elohim spoke all these words (וידבר אלהים את כל
הדברים האלה)."(Exod 20:1)

The writer of Deuteronomy would also feature the same basic
vocabulary, twice using the formal term "the Ten Words" (4:13,
10:4). Throughout his work, he would use the term "words" with
reference to the commands of God (4:2, 9, 10, 36; 5:5, 22(19);
6:6; 9:10; 10:2, 4; 11:18; 12:28; 13:1; 17:19; 18:18, 19;
27:3, 8, 26; 28:14, 58, 69; 29:8, 18; 28; 30:14; 31:12, 24,
28; 32:46). It is easy to see that this is a very marked
feature of the style of the book of Deuteronomy. By further
observation, the conceptual content of the term "word(s)" becomes
quite clear. We find the term used especially in the genitivus
appositionis (or epexegeticus) דברי התורה הזאת, "the words of
this law" (17:19; 27:3, 8, 26; 28:58; 29:28; 31:12, 24;
32:46). In the first instance of this expression, occurring in
the passage Deut 17:18-20, it is clear that the law to which
reference is made is the written law. Furthermore, in this
passage, we find some of the words which form a cluster together
with תורה and דבר throughout the book of Deuteronomy: חקים,
"statutes," מצוה, "commandment," משפטים, "ordinances," למד,
"learn," שמע, "hear," עשה, "do."

The clustering of the whole group of nouns in question is
well illustrated in Deut 4:1-14: חקים in Deut 4:1, 5, 6 and 14;
משפט in Deut 4:1, 5, 8 and 14; מצוה in Deut 4:2 and 8; תורה
in Deut 4:8; and דבר in Deut 4:2, 9, 10, 12 and 13.[2] The
significance of this for our purposes is that through observing
the constellation of words with which דבר is associated, we gain
further insight into the conceptual colouring of דבר.

The verbs in question are למד, "learn" in the qal and
"teach"in the piel,[3] שמע, "hear" and עשה, "do." The word למד
is not found in the first four books of the Torah, a simple but

remarkable fact; thus it is a feature of the thinking of the
Deuteronomist. In the book of Deuteronomy, שמע and עשה are
associated so closely that one is led to think that the "doing"
should be the normal and natural consequence of the "hearing."[4]
The Deuteronomic use of these three verbs, as well as their
relationship to some of the nouns with which we have been concerned, is easily observed in Deut 5:1-6 and 5:22-6:3. Deut
5:1-6 introduces the Ten Words, and Deut 5:22-6:3 comes between
the Ten Words and the prayer "Hear O Israel. . . "; as such
these are among the basic passages of the book:

> Hear (שמע) Israel, the statutes (חקים) and the ordinances
> (משפטים) which I speak in your ears today, and you shall
> learn (למד) them and be careful to do (עשה) them.
> These words (דברים) the Lord spoke. . . We will hear
> (שמע) and do (עשה). . . I will tell you all the com-
> mandment (מצוה) and the statutes (חקים) and the ordin-
> ances (משפטים) which you shall teach (למד) them. . .
> You shall be careful to do (עשה) as the Lord your God
> has commanded you. . . This is the commandment (מצוה),
> the statutes (חקים) and the ordinances (משפטים) which
> the Lord your God has commanded me to teach (למד) you
> that you may do (עשה). . . Hear (שמע) therefore, Israel,
> and be careful to do (עשה). . . (5:1, 22, 27, 31, 32;
> 6:1, 3)

Let us review the vocabulary in question in Deut 4:1-2:

> And now, Israel, hear (שמע) the statutes (חקים) and
> the ordinances (משפטים) which I teach (למד) you,
> and do (עשה) them, that you may live, and go in and
> take possession of the land which the Lord, the God
> of your fathers, gives you. You shall not add to
> the word (דבר) which I command you, nor take from it;
> that you may keep the commandments (מצות) of the
> Lord your God which I command you.

Here, מצות and דבר are practically synonymous. These are taught.[5]
The people are exhorted to hear and do the commandments[6] - to
hear and do the Word.[7] If one may judge on the basis of fre-
quency, in the book of Deuteronomy it is the doing of the
Commandments, the doing of the Words which is stressed. Throughout the Pentateuch, God speaks in the imperative as the com-
manding God who forbids and permits. The Word must become man's
deeds, and the Word empowers man for the deeds: "But the Word

(הדבר) is very near you; it is in your mouth and in your heart for its doing (לעשתו)" (Deut 30:14).

The association of the words תורה and דבר is found in various places throughout the Hebrew Bible. In II Kgs 22:8-23:3 (and parallel: II Chr 34:14-31[8]) the word דבר is used in such a way that it clearly has the meaning-content of what is to be done: it is the "word of the Law," the "word of the covenant."[9] It is apparent that in the phrases in this passage, again we have the genitivus appositionis; hence the word דבר receives meaning from those words to which it is bound as regens: תורה and ברית; and the דבר יהוה, "word of the Lord," is His imparted Word.

In the account of the presentation of the law at the watergate in Neh 8:8-13, the word דבר has the same weight:

> And they read from the book, from the law of God
> (בתורת האלהים) clearly, and they gave the sense. . .
> All the people wept when they heard the words of the
> law (דברי התורה). . . they had understood the words
> (דברים) that were declared to them. On the second
> day the heads of the fathers' houses of all the people,
> with the priests and the Levites, came together to
> Ezra the scribe in order to study the words of the
> law (דברי התורה).   (Neh. 8:8, 9, 12, 13)

Examples of the words דבר and תרוה used as parallels can be observed in the prophetic books, for example in Isa 1:10:[10]

> Hear the word of the Lord (דבר יהוה), you rulers of
> Sodom! Give ear to the law of our God (תורת אלהינו),
> you people of Gomorrah!

Ps 119 is assumed to be didactic poetry of the post-exilic period, bearing the influence of Deuteronomistic theology and wisdom instruction.[11] This Psalm presents a meditation in which we find the familiar attitude toward דברך, תורתך and מצותיך, "thy word," "thy law," and "thy commandments." These concepts are featured most often standing in final position in a stich. They are repeated and interchanged poetically throughout the Psalm. Let us observe this parallel treatment:[12]

And I keep thy Law.	ואשמרה תורתך
I promise to keep thy words.	אמרתי לשמר דבריך

I hasten to keep	חשתי. . .לשמר
thy commandments.	מצותיך
I hate double minded men,	סעפים שנאתי
but I love thy law.	ותורתך אהבתי
Thou art my hiding place	סתרי ומגני אתה
and my shield;	
I hope in thy word.	לדברך יחלתי
Depart from me, you evildoers,	סורו ממני מרעים
that I may keep	ואצרה מצות אלהי
the commandments of my God. (vv 55b, 57b, 60 and 113-115)	

Through such usages, we note the close conceptual proximity of

דבר, תורה and מצוה in the poetic and popular mind. This is to be

seen again in Prov 13:13-14a:[13]

He who despises the word	בז לדבר יחבל לו
brings destruction on himself,	
but he who respects the	וירא מצוה הוא ישלם
commandment will be fulfilled.	
The law of the wise is a	תורת חכם מקור חיים
fountain of life. . .	

The concepts of דבר, תרוה and מצוה are almost always trans-

lated λόγος, νομός and ἐντολή in the LXX; and we find these

Greek words used continuously in the Apocrypha. There are

striking literary parallels involving νομός and ἐντολή in the

Book of Sirach, for example Sir 45:5:[14]

(God) gave him (Moses) the commandments (ἐντολάς) face
to face, the law (νόμον) of life and knowledge.

These same two words, νομός and ἐντολή, are to be found at Wis

16:6 in the succinct expression, ". . . to remind them of thy

law's command (ἐντολῆς νόμου σου)."

We have noted examples of the parallels of "law" and "word"

in the prophets, and examples of "law" and "commandments" in

Proverbs, Sirach and Wisdom. Of the three words, apparently, it

was "law" which was, very subtly, an important and pivotal con-

cept both in the prophets and the wisdom writers. It was man-

ifestly the important and pivotal concept in I and II Maccabees.[15]

Matthias' exhortation (I Macc 2:49-69) was one of zeal for the

law; the martyrdoms are recounted as an "example of how to die

a good death willingly and nobly for the revered and holy laws"

(II Macc 6:28). The supremacy of the Law here is much as it is in the Pseudepigrapha.

The whole Jewish world which produced the Apocrypha and
Pseudepigrapha was intensely conscious of the supremacy of the
Law. Though some writers have tried to posit a difference on
this matter between "apocalyptic Judaism" and "legalistic
Pharisaism,"[16] it might be better to accept a more moderate
view:

> While there is a difference of emphasis in apocalyptic
> and Pharisaic circles, nevertheless, there was no cleavage
> between them; and in their attitude to the Law they were
> at one; indeed, some of the apocalyptists were probably
> as strict in their adherence to the Law as were the
> Pharisees themselves, and we can be fairly sure that
> what the former would have to say about the Law would,
> usually at least, command the assent of the latter.[17]

We agree that a common esteem for the Law is to be found in the
vast pseudepigraphic literature. The following remarks will
suffice to illustrate the centrality of the Law in these works.

The Book of Jubliees,[18] although it is a midrash on Genesis
and Exodus, opens with a detailed haggadic conversation between
God and Moses on Mount Sinai; the theme of this account is
given in the first statement: "This is the history. . . as the
Lord spoke to Moses on Mount Sinai when he went up to receive
the tables of the law and of the commandment."[19] Sinai is the
centre of all knowledge; ultimately the Law is the consummation
of knowledge. The whole Book of Jubilees is based on this
principle.

The primary concern of the Letter of Aristeas[20] is with the
Law, the account it its translation into Greek being the climax
and finale of the work (301-322).

In Book III of the Sibylline Books[21] we find exhortations to
"eschew unlawful service: serve the living God"(763); and
"unlawful" in the context of Book III apparently means what is
other than the Law of God of Sinai (cf. 256). This is "a holy
law" (768), "the holy law of the immortal God" (600).[22]

A Further Discussion of Terminology:
the "Words," the "Commandments" and the
"Law" in the Targums, Other Early Jewish
Tradition, and in the Qumran Literature

In the targumic traditions there are several contexts in
which there is mention of the "Ten Words" in addition to those in
which the phraseology is a direct translation of the Hebrew.[23]
The most significant context is in the addition of a sentence to
the last verse (v 25) of Exodus 19 by way of rounding out that
verse and introducing chap. 20:[24]

	Tg. Ps.-J.
Draw near and receive the Law with the Ten Words.	קרובו קבילי אורייתא עם עשרתי דיבריא
	CTg F
Draw near and receive the Ten Words.	קריבו קבילו עשרתי דביריה

Tg. Ps.-J. gives us a targumic exegesis of Deut 1:18. Deut 1:18
reads: "And I commanded you at that time all the things/words
(דברים) that you should do"; however in Tg. Ps.-J., the word
דברים is made to refer specifically to the Ten Words (as shown by
the addition of the adjective עשרא, "ten"), and the general tone
of the Hebrew is particularized:

And at that time I decreed (to) you all the Ten Words which you are to practice about judgements of money and judgements of life.	ופקידית יתכון בעידנא ההיא ית כל עשרא פתגמיא דתעבדון ביני דיני ממונא לדיני נפשתא

The power of the dynamic Word is expressed in the targumic
description of its activity in pronouncing the first and second
of the Ten Words. Tg. Neof. Deut 5:6 reads:

The first Word, when it went out from the mouth of the Holy One, may His Name be blessed, was like shooting stars and lightening, and like torches of fire to the right, and a torch of fire to the left. It flew and winged swiftly through the air of the heavens, and returned, and encircled	דברה קדמיה כד הוה נפק מן פם קודשא יהא שמיה מברך היך זיקין והיך ברקין והיך למפדין דנור מן ימיניה ולמפד דאשה מן שמאליה פרח וטייס באויר שמיא וחזר ומקף

the camps of Israel, and	על משיריתון דישראל
it returned, and was engraved	וחזר ומ(תה)קק
on the tablets of the covenant,	על לוחי קיימה
and it cried out thus and said:	וכן הוה צול ואמר
My people, sons of Israel,	עצי בני ישראל
I am the Lord your God	אנא הוא ייי אלהכון
who redeemed (you) and led you	די פרקית ראפקית יתכון
out redeemed from the land	פריקין מן ארעה
of Egypt, from the bondage	דמצרים מן בית שעברד
of slaves.	עבדיה

Tg. Neof. Deut 5:7 introduces the second Word by repeating the
same thing exactly. In Tg. Neof. Exod 20:2 and 3, the phraseology is almost the same, just a little more elaborated. Tg.
Ps.-J. Exod 20:2-3 is similar; however this targum does not
repeat this haggadah in Deuteronomy 5.

Another example of targumic work which we might mention
occurs at Exod 15:24-26; here the Hebrew speaks of Moses'
casting a tree into the waters and their becoming sweet. Apparently there were targumists who wished to guard against at-
tributing any power at all to the tree. In v 25, Tg. Neof. and
MS P read that Moses wrote on the tree מלה דאוריתא, "a word of
the law," then cast it into the waters which were then sweetened.[25]
The power of the Word was no new concept; Deut 30:14 had spoken
of nearness of the Word to man for him to carry it into deeds.
The fragment targum tradition (MSS V (N, ed. B) Tg. Neof. and
Tg. Ps.-J.) gives the verse in full with only slight embellish-
ment; this would probably indicate the importance of this verse
during the earlier days of targumic activity.

From observation of these several examples of the activity
of the targumists, in their proper contexts, it can readily be
said that the "Word(s)" primarily meant to them the very kernel
of their Torah, the Law as written in Exod 20:2-17 and Deut 5:
6-21(18); and then, by extension, the whole Torah.

As we have seen, the phrase דברי התורה, "words of the Law"
had its beginnings in Deuteronomy, and then was to be found in
later books of the Hebrew Bible. By the time of the targumists,
especially the composers of Tg. Neof. Deuteronomy, the "Law" was

receiving increased attention and becoming a central concept in
their thought patterns. Thus the word אוריתא, "the Law," could
be introduced into the text where it could add the clarity of
specification or even just a sonorous rounding-out of a phrase.

Some examples of this type of targumic activity are as
follows. First, where the Hebrew text has מצות, "commandments"
at Deut 4:40, 5:29 and 8:6, Tg. Neof. reads מצוותה דאורייתה,
"commandments of the Law";[26] furthermore both Tg. Neof. and Tg.
Ps.-J. use this expression at Deut 15:4.[27]

Second, where Deut 30:11-14 presents four sentences with
their subjects in parallel (v 11: המצוה; v 12: הוא; v 13: הוא;
v 14: הדבר), the tradition of the fragment targums makes the
pronoun subjects specific with the addition of the word אוריתה,
"the Law"; thus MSS V (N, ed. B) and Tg. Neof.[28]

Third, the concept of "learning" and "teaching" in the
sphere of religious knowledge had come to the fore in the book
of Deuteronomy which introduced the verb למד,[29] a word not
found in previous books of the Pentateuch. The Aramaic translation for this is אלף. Now, there are two words, each of which
is hapax legomenon in Deuteronomy (and in the Pentateuch), מוסר
and לקח used substantively; these have been translated using
the same Aramaic root in substantive form:

Deut 11:2	Tg. Neof.[30]
את מוסר יהוה אליכם	ית אולפן אורייתה דייי אלהכון
the teaching of	the teaching of the Law of
the Lord your God.	the Lord your God.

Deut 32:2	MS V (N and ed. B)[31]
לקחי	אולפן אורייתי
My teaching (i.e. God's)	My teaching of the Law

Apparently for the sake of avoiding any misunderstanding, the
translators have added the word אורייתה, "the Law," and we thus
have the expression אולפן אורייתה, "the teaching of the Law,"
which would be found as a cliché especially in Tg. Neof.
Deuteronomy.

This cliché is utilized to avoid what the targumists considered might be too personal a relationship with the trans-

cendent יהוה. When the Hebrew text has "love/loving (אהב) the

Lord your God," in Tg. Neof. we will find an expansion, typical

examples of which are to be seen in Deut 11:1 and 10:12:[32]

Deut 11:1   Tg. Neof.

ואהבת את יהוה אלהיך   ותרחמון ית אולפן

                       אורייתה דייי אלהכון

You shall love the   You shall love the teaching

Lord your God.   of the Law of the Lord your God.

Deut 10:12   Tg. Neof.

לאהבה אתו   למרחום ית אולפן אורייתא

to love Him.   to love the teaching of the Law.

Furthermore, when the Hebrew reads "cleave/cleaving to Him," in

Tg. Neof. we find a similar expansion, for example, Deut 10:20.[33]

Deut 10:20   Tg. Neof.

ובו תדבק   ובאולפן אורייתה תתבקון

And to Him you   And to the teaching of the

shall cleave.   Law you shall cleave.

Similarly with the clause ". . . forget (שכח) the Lord your God";

for example at Deut 8:14:[34]

Deut 8:14   Tg. Neof.

ושכחת את יהוה אלהיך   ותנשון ית אולמן אורייתה

                       דייי אלהכון

... and you forget   ... and you forget the

the Lord your God.   teaching of the Law of

                      the Lord your God.

There are two other instances in Tg. Neof. of a similar use of

the cliché after other verbs: שבק, "forsake" at Deut 28:20, and

חזר, "return" at Deut 30:2. The total of occurrences of the

words אולפן אורייתה introduced in this way into Tg. Neof.

Deuteronomy is twenty. Thus the concept of the "Law" which is

taught is highlighted.

The phrase אולפן אוריתי, "My teaching of the Law," is

utilized by the targumists to reverently replace the first

person objective pronoun when God is the speaker; examples

from Exodus and Leviticus:[35]

Exod 19:4   Tgs. Neof. and Ps.-J.

                       MSS V, P (N and ed. B)

ואם לא תשמעו לי   וקרבית יתכון לאולפן אורייתי

... and brought   ... And brought you to My

you to Myself. . .   teaching of the Law.

Lev 26:14	Tg. Ps.-J.	Tg. Neof.
ואם לא תשמעו לי	ואן לא תיצבון למדמע לאולפן מאלפי אורייתי	ואן לא תשמעון לאולפן אורייתי
If you will not hearken to Me...	If you will not be erect to hear the teaching - My teachers of the Law. . .	If you will not hear My teaching of the Law. . .

The poetic narrative of the oracle of Balaam at Num 24:3-9
gave the targumists occasion for their poetic freedom;   they
introduced an accent on the Law. Tg. Ps.-J. Num 24:6 has:

The house of Israel. . made strong by the teaching of the Law. . .	בית ישראל. . . מתגברין באולפן אורייתא. . .

MSS V, P (N and ed. B) have this variation:

. . . as shall be their cities, giving forth scribes and teachers of the Law.	כד יהון קרייתהו מפקן ספרין ומלפי אורייתא

Another variation: Tg. Neof. Num 24:6:

. . . so shall their cities be, producing sages and sons of the Law.	כדן יהוון קורייהון מפקן חכימין ובני אוריית

By turning to these examples from Exodus, Leviticus and Numbers,
we see how the accent on the Law, apparently characteristic of
the fragment targum tradition of Deuteronomy, came to find a
place in other targumic material. Even if the primary motive
was to use a known and suitable phrase to avoid what seemed an
over-familiarity with God, the secondary effect was a spreading
of a way of thinking which held the Law to be of greater and
greater importance.

We have been considering the concepts of "words" and "Law"
in the targumic traditions. Each of the members of the genitivus appositionis דברי התורה, "the words of the Law," of Deuteronomy, taken separately, carries the full connotation of the
written words given at Sinai/Horeb. While both concepts come
from the Hebrew text, the targums (especially Tg. Neof. Deuteronomy) highlight the word אוריתה, "the Law." What was called
the "Word of the Lord" at Deut 5:5 is called "the Law" in the

haggadah at Deut 1:1 in the fragment targum tradition.[35] The

ideas we have been discussing are aptly illustrated by the

opening words of the targumists' speech of Moses:

From MS V Deut 1:1

Behold, in the wilderness,	הלא במדברא
at Mount Sinai, the Torah	וטורא דסיני
was given to you. . .	איתיהבת לכון אורייתא

As we have seen, there is emphasis in the targums on loving the

teachings of the Law, cleaving to them, not forgetting them, and

hearing them. But this is not all; there is the matter of ob-

serving them. By prefixing conditional clauses to Deut 15:11 in

MS V (N and ed. B), the sense of the verse is altered.[36] The

simple reference in the Hebrew text to there being poor people in

the land is changed; now, whether there are poor or not becomes

contingent upon observance of the Commandments of the Law.

According to MS V:

If Israel would keep the	אין נטרין הינון ישראל
Commandments of the Law,	מצוותא דאורייתא
there would be no poor	לא יהווי בהון מיסכי[נון]
among them; but if they	ברם אין שבקין הינון
forsake the Commandments	מיצוותא דאורייתא
of the Law, the poor will	לא פסקין מיסכיניא
not cease from the midst of	מגו ארעא
the land.	

Similarly at Deut 17:18, there is a subordinate clause referring

to the king's sitting on the throne of his kingdom; however in

Tg. Ps.-J. this becomes the main clause; then the condition for

sitting on the throne is being pleasing to God with respect to

the Law:

And it shall be (that) if	ויהי אין נייח הוא
he is pleasing in the	במצוותא דאורייתא
Commandments of the Law,	יתיב לרוחצן
he shall sit in security on	על כורסי מלכותיה
the throne of his kingdom.	

A third example of this type of targumic activity is seen at

Deut 32:30 in MS V (N and ed. B) and Tg. Neof. In MS V:

When Israel toiled in the (study	כד הוון ישר אל
of the) Law and observed the	לעיין באוריתא ונטריו
Commandments, one of them would	פוקודי הוה חד
rout a thousand. . .	מינהון [רד]ף אלף. . .

Thus by altering the syntax of the sentence (and the sense), the
theology prevalent at the time of the production of the targums
was introduced; good fortune or ill depended upon the observance
of the Law or its neglect. Moreover, there were a variety of
verbs which could express the ramifications of "hear and do"; in
the above example, "toil (in the study) and observe." An example
similar to the preceding occurs in the fragment targum tradition
at Deut 33:29. According to MS V:[37]

Sons of Israel, when you toil	בני אשר אל כד תיהוון
in the Law and observe the	לעיין באורייתא ונטרין
Commandments, you shall tread	פיקודיא על פורקת
on the necks of their kings.	מלכיהון תיהוון דרסין

Besides appearing in the interpretation of passages, "toil (in
the study) and observe" appears independently in some of the
haggadic passages of the targums. It was held to be so basic
that it found a place in interpreting the story in Genesis 3. To
illustrate, the following are excerpts from MS V:[38]

And it shall be, when	ויהווי כד יהוון
the sons of the woman	בניי דאיתתא
toil in the Law and	לעיין באוריית[ן]
do the ordinances,	ועבדין פיקודייא
they will aim and	יהוון מתכווניןֿ
smite you on your	ומחיין יתך לרישך
head and kill you.	וקטלין יתך
And when the sons of	וכד ישבקון
the woman forsake the	בנייא דאיתתא
Commandments of the	מצותא דאוריתא
Law and do not do the	ולא יעבדון
ordinances, you will	פיקודיא
take aim and bite them	חהוי מתכוון
on their heels and	ונכית יתהון בעקביהון
afflict them.	וממרע יתיה

Two thousand years be-	קדם עד לא יברי עלמא
fore He created the world,	תרין אלפין דשנין
He created the Law.	ברא אורייתא
He established Gehenna	ואתקן גיחנם
and the Garden of Eden.	וגינתא דעדן
He established the Garden	אתקן גינת עדן
of Eden for the righteous...	לצדיקייא. . .
because they observed the	על די נטרו
Commandments of the Law	מצוותא דאורייתא
in this world.	בעלמא הדין

He established Gehenna | אתקן גיהנם
for the wicked. . . | לרשיעייא. . .
because they did not | על די לא נטרו
observe the Commandments | מצוותא דאורייח[ ]
of the Law in this world. | בעלמא הדין

In the first passage the balanced "toil (in the study) and do"
is seen; yet in the second, it is the second part of the conceptual pair, "observe" that is stressed.

Another haggadah featuring the necessity of observance of
the Law by linking this to eschatological consequences is found
at Gen 15:17 in Tg. Neof., MSS V, P (N and ed. B). The literary context is a revelation to Abraham as he passed between
the parts of the divided animals. Citing MS V:

And behold Gehenna. . . | . . . והא גיהנם
into the midst of which | דבגווה
the wicked fell | יפלון רשיעיא
because they rebelled | על דמרדו
against the Law during | על אורייח[א]
their lives in this world. | בחייהון בעלמא הדין
But the righteous, | וצדיקיא
because they kept it | על דאנטרן יתה
under oppression, will be | מן עקתא
saved from it (Gehenna). | ישתיזבון

We can make further observations: the haggadah contrasts those
who observe the commandments of the Law and those who do not in
terms of their ultimate destinies in the next world; it also
specifies the meaning of the terms "the righteous" and "the
wicked (the evil)" in terms of observing the commandments of the
Law or forsaking them. These ideas are basic in the conceptual
world evidenced in the targums and in the tannaitic midrashim.

Among the tannaim the practical equivalence of the meaning
of "the Law" and "the Commandments" is easy to recognize. For
all practical purposes, it is spelled out in Sipre Num 111:[39]

Whoever transgresses | מה העובר
all the commandments | על כל המצות
breaks off the yoke, | פורק עול
annuls the covenant and | ומפו ברית
misrepresents the Law. | ומגלה פנים בתורה
So also he who trans- | אף העובר
tresses one commandment | על מצוה אחת
breaks off the yoke, | פורק עול

annuls the covenant and	ומפר ברית
misrepresents the Law.	ומגלה פנים בתורה

Furthermore, the vocabulary range of equivalents is broadened;
here the "yoke" and the "covenant" are included. Another important equivalent in Mekilta, Sipra and Sipre is the "will" of
God; in Sipra and Sipre this is spelled out in parallelisms,
for example, Sipre Deut 306:[40]

If a man does the Law	אם עשה אדם תורה
and does the will of his	ועשה רצון
Father in Heaven,	אביו שבשמים הרי
behold, he is like	הוא כבריות של מעלה. . .
mankind on high. . .	

In Sipre Deut 48,[41] there is a considerable passage (attributed
to Aqiba) on the disciple and his acquiring דברי תורה, "the
words of the Law." In this passage, the "words of the Law" is
the subject of many similes, being compared to living waters,
wine, oil and honey in their beneficial effects. Here our
attention is attracted to the "words of the Law"; yet our
attentiveness is sharpened yet more in Sipra 112c and 115d - each
detail is important:[42]

We learn that the Law was	מלמד שניתנה התורה
given: its rules, its	הלכותיה ודקדוקיה
explanations and its	ופירושיה
interpretations by the	ע"י משה מסיני
hand of Moses from Sinai.	

These are the commandments.	אלא המצות
No prophet ever has the	אין נביא רשאי
power to change a word.	לחדש עוד דבר מעתה

This material was not novel in Sipra; there is a conceptual
parallel in the conclusion of Tg. Ps.-J. on Leviticus:

These are the precepts which	אלין פקודיא
the Lord prescribed Moses,	די פקיד ייי ית משה
and one may not compromise	ולית אפשר
a single (item) of it in	לחדתא בהון מידעם
any way. And he prescribed	ופקידימון מטול
them to be shown to the sons	לאחוואותהון
of Israel on Mount Sinai.	לות בני אשראל
	בטוורא דסיני

This attitude of precision with respect to the Law is especially

highlighted by the location of these comments. In Tg. Ps.-J.
the above was introduced into the translation of the last verse
(27:34) of the book of Leviticus; in Sipra the citations we have
made are from the last pages of that work, the second obviously
being a comment attached to Lev 27:34.

In ²Abot, the term "Law" is used comprehensively, both the
written and oral Law; and it is the chief concept of the
treatise. Just as in Jubilees, in ²Abot the authority of the Law
is emphasized by presenting it as having come from Sinai; the
first line is "Moses received the Law from Sinai and committed it
to Joshua, and Joshua to the Elders. . . " Although "the Law" is
the more frequent expression in ²Abot, the expression "the words
of the Law" has received explicit attention: "To gain the words
of the Law is to gain the life of the world to come."[43]

Now we come to the verbs of "saying" and "doing" with reference to the Law. The first words of Num 23:19, לא איש אל, "God
is not a man. . ." might have made a commentator with anti-
anthropomorphic tendencies look more closely: the targumists
(Tgs. Onq., Ps.-J., Neof., MSS V, P (N and ed. B) altered it:
"the word of God is not like the word of the sons of man." Then
the targumists continued to make the verse absolutely unambig-
uous, and this involved lengthening it somewhat. In MS V:[44]

Not like the word of the	לא [כ]מימ[ר] בני
sons of man is the word	אינשא הות מימרי[ה]
of the living God;	דאלהא חייא
nor like the words of	ולא כעובדיהון
the sons of man are the	דבמי אינש
works of God.	עובדוי אלהא
The sons of man say,	בני אינשא אמרין
but do not; they	ולא עבדין
decree but do not fulfil.	גזרין ולא מקיימין
And they go back and	וחזרין וכפרי[ן]
deny their words.	במיליהון
But God says and does;	ברם אלהא אמר ועבד
He decrees and fulfils;	גזר ומקיים
and His decrees are	וגזירתוהי קיימין
established for ever.	עד לעלם

This clarification, built upon Num 23:19, could well have had a wide influence; the exhortations on "saying" and "doing" are quite explicit.

The theme of "word and works" continued in other early Jewish literature.[45] We recall the sentence from ᵓAbot 1:17, attributed to the sons of Rabbi Gamaliel (who died only a few years after the fall of the Temple):[46]

Not the expounding (of the Law) is the chief thing but the doing of it.	ולא המדרש הוא העיקר אלא המעשה

The writer of Sipra 110c is emphatic:[47]

If you follow my statutes and heed by precepts and do them, learning in order to do, not learning in order not to do, for he who learns (and) who does not do, it would be better for him that he were not created.	אם בחוקותי תלכו ואת מצותי תשמרו ועשיתם אותם הלמד לעשות לא הלמד שלא לעשות שהלמד שלא לעשות נוח לו שלא מברא

Under the name of R. Eleazar of Modin, a tanna from the end of the first century, we have the following in Sipre Deut 40:[48]

R. Eleazar of Modin said, a book and a sword descended, tied together from heaven. He said to them, if you do Torah which is written in this (book), behold you will be delivered from that; if not, behold you will be struck by it.	רבי אלעזר המודעי אומר, ספר וסייף ירדו כרוכים מן השמים, אמר להם, אם עשיתם את התורה הכתובה בזה, הרי אתם נצולים מזה, ואם לאו הרי אתם לוקים בו.

Using the same pattern of writing, another presentation of the same thing was transmitted under the name of R. Simeon b. Yohai of the mid-second century A.D. in Sipre Deut 40.[49] In Sipre Deut 48, there is a passage (given anonymously) which sets the perspective with respect to learning, keeping and doing the Law:

If one (merely) learns the Law, behold (he has fulfilled) one commandment; if he learns and keeps (what he has learned), behold (he has fulfilled) two commandments; if he learns and	למד אדם תורה הרי מצוה אחת למד ושמר הרי בידו שתי מצות למד ושמר ועשה

keeps and performs, there is   אין
no one more meritorious.   [50]למעלה הימנו

The perennial rabbinic attitude, from its earliest roots, has been aptly summarized:

> Considering the enormous stress which the Rabbis laid
> upon the study of the Law, it is remarkable that many
> of them thought that doing was still more important
> than learning; or, again, that if learning was more
> important than doing, this was only because it was
> primary, seeing that, without a basis of study, doing
> could hardly be maintained and continued.[51]

As in Deuteronomy where the verbs "hear" and "do" were joined in the same mandate, the tannaim saw the latter verb as an imperative consequential upon the former. Given the principle, it would be expounded by various illustrations. First, a passage preserved in ᵓAbot 3:18 and also in ᵓAbot R. Nat. 22:[52]

> And again, R. Elazar, the son of Azariah, used to say,
> 'Where there is no wisdom, there is no fear of God.
> Where there is no fear of God, there is no wisdom.
> He whose wisdom exceeds his works, to what is he like?
> To a tree whose branches are many but whose roots are
> few; and the wind comes and plucks it up and over-
> turns it upon its face, as it is said, And he shall
> be like a lonely juniper tree in the desert, and shall
> not see when good comes; but shall inhabit the
> parched places in the wilderness, a salt land and
> not inhabited (Jer 17:6). But he whose works exceed
> his wisdom, to what is he like? To a tree whose
> branches are few, but whose roots are many, so that
> even if all the winds in the world come and blow upon
> it, it cannot be stirred from its waters; and that
> spreads out its roots by the river, and shall not
> perceive when heat comes, but his leaf shall be green;
> and shall not be troubled in the year of drought,
> neither shall cease from yielding fruit (Jer 17:8).'

A similar parable illustrating the point is found attributed to R. Elisha ben Abuyah (who lived at the end of the first century and in the early second century A.D.) in ᵓAbot R. Nat. 24:[53]

> Elisha ben Abuyah says: One in whom there are good
> works, who has studied much Torah, to what may he
> be likened? To a person who builds first with stones
> (אבנים) and afterward with bricks (לבנים); even when
> much water comes and collects by their side, it does
> not dislodge them. But one in whom there are no

good works, though he studied Torah, to what may he
be likened? To a person who builds first with bricks
(לבנים) and afterward with stones (אבנים); even when
a little water gathers, it overthrows them immediately.

This passage has three features: the point illustrated, the
building context, and the play on words.[54]

The overall impact of the available material clarifies the
idea that hearing, saying, studying, learning the Law were considered but preliminary to observing, doing the Law; and this
was stressed.

In the extant Qumran literature, explicit references to the
Law of Moses are not numerous, even if there is implicit refer-
ence to it throughout it. The position of the community of
Qumran with respect to the Law is made absolutely plain in
I QS 5:8-9 (the Manual of Discipline):[55]

(Each member shall) return	יבוא בברית אל
to the covenant of God in	לעיני כול המתנדבים
the presence of all the	ויקם על נפשו
members, and stand upon his	בשבועת אסר
life in a binding oath to	לשוב אל תורת מושה
return to the Law of Moses	ככול אשר צוה
in accordance with all that	בכול לב ובכול נפש. . . .
it commands with all (his)	
heart and with all (his) soul...	

The Law was paramount and each word had to be kept (I QS 8:22-
23):[56]

(Each member). . . who	. . . אשר יעבר
transgresses a word of	דבר מתורת מושה
the Law of Moses, either	ביד רמה או ברמיה
blatantly or deviously,	ישלחהו מעצת היחד
is expelled from the	ולוא ישוב עוד. . .
"plantation of the elect"	
and he shall never return...	

In a list of obligations in the allied Zadokite Document from
Cairo, CD 6:14-7:4, the obligation of keeping the Law comes
first (CD 6:14):[57]

Behold, if they do not hearken	חנם אם לא ישמרו
(i.e. they must hearken) to do	לעשות כפרוש התורה...
according to the separation (i.e.	
explicit injunctions) of the Law...	

110

CD uses the expression "Commandments of God" to express the same
basic moral imperative as "the Law." The שמר, "keeping" or
לא שמר, "not keeping" of it was of consummate consequence:

CD 2:18[58]

The Watchers of heaven fell. . . נפלו עירי השמים
because they did not keep the . . . אשר לא שמרו
commandments of God. . . מצות אל

CD 3:2[59]

Abraham. . . (was accounted)
a[s Fr]iend (of God) . . . אברהם . . . וי]ל או[הב
because of his keeping the בשמרו מצות אל
commandments of God. . .

CD 3:12-13[60]

But to those who held fast ובמחזיקים במצות אל
to the commandments of God, אשר נותרו מהם
which made them a remnant, הקים אל את בריתו
God established His
covenant. . .

The basic orientation of the community might be said to be its
insistence not merely upon hearing the "correct" interpretation
of the Law, but upon keeping the Commandments, doing the Law, as
"men of perfect holiness" (IQS 8:20).[61]

The "Words," the "Commandments" and the
"Law" in the Early Church and in the
Gospel of Matthew

The word "law" is common in the NT texts; throughout the
epistles of Paul, the understanding of the proper use of the
"Law" was thematic. However, Paul also uses "Commandments" in a
morally equivalent sense: "So the Law is holy, and the commandment is holy and just and good" (Rom 7:12). Nevertheless, for
Paul, "Law" is the conceptually comprehensive term to which
"Commandments" and "word" are closely allied: "Every commandment (ἐντολή). . . is summed up in this word (ἐν τῷ λόγῳ) 'You
shall love your neighbour as yourself'" (Rom 13:9); again, "For
the whole Law (ὁ πᾶς νόμος) is fulfilled in one word (ἐν ἑνὶ
λόγῳ), 'You shall love your neighbour as yourself'" (Gal 5:14).
The simple equivalence of the λόγος and the νόμος is apparent in

the epistle of James: "If you judge the Law, you are not a doer of the Law (ποιητὴς νόμου). . . (Jas 4:11); "Be ye doers of the Word (ποιηταὶ λόγου), not hearers only" (Jas 1:22).

Paul has the same orientation in Rom 2:13: "for it is not the hearers of the Law (οἱ ἀκροαταὶ νόμου) who are righteous before God, but the doers of the Law (οἱ ποιηταὶ νόμου) who will be justified." James stresses the doing of the Law: "But be doers of the Word, and not hearers only, deceiving yourselves. .. so faith by itself, if it has no works, is dead. . . you see that a man is justified by works and not by faith alone. . . For the body apart from the spirit is dead, so faith apart from works is dead" (Jas 1:22-25, 2:17-26). The deeds are also stressed in I Peter with the remark that the Father "judges each one impartially according to his deeds" (I Pet 1:17). The same thoughts recur in Revelation: the dead are judged "by what they had done" (Rev 20:12-13; cf. also 14:13, 18:6, 22:12).

In Matthew we find both (1) the normal acceptance of the hearing and the doing, and (2) a situation in which their mutual relationship is upset. In chap. 23, scribes and Pharisees are confronted as remiss in the doing but able to tell men what they should do, the implication being that they have indeed heard. The introduction to Matthew chap. 23 (vv 1-3) is unduplicated in the other Synoptics:

Then Jesus said to the crowds and to his disciples, 'The scribes and Pharisees sit on Moses' seat; so practice and observe whatever they tell you, but not what they do; for they preach but do not practice.

Τότε ὁ 'Ιησοῦς ἐλάλησεν τοῖς ὄχλοις καὶ τοῖς μαθηταῖς αὐτοῦ λέγων, 'Επὶ τῆς Μωϋσέως καθέδρας ἐκάθισαν οἱ γραμματεῖς καὶ οἱ Φαρισαῖοι. πάντα οὖ̓ν ὅσα ἐὰν εἴπωσιν ὑμῖν ποιήσατε καὶ τηρεῖτε, κατὰ δὲ τὰ ἔργα αὐτῶν μὴ ποιεῖτε· λέγουσιν γὰρ καὶ οὐ ποιοῦσιν.

What was lacking in the deeds of the scribes and Pharisees addressed was precisely pinpointed in Matt 23:23:

'Woe to you, scribes and Pharisees, hypocrites! for

Οὐαὶ ὑμῖν, γραμματεῖς καὶ Φαρισαῖοι ὑποκριταί, ὅτι

| you tithe mint and dill and cummin, and have neglected the weightier matters of the Law, justice and mercy and faith; these you ought to have done, without neglecting the others. | ἀποδεκατοῦτε τὸ ἡδύοσμον καὶ τὸ ἄνηθον καὶ τὸ κύμινον, καὶ ἀφήκατε τὰ βαρύτερα τοῦ νόμου, τὴν κρίσιν καὶ τὸ ἔλεος καὶ τὴν πίστον° ταῦτα δὲ ἔδει ποιῆσαι κἀκεῖνα μὴ ἀφιέναι. |

This material is part of a series of maledictions common to Matthew 23 and Luke 11 which vary in order and detail.[62] In parallel material in Matt 15:1-20 and Mark 7:1-23, we find a similar torrent of invective. In this material, the failure to do the Commandment of God, the Word of God, is pinpointed in Matt 15:1-9:

| 'And why do you trans- gress the Commandment of God for the sake of your tradition?. . . And you have made void the Word of God for the sake of your tradition. . . teaching as doctrines the precepts of men.' | Διὰ τί καὶ ὑμεῖς παρα- βαίνετε τὴν ἐντολην τοῦ θεοῦ διὰ τὴν παράδοσιν ὑμῶν;. . . καὶ ἠκυρώσατε τὸν λόγον τοῦ θεοῦ διὰ τὴν παράδοσιν ὑμῶν. . . διδάσκοντες διδασκαλίας ἐντάλματα ἀνθρώπων. |

Thus Matthew stated the basic problem with reference to the words and deeds of the scribes and Pharisees in 23:1-3, and in 23:23 and 15:1-9 reinforced this with material adapted from two proximate literary traditions. In criticising the lack of balance in the words and deeds of the scribes and Pharisees, there is the implicit instruction to the disciples to be people in whom the balance is manifest.

The balance of word and deed is set before Matthew's readership as the culmination of the whole Gospel in the last verse, 28:20:[63] "teaching them to observe (διδάσκοντες αὐτοὺς τηρεῖν) all that I have commanded you. . ." Here the observing is directly consequent upon the teaching. The vocabulary shift is quite explicable. The original imperative in the Pentateuch was to hear and do the Commandments; the Book of Deuteronomy intro-duced the term למד, "teach/learn"; the expression אולפו אורייתי,

"My teachings of the Law" was popular in the fragment targum
tradition, and is most frequent in Tg. Neof. Deuteronomy. The
importance of proper teaching and teachers is stressed throughout
Paul's letters (cf. as examples Rom 16:17, I Tim 4:3, Tit 1:1-9).

The word διδάσκω is used by Matthew at several key points in
the book.[64] The position in the final verse of the book, of
course, is noteworthy: Matt 28:18-20 draws the whole book to a
focal point and makes this focal point the starting point of the
commission of future discipleship. Further, the word διδάσκω
appears in the last pericope of the narrative (chaps. 1-4) in
preparation for the Sermon on the Mount. Again, the importance
of teaching and learning[65] is stressed in the presentation of the
Sermon on the Mount. In Matt 5:1-2 the formal teaching-situation
is presented: ". . . when he sat down, his disciples (μαθηταί
lit.: learners) came. . . and he taught (διδάσκω). . . " Matt 7:
28-29, the postscript of the Sermon on the Mount, carries the
same emphasis: ". . . the crowds were astonished at his teaching
(ἐπὶ τῇ διδαχῇ[66]) for he taught (διδάσκω) them as one who had
authority. . ." The setting as teaching-situation could not have
been spelled out more clearly; by this means Matthew labels the
material in chaps. 5-7 and highlights it in the context of the
whole Gospel.

The second part of our discussion arising from Matt 28:20 is
concerned with the second verb of διδάσκοντες αὐτοὺς τηρεῖν:
τηρεῖν, "to observe." We can start by reviewing the usage of שמר
in Deuteronomy. Observe Deut 7:11:

You shall observe the Command-	ושמרת את המצוה
ment, the statutes and the	ואת החקים ואת המשפטים
ordinances which I command you	אשר אנכי מצוך העום
this day, to do them.	לעשותם

Here we have what seems to us an awkward sequence of verbs
(שמר לעשות) yet a very common one in Deuteronomy (4:6; 5:1, 32;
6:3, 25; 8:1; 11:22, 32; 12:1; 13:1; 15:5; 16:12; 17:10;
19:9; 24:8; 26:16; 28:1, 15, 58; 31:12; 32:46). It is possible that the expression did not always have to be spelled out

in full because of the doing (עשה) being implied in the observing (שמר). The word שמר with a direct object such as
"commandments" or "words" and without a further completing verb
is found at Deut 4:2, 40; 6:2; 7:9; 11:8; 13:19; 26:17, 18;
27:1; 30:10, 16. There are instances of a direct object such as
"commandments" for the verb עשה: Deut 26:16; 27:10; 30:8; and
frequently עשה with pronoun objects of which the antecedent is
"commandments" or an equivalent expression.[67] Thus the contexts
of the verbs שמר and עשה in Deuteronomy are quite consistent:
observe the commandments, do the commandments.

The commission in Matt 28:20 is to the disciples in view of
the wider audience; the commission in Deut 5:31-32 is to Moses
in view of the whole people; these read very much the same way.
Deut 5:31-32:

. . . all the commandments	כל המצוה
and the statutes and the	והחקים והמשפטים
ordinances which you (Moses)	אשר תלמדם
shall teach them (the people)	
that they may do (them)...	ועשו . . .
You shall be careful to do	ושמרתם לעשות
as the Lord your God has	כאשר צוה יהוה
commanded you.	אלהיכם אתכם

One might suspect that Matt 28:20 was patterned after this commission in Deuteronomy.

We recall that the observance (נטר) of the Commandments was
the subject of haggadic additions in the fragment targum tradition. Observance of the Law was requisite for blessing in this
world, "no poor among you," according to Tgs. Ps.-J., Neof., MSS
V (N and ed. B) at Deut 15:4-11; study of the Law and observance
of the Commandments was requisite for victory over alien kings
according to MSS V (N and ed. B) at Deut 33:29. Observance of
the Law was also requisite for eschatological blessing: the
Garden of Eden was established for those who observed the Commandments of the Law in MSS V, P (N and ed. B) at Gen 3:24.

In the NT books, the verbs τηρέω and φυλάσσω frequently
stand with "words," "commandments," etc. as direct object: τηρέω

is used in this way in Revelation, James, Paul, John, Acts and
Matthew;[68] φυλάσσω in Paul, John, Acts and the Synoptics.[69]
There is only one pericope common to the three Synoptics in which
keeping (φυλάσσω) the commandments is the point at issue, the
story of the rich young man (Matt 19:16-22, Mark 10:17-22, Luke
18:18-23). It would seem that Mark and Luke had the story from
a common tradition, but Matthew's edition diverges. By using
both φυλάσσω and τηρέω in the same passage, Matt 19:17 and 20
(Mark and Luke use only φυλάσσω here.), Matthew points up their
acceptance as synonyms when used in the same type of context;
they both carry the significance of the Deuteronomic שמר.[70] The
two remaining contexts of Matthew's use of τηρέω, "keeping" the
dictates of God and of Jesus are 23:2-3 and 28:18-20, the opening
of the sermon material of chaps. 23-25 and the final text of the
Gospel. In 23:3, the imperative τηρεῖτε stands in synonymous
parallelism with ποιήσατε.

Thus the עשה, "do" and שמר, "observe" of Deuteronomy (נטר,
"observe," emphasized in the targumic tradition) have as object
"commandments," etc.; the NT writers have φυλάσσω and τηρέω,
"observe/keep."[71] In Matthew it is clear that φυλάσσω and τηρέω
are equivalent, and that these basically mean the same as ποιέω
in the context of doing the Commandments, Words, etc.

Finally, doing (ποιέω) and teaching (διδάσκω) the Commandments (the Law and the prophets) is commanded in the pivotal
passage, Matt 5:17-20. In Matt 7:12, the Golden Rule turns upon
doing (ποιέω), and Matthew comments that this Rule simply is "the
Law and the prophets"; because the concepts in this verse resume
those in 5:17-20, it can be suggested that 7:12 was placed where
it is so that the two passages would open and close the central
core of the Sermon on the Mount, a suggestion of inclusio.
Hearing (ἀκούω) and doing (ποιέω) the words of Jesus is the mandate of Matt 7:24-27, the final pericope of the Sermon on the
Mount. We cannot fail to observe how Matthew, in structurally
important passages, has faithfully presented in Greek both the

verbs (hear, observe, do, teach) and the nouns (Words, Commandments, Law) which were basic in the Pentateuch, especially in
Deuteronomy, and amplified in the targumic traditions, in ex-
pressing man's relationship to the Word(s) of God.

Conclusion: the "Words," the "Commandments"
and the "Law" in Matt 7:24-27

The final parable of the Sermon on the Mount (7:24-27) is
important since it contains a recapitulation of the concepts
fundamental to the understanding of the code of living presented
in the Sermon on the Mount. Since this is the case, in studying
it, other important aspects of the Sermon on the Mount are drawn
into consideration, especially Matt 5:17-20. Hence the plan of
this portion of our work is to draw our outline from the concepts in this final parable and discuss some of the key themes
of the Sermon on the Mount in the light of their situation in the
Gospel of Matthew and in Jewish tradition.

First, λόγοι, "words": this recalls the use of the term in
the Pentateuch, especially Deuteronomy where its most exalted and
specific use is for the Ten Words. It also recalls those words
which, in the prophetic and wisdom literature, had been accepted
as its primary synonyms, "commandments" and "the Law." The "Law"
meant the Decalogue, and then it could also mean the whole Pentateuch; and both the details of the written Law, and the extent
to which the unwritten Law was included was pondered by the
writers of the Pseudepigrapha and early midrashim. The term
"Law" had grown in popularity; this is very obvious in the targums (especially Neof. Deuteronomy) and in the tannaitic midrashim. Matt 7:24-27 features the term λόγοι, and is the finale
to the presentation of the "Law" in chaps. 5-7. But Matthew de-
picts Jesus as very specifically presenting μου τοὺς λόγους
τούτους, "these words of Mine." The Sermon is presented as
His words, His Law.

Second, ἀκούω and ποιέω, "hear" and "do": this recalls the presentation of the Ten Words in Deuteronomy and the response to them: "Hear. . . and be careful to do them" (Deut 5:1); "We will hear and do it" (Deut 5:27). However, ἀκούω and οὐκ ποιέω, "hear and not do" was a problem subsequently encountered. The שמע, "hearing/obeying" or on the other hand סור, "turning aside" were what would result in the blessing or the curse in Deut 11:27-28. The fragment targums and Tg. Ps.-J. overtly describe the righteous destined for the Garden of Eden as those who "study the Law and do the Commandments," and the wicked destined for Gehenna as those who "did not observe the Commandments in this world." The crucial thing is the observance; this was very widely held among the tannaim; this is precisely the point made in Matt 7:24-27.

Third, the similes: the man who "does my words" is compared to a man who built on the rock (ἐπὶ τὴν πέτραν), and the man who "does not do. . . " is compared to a man who built on the sand (ἐπὶ τὴν ἄμμον). Whereas in the parable of Elisha ben Abuyah (above p. 108) there was the play on the words אבנים, "stones," and לבנים, "bricks" which, as it were, bound the passage together, this word-play would be lost in Greek. Now, Matthew has used exact repetition extensively in vv 24 and 26 and in vv 25 and 27 for binding his passage together; because of this the contrasting words, which are not repetitions, stand out. Luke's 6:47-48 is quite descriptive, but in the contrasting v 49 the parallel is very abbreviated; v 49 gives the key words and phrases, but the detail is omitted. With less sharp contours, Luke's contrasts are a little dulled. The difference in style between Matt 7:24-27 and Luke 6:47-49 can be illustrated with the opening words of Matt 7:24 and 26, Luke 6:47 and 49:

```
Matt 7:24 Πᾶς οὖν ὅστις            ἀκούει μου       τοὺς λόγους
Matt 7:26 καὶ πᾶς ὁ               ἀκούων μου       τοὺς λόγους
Luke 6:47    πᾶς ὁ ἐρχόμενος πρός με καὶ ἀκούων μου τῶν λόγων
Luke 6:49         ὁ                δὲ ἀκούσας
```

Matt 7:24 τούτους καὶ ποιεῖ   αὐτους. . .
Matt 7:26 τούτους καὶ μὴ ποιῶν αὐτους. . .
Luke 6:47   καὶ ποιῶν   αὐτους. . .
Luke 6:49   καὶ μὴ ποιήσας. . .

Matthew's precision and repetition of pronouns indicates his explicit intention to make repetitions; he had a purpose for it.
It seems that Matthew was not only repeating a pericope entailing
certain contrasts, but for him, the wording was important too.
This attention to details of wording continues throughout
Matthew's passage. He stands ἀνδρὶ φρονίμῳ in contrast to ἀνδρὶ
μωρῷ; but Luke lacks the two striking adjectives. It would seem
that of the two evangelists who use this pericope, it was Matthew
who judged the wording to be integral to the material, and that
the desired poignancy depended upon the wording.

Finally, the pericope of the two builders stands at the end
of the Sermon on the Mount. If the Sermon on the Mount stands as
a presentation of the Law of the Gospel, one might expect a re-
flection of covenant form with the blessing and the curse as one
of the last elements. If the pericope of the two builders is
intended to convey this, it does so in language somewhat gentler
than the overt ראה אנכי נתן רפניכם היום ברכה וקללה, "Behold I
give you today a blessing and a curse" (Deut 11:26); a blessing
and a curse, the one or the other contingent upon whether or not
the commandments are obeyed; this opens the final passage (Deut
11:26-32) of the great parenesis of the book of Deuteronomy
(chaps. 5-11).

We might well stop to consider the targumic treatment of
Deut 11:26ff. (for the treatment of the finale of the greatest
sermon in the Torah might well aid us in our understanding of
the finale of the Sermon on the Mount). Although the poignant
concepts of the blessing and the curse remained firm, at the
same time various targums attest to a certain reluctance to say
"curse." First, at Deut 11:26, 27 and 28, the Hebrew text has
והקללה... את הברכה... ברכה וקללה, "a blessing and a curse ...
the blessing ... and the curse"; however Tg. Ps.-J. reads:

119

וחילופה יח בירכתא ... וחילופה, "the blessing and the contrary
... the blessing ... and the contrary." In v 28, MSS V (N and
ed. B) are similar to Tg. Ps.-J. Second, at Deut 30:1, Tg.
Ps.-J. reads: ברבתא וחילופה, "blessings and their contraries,"
and Tg. Neof.is similar: סדר ברכתה וחילופיהון, "the order of the
blessings and their opposites." Third, at Deut 30:19, Tg. Ps.-J.
alone reads ברכתא וחילופה, "the blessing and the contrary."
These are the only three instances in Deuteronomy of the expression "blessing(s) and curse(s)"; and these are the three
places where the targumists softened the language.[72] The curse
list of Deut 27:15-26 is mollified in the fragment targums and
in Tg. Ps.-J. by preceding the initial curse with a blessing;
and Tg. Ps.-J. goes a step further by preceding the final curse
with a blessing as well. Whereas the Hebrew text hurls its ארור
"cursed be" without relief in every verse in Deut 27:15-26, these
targums open the passage by preceding v 15 with a blessing:
בריך יהוי גברא דלא . . . , "blessed be the man who does not. ..";
this blessing is simply an almost verbatim reverse of v 15.[73]
In Tg. Ps.-J. the final poignant recapitulating curse (27:26) is
also prefaced by a blessing written as the reverse of the verse,
so that we find:

Blessed is the man who	בריך יהוי גברא די יקים
confirms the words of this	ית פתגמי אורייתא הדא
law by doing them. . .	למעבדהון . . .
Cursed is the man who	ליט יהוי גברא דלא יקים
does not confirm the words	ית פתגמי אורייתא הדא
of this law in doing them.	למעבדהון
And they will all answer	הוון עניין כלהון כחדא
together and say, Amen.	ואמרין אמן

To sum up: the blessing comes first, before the curse in
the final passage of the great parenesis in Deut 11:26-32. The
targumists place a blessing before the curses of Deut 27:15-26.
They also soften the language, removing the word "curse" from
Deut 11:26-28 and 30:1 (Tg. Ps.-J. also at Deut 30:19). The
fortunate comes before the disastrous in the parables of R.
Elazar and Elisha ben Abuyah. The fortunate comes before the

disastrous in the final parable of the Sermon on the Mount, Matt
7:24-27 (Luke 6:46-49).

The pattern of the blessing then the curse is not limited
to this pericope in Matthew; it is one of the redactional
patterns of the book. If one views the whole book as one great
symmetrical structure,[74] the sermon material of chaps. 5-7 is the
counterpart of the sermon material of chaps. 23-25. The beatitudes (μακάριοι. . .) which open chap. 5 have their foil in the
woes (οὐαί. . . - perhaps a softer word than κατηραμένοι) of 23:
13-36; a detailed comparison shows some elements of these woes
to be in reverse order of the same elements in the Beatitudes:[75]

8. theirs is the Kingdom of heaven (5:10)	1. you shut the Kingdom of heaven (23:13)
7. sons of God (5:9)	2. child of hell (23:15)
6. they shall see God (5:8)	3. blind...blind...blind (23:16, 17, 19)
5. mercy...merciful (5:7)	4. mercy (23:23)
4. hunger and thirst (5:6)	5. the outside of the cup and the plate (23:25)
2. those who mourn (5:4)	6. tombs... dead men's bones (23:27)
3. they shall inherit the earth (5:5)	7. that upon you may come all the righteous blood shed upon the earth (23:25)

In the overall structure, the blessings occur in the first and
the woes in the last great sermon of the book. Not only are the
openings of Matt 5-7 and 23-25 thus complementary, but the
finale of each spells out the judgement upon those who "do"
(ποιέω in Matt 7:24 and twice in 25:40) and those who "do not do"
(οὐκ ποιέω in Matt 7:26 and twice in 25:45). The blessing (Come
ye blessed. . . οἱ εὐλογημένοι) and the curse (Depart, ye cursed
. . . κατηραμένοι) of Matt 25:34 and 41 are explicit; in Matt
7:24-27 they are implicit in somewhat softened, just slightly
refined language, ἀνδρὶ φρονίμῳ. . . ἀνδρὶ μωρῷ, "like a prudent
man. . . like a foolish man."

The blessing and the curse are the last elements of the
covenant form; in Matthew they have a clear eschatological impact. As the last elements they are contingent upon the central

element, the laws of the sovereign prescribed for the doing. In
Matt 7:24-27 this main element is summarized as μου τοὺς λόγους,
"my words." Those "words" would then be taken in apposition to
the whole Sermon on the Mount, or wider still, the whole of the
Gospel of Matthew, or wider still, the full heritage of the early
Church of the words of Jesus.

"Vacuous"/"Vitiated" and "Salt" in the
Hebrew Pentateuch, LXX and Early Jewish Tradition

Deut 32:6 is the only place in the Pentateuch where the word
נבל is hurled at the assemply of Israel[76] - albeit with the
modicum of reserve suggested by the use of the rhetorical question. The suggestion of stark sin, of being vacuous, stands out
as unusually strong language.[77] Not only is there poignancy in
the use of the word נבל, but also poignancy arising from the fact
that what is predicated of אל, "God" (32:4) and what is predicated of the reproached עם, "people" (32:6) stand in sharp contrast. Deut 32:4b-6:

God of faithfulness	אל אמונה
and without wrong,	ואין עול
Righteous and straight (is) He.	צדיק וישר הוא
(The people) has destroyed (i.e.	שחת לו. . .
vitiated) itself with respect to Him. . .	
Do you thus requite the Lord,	ה־ליהוה תגמלו־זאת
foolish people, and not wise?	עם נבל ולא חכם
Is He not your Father who created you	הלוא־הוא אביך קנך
who made you and established you?	הוא עשך ויכננך

(Note the syntactical parallel of אל אמונה ואין עול in v 4 with
עם נבל ולא חכמ in v 6. Note also צדיק predicated of God - but
not of the people.) A review of the later passages of the Hebrew
Bible in which the נבל-root occurs is useful for observing how
its meaning was clarified, made quite specific. To be brief, in
each of the three texts, Isa 32:5-6, Ps 14:1 and par. Ps 53:2,
we observe the double evil of the fool, error with respect to
knowledge of God and error in practice, abominable deeds.
The LXX translators usually use the root ἀφρο- for נבל/נבלה.

However, only at Deut 32:6 and Isa 32:5-6 is the word μωρός used
to translate (ה)נבל; the passages in which these occur are
hortatory addresses to the people of Israel. It seems that, at
the time of the translations, μωρός was a word to be used with
care.[78] The עם נבל of Deut 32:6 was sensed as sufficiently
unique by the LXX translators that they used the scathing adjective μωρός. (No word of this root is used anywhere else in
the LXX Pentateuch.)

Deut 32:6b-7 goes on to spell out the mentality of the
people which is נבל/μωρός: without a working concept of God as
Father and Creator, basically uninstructed by the זקנים/πρεσβυτ-
έροι, "elders." Deut 32:4-5 had already spelt out the behaviour
of the people which is נבל/μωρός. The context, an exhortation
to Israel in the face of corrupt behaviour and in the face of
basic ignorance with respect to God, contributes to the meaning
of עם נבל. The LXX translator pinpointed and highlighted this
through his style and vocabulary: Θεὸς πιστός. . . δίκαιος. . .
λαὸς μωρός.

The עם נבל of Deut 32:6 appears in the fragment targum tradition as אומא טפשא,[79] "a dull/obdurate people," a people to be
decried as foolish. Tg. Ps.-J. shows an expansion:

The people which are obdurate   עמא דהוון טפשין
and have befogged/obfuscated[80]   וקבילו אורייתא
the Law.

The obduracy consisted in a basic ignorance with respect to the
Law, that is, with respect to God. The same point is rather
clearly made in Sipre Deut 309 in commenting on Deut 32:5:[81]

Whoever causes Israel to be   ומי גרם לישראל להיות
decayed or obdurate, they   מנובלים ומטופשים
have not become wise in   שלא הוחכמו בדברי תרוה
the words of the Law.

In order to understand the words שחת לו of Deut 32:5, we shall
pause to consider the meaning of the verb שחת in the Pentateuch.
First, שחת in Genesis and Exodus. The verb שחת is found in the
flood story and the story of Sodom and Gomorrah. In both of
these, it was a question of being absolutely corrupt (שחת),

therefore of being absolutely destroyed (שחת). From these two
contexts we learn the unequivocal meaning of the verb. Exod 32:7
has the verb שחת in the piel without direct object: "for your
people has acted corruptly (שחת)." Considering the force of the
verb, one might infer that the action was one by which the people
was destroying itself; v 8 gives the means of the people's self-
vitiation: turning aside from the way and making the molten calf.
Exod 32:7 is echoed in the central parenesis of Deuteronomy (9:12)
The theme is again taken up in chap. 4 where the people is warned
not to act corruptly (vitiate itself) by making a graven image
(vv 16 and 25). Considering the strength of the verb and especially its impact from usage in the context of idolatry in Deuteronomy, we can turn to Deut 32:5.

In Deut 32:5, the clause שחת לו, "(the people) has destroyed
(vitiated) itself with respect to Him" is brief and to the point.
The parallel clause is given as a plain negative: לא בניו, "they
are not His children." Although v 5 continues in general terms,
it can be understood quite well in the light of Deut 31:29 where
the verb שחת is made specific, that is, in turning aside from the
way which Moses had commanded. (The verb שחת makes a stark contrast for the verbs of v 6, קנה, עשה and כון.)

The targums of the Pentateuch reflect a tradition of interpretation of the verb שחת in the piel or hifil[82] when it has no
direct object. At all six of the occurrences where this is the
case, Tg. Ps.-J. supplies a direct object: אורחתהון at Deut 9:12;
עבודיכון at Deut 4:16, 4:25, 31:29; עבודיהון at Exod 32:7; and
עבודיהון טביא at Deut 32:5. Tg. Neof. agrees with Tg. Ps.-J. at
Deut 4:16 and 4:25; at 9:12 it supplies the direct object
עיבדהון.[83] The sense in these targums is that the people have
vitiated their (good) deeds of efficacy.

The שחת לו of Deut 32:5 was apparently so in need of an
explanation that there was an opening for the fragment targum
tradition to develop one;[84] MS V reads:[85]

The sons have vitiated their   חבלחו בנייא עובדיהון
works;

but it is not <u>before Him</u>[86] ולא קודמוי
(that) they have corrupted... חבילו
but rather, <u>themselves</u>. אלא להון
And because they have ועל די חבילו
vitiated (themselves),
a blemish will be placed מומא
upon them. יתיהב בהום

The consequence of such self-destruction is spelled out in the
remainder of the verse. <u>Tg. Ps.-J.</u> and <u>MS</u> V respectively read:[87]

An insidious generation which דרא עוקמנא
have changed their deeds, so דאשנין עובדיהון
the order of judgement of the ואוף סדר דינייא
world shall be changed with דעלמא
respect to them. אישתני עלהון

An insidious and twisted דרא עוקמא ופתלנא
generation which has changed דשני עובדוי
its deeds, so the orders (of ואוף סידריה
judgement) of the world shall דעלמא
be changed with respect to it. אשתני עלוי

Here, whereas one might have expected the penalty to be in terms
of judgement in the world to come, it is in terms of the judgement of this world.

There are other Hebrew verbs with similar connotations. The
hifil of the verb נוא: forbid, avert, hinder, refuse, frustrate;
the hifil of the verb פרר: break, dissolve, violate, frustrate,
annihilate, annul. The verb פרר: in the Pentateuch usually
occurs in the context of "breaking My covenant";[88] one quickly
senses the meaning to be "vitiating My contract" (to use the
appropriate parlance of modern business English). Both of these
verbs are found repeatedly in the chapter on the validation and
voiding of vows, Numbers 30: נוא four times, and פרר five times.
In Numbers 30, <u>Tg</u>. <u>Onq</u>. uses בטל for translating פרר (but not
נוא); but <u>Tg</u>. <u>Ps.-J</u>. does not show a distinction: בטל is found
for either or both of the Hebrew verbs in question; and in
material added in the course of Numbers 30, the verb בטל also
occurs. <u>Tg</u>. <u>Neof</u>. has בטל for the translation of both verbs,
consistently. Thus in Numbers 30, <u>Tgs</u>. <u>Onq</u>., <u>Ps.-J</u>. and <u>Neof</u>.
show quite different patterns of occurrence of the verb בטל,
and the latter two show a preference for this verb.[89]

The חק עולם, "perpetual statute" which gave the Levites the
right to the food-offerings (Numbers 18[90]) is given a slight explanation in a literary parallel at Num 18:19: חק עולם ברית מלח
עולם - "a perpetual statute, a perpetual covenant of salt." However, this biblical explanation apparently itself needed further
explanation in the mind of those who commented upon this phrase
in Tg. Ps.-J. There the reading is:

It (i.e. the statute) shall	ולא יתבטיל
not be voided as the salt	הי כמלחא
which seasons the flesh of the	דמבסים בשר
statutory offerings; it is	קורבניא דקיים
before the Lord perpetually.	עלם הוא קדם ייי

Here we have a significant complex: (1) the verb בטל; (2) the
implication that מלח, "salt" could be made void in the process of
the sacrifice, and this (3) in an expression posed as a foil to
accent the essential and permanent character of the חק עולם.

There is a close connection between "salt" and "covenant."[91]
We can view Lev 2:13 as a verse in which word-patterns were established which would subsequently be repeated. It reads, "And
all your cereal offerings you shall salt with salt (במלחא תמלח).
And you shall not abolish the salt of the covenant of your God
(ולא תבטל מלח קיים אלהך) from your cereal offering. With all
your offerings you shall offer salt." Tg. Ps.-J. prefaces Lev
2:13b thus: "And you shall not abolish the salt of the covenant
of your God from your cereal offering because the twenty-four
gifts of the priests are appointed with a covenant of salt
(בקיים מילחא) for which reason. . ." So, in this verse in Tg.
Ps.-J. there are the two expressions מלח קיים and קיים מילחא,
"salt of the covenant" and "covenant of salt." It is possible
that the targumists had an appreciation of the connection between the two expressions and drew the latter from Num 18:19[92]
for use in the addition to Lev 2:13. It is quite probable that
it was a question of genitivus epexegeticus, and that the regnum
and the regens of the bound form could be interchanged for
poetic purposes. That the characteristics of salt were taken

for describing the characteristics of the covenant is evident in
Sipre Num 118 in its comment upon Num 18:19:[93]

It is a covenant of salt	ברית מלח
perpetually before the Lord.	עולם היא לפני ה'
The writing was concluded,	כרת הכתוב
a covenant with Aaron with	ברית עם אהרן
respect to a wholesome thing,	בדבר הבריא
and not only this, it makes	ולא עוד אלא
other things wholesome.	שמבריא את אחרים

If "salt" was a standard metaphor for anything, it was a metaphor
for the permanence of the covenant;[94] here another attribute of
salt is brought forward, "wholesomeness." Both are applied to
God's covenant. Covenant effects wholesomeness; the Torah
effects savour. This is presented in Sipre Deut 37[95] in the
course of a play on words, תבל - תבל:

> R. Simeon ben Johai said: תבל (world): that is the
> land of Israel, as it is said, 'playing in the תבל
> (world) of His land' (prov 8:31). Why was its name
> called תבל (world)? Because it was be-תבל-ed (seasoned)
> above all. For as to all other lands, there is in one
> what is lacking in another, and in this one what is
> lacking in that one; but in the land of Israel nothing
> at all is lacking. . . תבל (world): that is the land
> of Israel. Why was its name called תבל (world)? On
> the basis of the תבל (spice) which is in its midst.
> What is the תבל (spice) which is in its midst? That
> is the Law, as it is said, 'Among the nations there
> is no Law' (Lam 2:9). . . .

The first part of this highly developed passage is given under
the name of R. Simeon ben Johai, a tanna of the mid-second
century. It is possible that the sophistication alone belongs
to that tanna who utilized and transmitted an old play on words.[96]
The second part of this passage (after our ellipsis) is given
anonymously, the possible implication being that it contains
elements older than the first part.

The Law would have an effect upon those who studied it, as
salt has an effect on its milieu. To this, allusions are made
in several places in early Jewish literature. In Derek Erez
Zuta, Kalla rabbati (probably commenting on the former text) and
Kidd. 29b, the disciple of the Scribes (student of Torah) is

described as זריז וממולח, "industrious and bright," literally
"industrious and salted."[97] It is the cumulative witness of
precisely the same phrase which leads to positing it as a terminus technicus which can be considered as well established by
the time of the writing of the sources in which it has been
transmitted to us. This evidence suggests an early date of
origin, and a good possibility that it could have been known in
the period of the Second Temple.[98] The opening words of Derek
Erez Zuta are worth noting:[99]

The ways of the disciples	דרכן של תלמידי חכמים
of the wise: poor and humble	הניו ושפל רוח
of spirit, industrious and	זריז וממולח
salted, suffering insult	עלוב ואהוב לכל אדם
yet loved by all men.	

"Vacuous"/ "Vitiated" and "Salt" in the
Early Church and the Gospel of Matthew

The words μωρός and μωραίνω are used in the NT by Matthew
(8 times), Luke (once) and Paul (8 times[100]). Its main meaning
is "foolish, stupid, vacuous," but in connection with taste:
"insipid, flat." It is remarkable that the word ἄφρων (and cognates) appears in Mark (once), Luke (3 times), Paul (11 times)
and I Peter (once), but never in Matthew. We recall that the
word נבל was usually translated ἄφρων in its occurrences in
general contexts in the LXX; but when Israel specifically was
addressed (Deut 32:6 and Isa 32:5-6) it was translated μωρός.
Thus Matthew is conspicuous in the consistent choice of μωρός
over ἄφρων. Matthew has chosen the word which would be the more
poignant in the ears of his knowledgeable Jewish audience. The
juxtaposed opposite of μωρός in Paul is ordinarily σοφός, "wise"
as it was in the LXX of Deut 32:6; the passages where these
occur are instructional and straightforward, Rom 1:18-23 and
I Cor 1:17-30.[101] In Matthew, the juxtaposed opposite of μωρός
is φρόνιμος, "prudent, wise"; the passages where these occur
are parables, Matt 7:24-27 and 25:1-12.[102] These passages are

about people's houses and lamps at the level of the story - and
on this level φρόνιμος could be seen as appropriate. Yet the
parables are about eschatological reality, and on this level
μωρός could be seen as appropriate.

It is to be noted that all of the occurrences of μωρός (and
μωραίνω) in Matthew are found in the two major blocks of sermon
material, chaps. 5-7 and 23-25. In chap. 23, eleven times the
scribes and Pharisees are addressed in an apostrophe - six times
as hypocrites, five times as blind, but only once (or twice[103])
as μωροί. Those addressed are fittingly described as foolish men
who ought to have known and done all the things of the Law, but
did not; they only observed the smaller precepts but not the
more weighty: ταῦτα (the weightier matters) ἔδει ποιῆσαι κἀκεῖνα
μὴ ἀφιέναι, "those you ought to have done without neglecting the
others" (Matt 23:23).

Here then, in Matthew 23, the meaning of the word μωρός is
made clear by the collection of examples.[104] We should also note
the similarity of context with Deut 32:6 and Isa 32:5-6. In all
three cases, the people addressed were the people of Israel who
ought to have known and observed the Law. The astuteness of the
LXX translators with respect to word and context (above p. 122)
has afforded us the basis of our understanding of the word μωρός
in Matthew 23. Jewish traditions, especially targumic traditions on Deut 32:5-6 bring further clarity to that understanding. Those who are μωροί are obdurate with respect to the
Law, and they have vitiated their (good) works of efficacy. To
sum up, such people are "not His (God's) children" and "not
wise" (Deut 32:5-6); which means that they have vitiated themselves as people, the consequence of which is adverse eschatological judgement (above pp. 122-124).

Matthew 24-25 is the finale of the sermon material in the
Gospel of Matthew; it is made up of a series of pericopes of
eschatological tenor. The final words of Matthew 25, "eternal
punishment. . . eternal life," constitute the focal point to

which the materials tend; and in the light of these concepts they are to be studied. This is the eschatological dimension of the two ways.

In Matt 25:1-12 we have the parable of the maidens awaiting the marriage feast, in the course of which Matthew terms them φρόνιμοι (vv 2, 4, 8 and 9) and μωραί (vv 2, 3 and 8). The contrast is strong indeed, strong in view of the eschatological urgency of the final sermon in which the passage stands. But we note that the contrasted words are counterpoised only three times. It was enough to have strongly alluded to "the blessed. . . the cursed" three times as the φρόνιμοι and μωραί, the "prudent" and "foolish"; the fourth contrast was αἱ φρόνιμοι. . . αἱ λοιπαὶ παρθένοι, "the prudent. . . the other maidens" (vv 9 and 11). This can be viewed in the light of the well-attested targumic preference for softening the second member of "blessed. . . cursed" to a rather indefinite expression, "the blessing and the contrary." Matthew's exegetical etiquette at this point, in accord with that of the targumic traditions, makes it clear that he had a full understanding of the sharpness of the term μωρός.

There are few occurrences of the word ἅλας (ἁλίζω, ἄναλος), "salt," in the NT. They are limited to the three passages of Matt 5:13, Mark 9:49-50 and Luke 14:34, with one further occurrence at Col 4:6.

The context of ממולח, "salted" in Derek Erez Zuta (above p. 127) exhibits both a conceptual context and a style of writing with which a reader of Paul is not unfamiliar. Observe Col 4:6: ὁ λόγος ὑμῶν πάντοτε ἐν χάριτι, ἅλατι ἠρτυμένος, εἰδέναι πῶς δεῖ ὑμᾶς ἑνὶ ἑκάστῳ ἀποκρίνεσθαι, "Let your speech always be gracious, seasoned with salt, so that you may know how you ought to answer everyone." In both this passage and the citation from Derek Erez Zuta, the concern is with the intelligent and kind deportment of the disciple due to his having been "salted," and with that deportment vis-à-vis "everyone."

We might recall Paul's description of the θεοῦ διάκονοι,
"servants of God" in II Cor 6:4-10; especially the list of contrasts in vv 8-10. Paul proceeds with antitheses: negatives
balanced by a simple καί and the contrary affirmatives (Derek
Erez Zuta has a simple ו). All three passages end on a comprehensive note: Derek Erez Zuta, כל אדם, "all men"; Col 4:6, ἑνί
ἑκάστῳ, "everyone"; and II Cor 6:10, πάντα, "everything."

Apparently, in Mark 9:49-50, there are three independent
sayings juxtaposed; and the catch-word is "salt." Verse 49
has long been an enigma, a crux interpretum, and is thought to
refer to the purifying fire of God's chastisements.[105] Verse 50
has the two facets already seen in Col 4:6 and Derek Erez Zuta:
concern with the deportment of the disciple (ἔχετε ἐν ἑαυτοῖς
ἅλα, "Have salt in yourselves," quite possibly reflecting the
pual participle ממולח[104]), and with that deportment vis-à-vis
others (καὶ εἰρηνεύετε ἐν ἀλλήλοις, "and be at peace with one
another"). The last word is the reciprocal pronoun with no
antecedent - hence the verse ends on the same comprehensive note
which we have observed in the other passages. The third occur-
ence of ἅλας in Mark 9:50a will be considered together with the
parallels in Luke 14:34 and Matthew 5:13.

Matt 5:13 and its Place in the Sermon on the Mount

As a parallel to Matt 5:13 (Mark 9:50a and Luke 14:34),
commentators[107] often cite from T.B. Bechoroth 8b: מילחא כי סריא
במאי מלחי ליה, "Salt if it has lost its savour, wherewith shall
it be salted?" This has the character of a proverbial saying and
occurs in a text purporting to transmit a late first century
story.[108] Thus it offers one reason to suggest that the three
Gospel texts (constructed with the same import and syntax)
provide sources of the same already-proverbial saying.

The precise wording of the saying must be accepted as fluid:

Matt: ἐὰν δὲ   τὸ ἅλας μωρανθῇ   ἐν τίνι   ἁλισθήσεται;
Mark: ἐὰν δὲ   τὸ ἄναλον γένηται, ἐν τίνι αὐτὸ ἀρτύσετε;
Luke: ἐὰν δὲ καὶ τὸ ἅλας μωρανθῇ   ἐν τίνι   ἀρτυθήσεται;
Bek.   מילחא כי סריא במאי מלחי ליה

The wording of the saying in Matthew, Mark and Luke varies
slightly (apparently due to two sources: Mark and Q). Yet the
final word, the verb of the second clause, shows agreement (the
same root) between Mark and Luke against Matthew; this is thought
to have arisen from the influence of one of the stages of Mark on
the final redaction of Luke. Moreover, in the introductory clause
καλὸν (οὖν) τὸ ἅλας, "salt is good," Mark and Luke agree against
Matthew, probably due to the same influence.[109] What is significant for our purposes is that both of the verbs in Matthew differ
from both of the verbs in Mark. We find it important to bear in
mind the common opinion proposed by source criticism which accepts
two proximate sources, Mark and Q; and not try to resolve these
into one hypothetical original.[110]

Of the significant words, only the first noun is standard:
ἅλας (Matthew, Mark, Luke), מלח (Bekorot). Only Bekorot and
Matthew repeat the initial root in the final verb: ἁλίζω and מלח,
while Mark reflects the initial root immediately in the first
clause: ἄναλον γένηται; these sources preserve the poetic touch
found in popular proverbs. (Luke does not have this touch; the
saying is given without repetition of roots: Luke's first verb is
as Matthew's, and his second is as Mark's.) It is then the verb
in the first clause in Matthew's rendition (and Luke's) that
stands out as strong in character and chosen with the purpose of
anticipating the interpretation of the saying.

It is possible that an awareness of the strong character of
the μωρός-concept played some rôle in the selection and arrange-
ment of the material within the Sermon on the Mount. To be
specific, immediately after the introductory Beatitudes, in the
opening verse of the sermon-proper, Matt 5:13 has μωρανθῇ (the
verb); in the final pericope of the sermon, the veiled eschatological parable of the two builders, Matt 7:26 has ἀνδρὶ μωρῷ

(the adjective);   in the overt eschatological material of chap. 5
in the exegesis of the commandment against killing, Matt 5:22 has
Μωρέ (the noun), a vocative which would cause την γέενναν τοῦ
πυρός, "the Gehenna of fire," to redound upon its speaker. These
words could not have been more unequivocal or direct. Thus the
root μωρ- is poised in all its forcefulness at 5:22; and it is
found in material placed in the initial and final positions of
the Sermon on the Mount (5:13 and 7:24-27). This type of word-
placing is not at all uncharacteristic of Matthew.[111] It would
not be going too far to suggest a possible poignant _inclusio_ here,
the significance of which we must seek to appreciate. The
literary features of Matt 5:13, then, are precise and carefully
chosen. We can easily deduce that there would have been cognate
usage and word play in the Semitic saying which Matthew's Greek
probably reflects: "You are the salt (מלח) of the earth (תבל);
but if the salt (מלח) has been made void (בטל or חבל; or less
likely נבל or קבל) wherewith shall it be salted (מלח)?"

In Matthew, the word γῆ occurs in the clause introducing the
saying: "You are the salt of the earth (γῆ)"; in Luke it occurs
in the commentary after the saying.[112] Was the Matthean "You
are the salt of the earth" based on an Aramaic saying such as
אתון מלחא דתבל?[113] Did the introductory clause of Matt 5:14,
"You are the light of the world (τοῦ κόσμου)" influence the
reading of the Aramaic? Was this how the introductory clause of
Matt 5:13 came to be "you are the salt _of the earth_" when it
might have read "you are the salt _which seasons_"?   Actually,
either reading would have been acceptable in the limited context
of Matt 5:13.   Either reading could find a parallel in the
context of _Sipre_ Deut 37 (above p. 126) in which the תבל
(world: land of Israel) was pre-eminently תבל (seasoned) with
all the goods of the earth, but notably the Torah. The significance of this discussion is that it presents the word תבל as one
which must be given serious consideration in our present enquiry,
and this Aramaic word becomes a condidate as possibly lying

behind the Greek γῆ. As such it would suggest even more word
play than the Greek could transmit.

The word בטל is found in Tg. Ps.-J. at Num 18:19. We have
already noted (above p. 125) that the verb בטל was used in implying that salt (מלח) could be voided (בטל) of its essence; and
this idea was found in an expression posed as a foil: salt could
be voided; the covenant could not be voided. Furthermore, we
see a preference in Tgs. Ps.-J. and Neof. for the use of the verb
בטל in translating both of the Hebrew verbs נוא and פרר which
occur repeatedly in Numbers 30 in the context of the annulling of
vows. Thus there is a good possibility that the word בטל lies
behind the Greek μωραίνω at Matt 5:13.

On the other hand, we must remember that the targumists
apparently thought that the Hebrew verb שחת was somehow incomp-
lete without a direct object, and thus the phrase שחת לו at
Deut 32:5 became susceptible of interpretation (above p. 124).
In the course of their interpretation, they used the verb חבל
repeatedly. First, the direct object was "works": thus we read:
חבילו בניא עובדהון, "the sons have vitiated their works."
Second, they added this idea: חבילו אלא להון, "they have corrupted
(rather) themselves." Third, the verb חבל without a direct object,
"vitiated (themselves)" is repeated. Thus in the fragment targum
tradition, the key word in the interpretation of Deut 32:5 is
חבל, and not just this, but the interpreters have spelled out
the concept of the people vitiating themselves. Thus there is
a good possibility that the word חבל lies behind the Greek
μωραίνω at Matt 5:13.[114]

There is another reason why either בטל or חבל (or even נבל
or קבל[115]) are good candidates as having stood here in the Semitic
saying which Matthew's words probably reflect; these words give
word play with תבל; and בטל has all three consonantal sounds in
common with תבל.

In the introductory clause, Ὑμεῖς ἐστε τὸ ἅλας. . . , the
first word Ὑμεῖς is emphatic; the clause is explanatory, and so

the salt-metaphor is not at all ambiguous. With assurance, we
can read the meaning of the saying "if you have been vitiated,
wherewith shall you be reconstituted?" Then it is natural to ask
about the "wherewith," the constituting factor, the dimension of
life without which a person is not of any worth as a person.
Starting with the Hebrew Bible, we have observed the close connection between the words "salt" and "covenant." "Salt," as
Jewish tradition explained, stood for the covenant in its permanence and in its capacity for making other things savoury;   the
Law was the spice in the midst of Israel.

On its opening page, Derek Erez Zuta transmits the saying
that the disciples of the wise should be ממולח, "salted." The
inference would be that wisdom consisted in being salted with
the covenant, the Law. In Sipre on Deut 32:5, we read ". . . wise
in the words of the Law," the opposite being obduracy. Tg. Ps.-J.
on Deut 32:6 speaks of obduracy with respect to the Law. When שחת
in the Hebrew text has no direct object, the targumic traditions
usually added עובדהון, hence "they have vitiated their works." At
Deut 32:5, as we have noted, the interpretation in the targum
traditions is "they have vitiated their works and also themselves."
We reach the conclusion that the "wherewith" which constitutes the
worthwhile dimension of the life of the sons of God is (1) the
covenant, the Law, the words of the Law, (2) their (good) works.
With these two factors are the sons of God constituted, (1) themselves vis-à-vis God, and (2) vis-à-vis one another.

At this point we turn to the Matthean postscript to the
saying. To be "thrown out" is an expression for eschatological
perdition, used more often by Matthew than by the other Synoptics
in this way. We find ἐκβάλλω used in direct speech at Matt 8:12
(par. Luke 13:28) and in obvious parables at Matt 22:13 and 25:30.
In the simile of the kingdom of heaven, Matt 13:47-50, we find
ἔξω βάλλω. . . βάλλω εἰς τὴν κάμινον τοῦ πυρός, "throw out. . .
throw into the furnace of fire." In the metaphor of the bad tree,
Matt 3:10 (par. Luke 3:9 and Matt 7:19) we find εἰς πῦρ βάλλω,

"throw into the fire." In the directives about the offending
member we find βάλλω εἰς γέενναν, "throw into Gehenna" (and
slight variants in Matt 5:29-30, 18:8-9 (par. Mark 9:45-47).
Thus this eschatological use of "thrown out" occurs in Mark and
Luke only in passages for which there is a parallel in Matthew;
but in Matthew in more passages than have parallels in Mark or
Luke. It would be natural to suggest that there is an eschatological hint in the use of ἔξω βάλλω in the sentence following
the salt-saying in Matt 5:13 and Luke 14:35; it would be natural
to suggest that Q had the expression in this sense, and that
Matthew, above all, would have been likely to incorporate this
into his Gospel. However, the immediate contexts in both Matthew
and Luke do not lend themselves directly to accommodating this
interpretation. Were they purposely constructed to veil this
interpretation? Luke speaks of unfitness for the land or for the
dunghill, but then tempts his readers to read meaning into his
words: "he who has ears to hear, let him hear." Matthew speaks
of the uneless substance's being "trodden underfoot by men" (cf.
Matt 7:6 for another similar use of this expression), but he has
already anticipated the interpretation of his words in his pre-
fatory remark, "you are the salt of the earth."

Immediately after the exegesis of Deut 32:5 in the fragment
targum tradition, the same tradition goes on to spell out the
consequence of the sons' having "vitiated their works (and of
having) vitiated themselves also." The consequence is that "the
order of judgement of the world shall be changed with respect to
them." The Synoptics, especially Matthew, tacitly support the
interpretation that "thrown out" in Matt 5:13 (and Luke 14:35)
has an eschatological nuance; this can be said with greater
assurance when the witness of the material referring to Deut 32:5
in the fragment targum tradition is taken into account.

Conclusion: Matt 5:13 and 7:24-27

Some features of Semitic style are attempted in the Greek of
Matt 5:13; the same saying, in the same style, is preserved also
in T.B. Bechoroth 8b in a text purporting to transmit a late
first century story. In Matt 7:24-27 we have observed parallel
constructions and repetition, an attempt to present the pericope
as though wishing to transmit an old familiar pericope which involved Semitic style. There was in fact a parable of two builders which was preserved under the name of Elisha ben Abuyah in
ᵓAbot R. Nat. 24 (above p. 108) in which the words denoting the
building materials, stones (אבנים) and bricks (לבנים) are similar-
sounding and repeated in a-b-b-a fashion. These literary devices
give coherence to the passage and make its lesson memorable.
These specific literary devices could not be transmitted in the
Greek language, hence Matthew's recourse to what devices he could
use. Here then we have a noteworthy point common to Matt 5:13
and 7:24-27; each is a masterly attempt at presenting an analogy or parable reflecting Semitic literary features.

A second feature common to Matt 5:13 and 7:24-27 is the
presentation of the dual imperative. Implicit in the word "salt"
in Matt 5:13 was the Law and (good) works, the two occupations
which gave the sons of God their identity as sons of God. In
Matt 7:24-27 this dual imperative is in the same terms as in
Moses' instructions for acceptance of the Commandments in Deuteronomy, hear and do. In Deut 5:1, 27, 6:3, the words are שמע,
"hear" and עשה, "do," with the accent on עשה, "do" in Deut 5:32
and especially in 6:25. This imperative was stressed in the
targumic tradition, a good example being found in the fragment
targum tradition on Gen 3:15, 22, 24. Those who "study the Law
and do the Commandments" are the ones who overcome the serpent
and are destined for Eden; those who "do not do the Commandments"
will be made ill by the serpent and are destined for Gehenna. In
the centuries which produced the targums, it was natural that
"hearing" the Law was expressed as "study" of the Law. The dual

imperative remained basically the same. It was also an integral
part of early Christian tradition, being spelled out in plain
terms by Paul who stressed the "doing" in Rom 2:12-23: "not the
hearers of the Law who are righteous before God, but the doers
of the Law who will be justified"; and by James (2:21-25):
". . . faith was completed by works. . . You see a man is justified by works and not by faith alone." The final pericope of
the Sermon on the Mount stands squarely in accord with Jewish and
Christian tradition with respect to the use of the verbs "hear"
and "do," ἀκούω and ποιέω. Both are required; the second is
crucial. From the fragment targum tradition we learned of the
proclivity for softening the language used when speaking of what
the Hebrew text calls the "curse." This softening was achieved
by the use of the parable with its similes in Matt 7:24-27, and
of the use of the common verb πίπτω, "fall." In Matt 5:13,
through the use of the salt metaphor, a softening is achieved,
and the verb is ἐξω βάλλω, "throw out."

The use of parable and metaphor also makes it possible to
indicate that the implied blessing or curse had ramifications
both in this world and in the world to come. The this-world
ramifications occupy a large portion of the book of Deuteronomy;
they are indicated, for example, in the fragment targum tradition
in Genesis 3 (the overcoming of, or being made ill by the snake)
side by side with the eschatological implication (Eden or Gehanna).
In the context of the Gospel of Matthew, Matt 5:13 can be read at
both levels; being constituted by or vitiated of the Law and
good works has consequences both in this world (the literal side
of the metaphor) and in the world to come (the implication).
Matt 7:24-27 also can be read at both levels; it is the Words
which must be heard and done; the consequences take place both
in this world (the literal side of the parable) and in the world
to come (the implication).

The most obvious point in common between Matt 5:13 and
7:24-27 is the use of the root μωρ-. The significance of this

root has been discussed at length. Even if the root καταρ-, "curse," was not used in the Sermon on the Mount, μωρ- could be said to be an unequivocal substitute (cf. Matt 5:22) with a manifest eschatological dimension. It is the eschatological dimension of this word which gives the greatest assurance that there are eschatological implications in Matt 5:13 and 7:24-27.

To summarize, Matt 5:13 and 7:24-27 have much in common. In the style and vocabulary of each of them, there are strong suggestions of a masterly attempt to produce in Greek some reflections of Semitic literary form to the extent that it is probable that polished Semitic material is reflected by each passage. Both passages have the root μωρ-, signifying a vacuous state with respect to knowledge of God and being non-productive of good works. Both passages contain the double imperative: Matt 5:13 requires that the disciples be salted and salt the earth; Matt 7:24-27 says the same thing without metaphor: plainly, "hear" and "do." The constitutive factor of salting is the Law and good works; the object of the hearing and doing is Jesus' "words" (in the formal sense of Law and Commandments) the doing of which is stressed. The use of the salt metaphor in Matt 5:13 and the use of the similes in the parable in Matt 7:24-27 create a softer language than if the plain language of "blessing and curse" were used; however the root μωρ- was used in both passages and it plainly implies the eschatological curse. Thus what lies behind the metaphor of Matt 5:13 means the same thing as that which stands out in Matt 7:24-27. The opening verse (after the introductory Beatitudes) and the closing pericope of the Sermon on the Mount have so much in common that one might suggest an inclusio - taking this term in a broad sense.

139

Notes

[1] Klaus Koch, in discussing literary types and formulas, explains that a modern form critic might call the decalogue an "apodictic series of prohibitions," but that there is a Hebrew name for the form: דבר, in the sense of the empowering word. Cf. Klaus Koch, The Growth of the Biblical Tradition: The Form-Critical Method (N.Y.: Charles Scribner's Sons, 1959) 9-10.

[2] Further examples of associations of these words:
חק, משפט and מצוה in Deut 5:31; 6:1-2; 7:11; 26:16-18.
חק and משפט in Deut 5:1; 11:32.
משפט and מצוה in Deut 8:11; 11:1 (also 30:16).
תרוה, חק and דבר in Deut 17:11. In the later additions to Deut:
משפט and תורה in Deut 33:10; מצוה and תורה in Deut 30:10.

[3] In the qal: Deut 4:10; 5:1; 14:23; 17:19; 18:9; 13:12, 13; in the piel: 4:1, 5, 10, 14; 5:31(28); 6:1; 11:19; 20:18 (30: 19, 20).

[4] Deut 5:1; 6:3; 7:12; 12:28; 13:19; 15:5; 26:16-17; 28:1-2; 28:13; 31:12 and 4:1.

[5] The "commandment" (מצוה) is what is to be taught (למד): Deut 5:31(28) and 6:1. The "words" (דבר) are what is to be taught (למד): Deut 11:19. The "words" (דבר) are to be inculcated (hapax שנן, piel): Deut 6:7.

[6] We find מצוה as the object of the verb עשה at Deut 6:25; 7:11; 8:1; 15:5; 19:9; 28:1 and 30:8; cf. also 6:1; 26:17; 27:10; 28:15; 28:45.

[7] For passages in which דבר "word(s) is object of the verb עשה "do," cf. Deut 13:1; 17:19; 28:58; 29:29; 30:14; 31:12; cf. also 4:13. The word דבר is object of both verbs שמע and עשה at Deut 12:28 and 27:26.

[8] Cf. also II Kgs 23:24-25.

[9] Cf. II Kgs 22:11, 13; 23:2, 3; II Chr 34:18, 21, 30, 31.

[10] Further examples: ". . . Out of Zion shall go forth the law (תרוה) and the word of the Lord (דבר יהוה) from Jerusalem" - Isa 2:3; also Mic 4:2. "The law of the Lord (תורת יהוה). . . this word (דבר הזה)" - Isa 30:9-12. "The law of the Lord (תורת יהוה). . . the word of the Lord (דבר יהוה)" - Jer 8:8 and 9. In the book of Daniel, דבר (9:12) is associated with תורה (9:10, 11 twice, 13).

[11] Ernst Sellin & Georg Fohrer, Introduction to the Old Testament (N.Y.: Abingdon, 1968) 292.

[12] Further examples of the use of these words in parallel:
מצוה and דבר: Ps 119:73b and 74b; 9b and 10b.
דבר and תורה: Ps 119:28b and 29b; 113b and 114b.
תורה and מצוה: Ps 119:34a and 35a; 60b and 61b; 18b and 19b; 97a and 98a; 143b and 174b; 142b and 151b.

[13] In the book of Proverbs there are further noteworthy
parallels of תורה and מצוה:
Prov 7:2: "Keep my commandments (מצותי) and you shall live, keep
my law (תורתי) as the apple of your eye."
Prov 6:32a: "For the commandment (מצוה) is a lamp, and the law
(תורה) a light."
[14] Further:
Sir 32:24: "He who believes in the Law gives heed to the Commandments." (ὁ πιστεύων νόμῳ προσέχει ἐντολαῖς.)
Sir 35:1: "He who keeps the law (νόμον) makes many offerings;
he who heeds the commandments (ἐντολαῖς) sacrifices a
peace offering."
Sir 45:17: "In His commandments (ἐν ἐντολαῖς αὐτοῦ) He gave him
(Moses) authority. . . to enlighten Israel with His
law (ἐν νόμῳ αὐτοῦ).

[15] I and II Maccabees stem from the same period as much of the
Pseudepigrapha: I Maccabees: 103-63 B.C.; II Maccabees: probably
around 100 B.C. Cf. Leonhard Rost, Judaism Outside the Hebrew
Canon: An Introduction to the Documents (Nashville: Abingdon,
1976) 79, 82.

[16] R. H. Charles, The Apocrypha and Pseudepigrapha, vol. 2,
vii. Charles is of the opinion that the two wings had an
"original and fundamental identity" with respect to devotion to
the Law, but that they did diverge.

[17] W. D. Davies, The Setting of the Sermon on the Mount, 140.

[18] For date, cf. above chap. 1, n. 29, p. 28.

[19] R. H. Charles, The Apocrypha and Pseudepigrapha, vol. 2, 11.

[20] The original composition of the Letter of Aristeas dates
from the early second century B.C.; cf. Charlesworth, The
Pseudepigrapha and Modern Research, 78.

[21] For date, cf. above chap. 1, n. 30, p. 28.

[22] Cf. also Book III, lines 284, 580 and 719.

[23] In the Hebrew text, mention of the "Ten Words" occurs at
Deut 4:13, 10:4 and Exod 34:28. With a sense of the importance
of the phrase, at Deut 4:13, Tg. Ps.-J. adds לוחי סמפירינון,
"tablets of sapphire." In the same vein, Tg. Ps.-J. speaks of
לוחי מרמירא, "tablets of marble" at Deut 9:9 and 10. At Deut
10:4, the targumic traditions do not elaborate. At Exod 34:28,
Tg. Ps.-J. simply adds the clause "which had been written on the
former tablets."
At Gen 24:22, the mention of the two bracelets weighing the
gold shekels provoked targumic activity. Tg. Ps.-J. has additional material in which we find the following:
תרין לוחיא דכתיבין בהון עישרתי דבירים. . .," ". . . the two
tablets on which were written the ten words."

[24] Tg. Neof., MSS V and P read as does CTg F (except for small spelling variations). Similarly N and ed. B.

[25] However, Tg. Ps.-J. reads so as to attribute the power to שמש רבא ויקירא, "the Great and Glorious Name."

[26] Tg. Neof. only.

[27] Further, Tg. Ps.-J. in additions at Deut 15:7 and 17:18.

[28] In MSS V (N and ed. B) and Tg. Neof., the reading in both vv 12 and 13 is היא אוריתא; MS P contains only v 12 wehre the reading is the same.

[29] Qal (learn) at Deut 4:10; 5:1; 14:23; 17:19; 18:9; 31:12, 13; Piel (teach) at Deut 4:1, 5, 10, 14; 5:31; 6:1; 20:18; 31:32.

[30] Similarly, Tg. Ps.-J.

[31] Tg. Neof. and Tg. Ps.-J.: אולפני.

[32] Cf. also Tg. Neof. at Deut 6:5; 11:13, 22; 13:4; 19:9; 30:6, 16, 20. The fragment targums have not retained these verses. Tg. Ps.-J. and Tg. Onq. follow the Hebrew.

[33] Cf. also Tg. Neof. Deut 11:22 and 4:4.

[34] Cf. also Tg. Neof. Deut 6:12; 8:11, 14, 19. In Tg. Ps.-J. the reading is "forget the fear (דחלת) of the Lord your God" in all four places.

[35] This haggadah is found in MSS P, V (N and ed. B), Tg. Neof. and Tg. Ps.-J.

[36] The condition is prefixed in three places, Deut 15:4, 7, and 11 (the beginning, the middle and the end of the whole passage) in Tg. Ps.-J.; thus the sense of the whole passage is altered to be consistent with the alteration of the final verse. Tg. Neof. has apparently been influenced by Tg. Ps.-J. in that the additional clauses appear in vv 4 and 11. However, v 11 shows a variation: whereas MSS V (N and ed. B) and Tg. Ps.-J. speak of keeping מצייתא דאורייתא, "the commandments of the Law," Tg. Neof. (consistent with its own cliché throughout Deuteronomy) has אולפן אורתה, "the teachings of the Law," and Tg. Neof. singularly adds ועבד פיקודיה, "and do the commandments" at this point.

[37] MS V Deut 33:29. In this passage, where MS V (N and ed. B) read נטר, "observe," Tg. Neof. reads עבד, "do," a small variation, but one characteristic of Tg. Neof. in its individual differences.

[38] On Gen 3:15 and 3:24. The same (with minor variations) is found in Tg. Ps.-J., Tg. Neof., MSS P, N (and ed. B).

[39] H. S. Horovitz, Siphre, vol. 1, 116.

[40] Finkelstein, Siphre, vol. 2, 341. Note further references

as we have offered above, pp. 17 and 18, and notes to chap. 1, 54
and 55, p. 30.

[41]Ibid., vol. 2, 110-111. Cf. also ibid., 112.

[42]J. H. Weiss, Sifra, 112c and 115d. On the subject of
minute detail, there is a fascinating sentence in Mekilta. Cf.
Lauterbach, Mekilta, vol. 3, 136-137: "Some say the Torah was
given with its tittles": יש אומרים באותיותיה נתנה תרוה .

[43]ʾAbot 2:7; the saying is attributed to Hillel. Cf. P.
Blackman, Mishnayoth, vol. 4, 500. In sayings of later tannaim
the thought is also found: ʾAbot 1:5, 3:2 (twice), 3:3 (twice);
cf. ibid. 491, 506, 507.

[44]So also Tg. Neof., MSS P, N (and ed. B). Tg. Ps.-J. gives
an even longer reading to incorporate further theological concerns.
Tg. Onq. definitely shows the influence of the fragment targum
tradition.

[45]See also Philo, above chap. 2, p. 43.

[46]P. Blackman, Mishnayoth, vol. 4, 495.

[47]J. H. Weiss, Sifra, 110c.

[48]Finkelstein, Siphre, vol. 2, 84.

[49]Ibid., 83:

Rabbi Simeon ben Yohai said:	רבי שמעון בן יוחי אומר
a loaf and a stick descended,	ככר ומקל ירדו כרוכים
tied together from heaven.	מן השמים אמר להם
He said to them: if you do	אם עשיתם את התורה
Torah, behold a loaf to eat;	הרי ככר לאכל ואם לאו
if not, behold a stick by	הרי מקל ללקות בו
which to be punished.	

[50]Finkelstein, Siphre, vol. 1, 113.

[51]C. G. Montefiore, Rabbinic Literature and Gospel Teachings
(1930; reprint: N.Y.: KTAV, 1970) 155.

[52]Cf. Schechter, Aboth de Rabbi Nathan, 75. The translation
is that of Montefiore in Rabbinic Literature and Gospel Teachings,
155.

[53]Schechter, Aboth de Rabbi Nathan, 77. The translation is
that of Judah Goldin, The Fathers according to Rabbi Nathan (New
Haven: Yale University Press, 1955) 103.

[54]A play on words in the context of the building-metaphor
was nothing new; there was one as early as the writing of Gen
11:3: והחֵמָר היה להם לחֹמֶר, "the bitumen was clay for them."

[55]Eduard Lohse, Die Texte aus Qumran, 16-18.

[56]Ibid., 30.

[57]Ibid., 78.

[58] Ibid., 68.

[59] Ibid., 70.

[60] Ibid., 70.

[61] Ibid., 30.

[62] Luke 11:29-41, par. Matt 23:25; Luke 11:42, par. Matt 23:23; Luke 11:43, par. Matt 23:6-7; Luke 11:44, par. Matt 23:27-28; Luke 11:46, par. Matt 23:4; Luke 11:47-51, par. Matt 23:29-36; Luke 11:52, par. Matt 23:13.

[63] The recapitulation of the Matthean themes in 28:20 has been discussed by a number of writers; cf. for example, Bornkamm, Barth, Held, Tradition and Interpretation in Matthew, 131-137; B. J. Malina, "The Literary Structure and Form of Matthew XXVIII 16-20," NTS 17, 1970, 87.

The study of J. D. Kingsbury (The Parables of Jesus in Matthew 13 [London: SPCK, 1969]) led him to the conclusions that chap. 13 is "the great turning point" of the whole book of Matthew (130-132); and that the unifying thought behind this chapter was "knowing and doing" the will of God (131). Thus both the final passage (28:18-20) and the central chapter (13) served a unified purpose in the book of Matthew.

[64] In Matthew: διδάσκω 14 times; cognates: διδασκαλία once, διδάσκαλός 12 times; διδαχή three times. The word διδάσκω occurs at a number of structurally important points throughout the book of Matthew; thus its importance in the thought of Matthew is stressed. Cf. Charles H. Lohr, "Oral Techniques in the Gospel of Matthew," CBQ 23, 1961, 427; J. D. Kingsbury, The Parables of Jesus in Matthew 13, 130-132.

[65] We recall that "teaching" and "learning" are words of the same root למד in Hebrew, and of the same root אלף in Aramaic. Although not of the same root in Greek, the logical relationship remains, so we complete note 63 above: in Matthew, μανθάνω three times, μαθητεύω three times, μαθητής 71 times.

[66] Matthew uses the same expression at 23:33.

[67] The word עשה sometimes has a direct object pronoun of which the antecedent is "Commandments," "statutes" or the like: Deut 4:5, 6, 14; 5:27, 31; 6:1, 3; 7:12; 17:19: 24:18, 22; 27:26; 30:13, 14.

[68] Eight times in Revelation, once in each of James, I and II Timothy, and Acts, 11 times in John, 6 times in I John, three times in Matthew.

[69] Twice in Paul, once in John, twice in Acts, twice in Luke (and once in each of Matthew and Mark in parallels to Luke).

[70] The following applies when the direct object is what is commanded (Words, commandments, etc.). The word שמר in the

Hebrew text is almost always φυλάσσω in the LXX; it is consistently נטר in Tg. Onq. In Hebrew, נטר occurs only twice: in the
MT of Canticles and is translated τηρέω in the LXX. However,
Dan 9:4: . . . God who keeps (שמר - τηρῶν) covenant and ḥesed with
those who love Him and keep (שמר - φυλάσσουσι) his Commandments."
(Note also Sir 29:1: ὁ ποιῶν ἔλεος. . . τηρεῖ ἐντολάς.) It would
appear that the שמר-concept had long been expressed in Greek with
φυλάσσω, but the fashion of using τηρέω in this way was appearing
in the very late literature. This fashion was apparently prevalent in the circles from which various of the NT writers came.

[71]Not only was this a very widespread idea in Jewish tradition but also was an integral part of the Christian tradition.
It is spelled out unambiguously in Rom 2:12-13: "All who have
sinned without the law will be judged by the law. For it is not
the hearers of the law who are righteous before God, but the doers
of the law who will be justified." James also writes plainly:
"Was not Abraham our father justified by works, when he offered
his son Isaac upon the altar? You see that faith was active along
with his works, and faith was completed by works, and the scripture
was fulfilled which says, 'Abraham believed God, and it was reck-
oned to him as righteousness'; and he was called the friend of
God. You see that a man is justified by works and not by faith
alone. And in the same way was not also Rahab the harlot justified by works when she received the messengers and sent them out
another way?" (Jas 2:12-25).

[72]Elsewhere the Hebrew קללה is translated with the Aramaic
לווטיה (Onq. לוטין).

[73]Thus Tg. Neof., Tg. Ps.-J., MSS V, P (N and ed. B).

[74]Cf. Charles H. Lohr, "Oral Techniques in the Gospel of
Matthew," 427.

[75]In Luke the woes occur right after the blessings (Luke
6:20-22, 24-26).

[76]Cf. context and Deut 31:30.

[77]The נבל-root is found only six times in the Pentateuch. The
qal of the verb (at Exod 18:18) is used just to signify wearing
oneself out from overwork; the piel of the verb (Deut 32:15) is
used to signify a strong disregard. The noun (Gen 34:7) stands in
parallel with the sin of Shechem against Dinah, and (in Deut 22:21)
with playing the harlot. The adjective at Deut 32:21 occurs in a
poetic passage which is quite informative as a context of the word
נבל: נבל בגוי . . . בלא עם . . . בהבליהם . . . בלא אל, "With 'no god'
. . . with their idols. . . with 'no people'. . . with a foolish
nation.

The concept of other gods as quite non-existent - "nothings"-
is well known. Here at Deut 32:21, then, the vacuous aspect of the
word נבל is observable. From just these five contexts, one can
observe a thought-pattern: immorality and idolatry, sin, is marked

by <u>vacuousness</u>.

[78]The same meaning with respect to lack of knowledge of God and abominable deeds again comes to mind with the mention of Shechem at Sir 50:26. Although μωρός was used 27 times in Sirach, the extant Hebrew has נבל only three times, for other Hebrew words are also translated by μωρός. (Cf. Rudolph Smend, ed., <u>Die Weisheit des Jesus Sirach</u> [Berlin: Georg Reimer, 1906] note esp. Sir 4:27, 21:22 and 50:26.) In Sirach, we do not have a formal address to the assembly of Israel; נבל occurs in third person singular contexts.

[79]Thus <u>MS</u> V; similarly <u>Tg</u>. <u>Neof</u>. (N and <u>ed</u>. B).

[80]Cf. <u>Tg</u>. <u>Onq</u>., <u>Tg</u>. <u>Ps.-J</u>. and CTg D Deut 28:29: בקבלא, "in darkness."

[81]<u>Sipre</u> Deut 309; Finkelstein, <u>Siphre</u>, vol. 2, 349.

[82]There are two occurrences in the qal, Gen 6:11, 12; for these translation without a direct object was not problematic.

[83]At the other three places in <u>Tg</u>. <u>Neof</u>. there is no direct object supplied, possibly due to the influence of <u>Tg</u>. <u>Onq</u>. which does not supply a direct object in any of the six places.

[84]Among the fragment targums, we do not have any evidence of their treatment of the verb שחת without a direct object anywhere other than at Deut 32:5.

[85]Similarly <u>Tg</u>. <u>Neof</u>. (N and <u>ed</u>. B).

[86]According to Michael L. Klein (<u>The Fragment-Targums of the Pentateuch according to their Extant Sources</u>. <u>Volume II: Translation</u> [Rome: Biblical Institute Press, 1980] n. 83, p. 183), "The word 'before' is added in the tg. to avoid implying that God would be harmed by the corruption of Israel."

[87]Similarly N and <u>ed</u>. B.

[88]Gen 17:14; Lev 26:15, 44; Num 15:31; Deut 31:16, 20.

[89]We note other occurrences of the verb in <u>Tg</u>. <u>Ps.-J</u>. At Gen 6:7: "I will blot out (MT: אמחה) man whom I have made. . . "; <u>Tg</u>. <u>Ps.-J</u>. has the reading אבטיל. At Exod 17:1 which speaks of the camp at Rephidim and there being no water for the people to drink, <u>Tg</u>. <u>Ps.-J</u>. has "Rephidim, a place where their hands <u>were</u> <u>devoid of</u> the commandments of the Law (אתרא דבטילו אידיהון ממצוותא דאוריתא) and the fountains were dry." (The idea of the necessity of having מצותא in one's hands is not unique here; cf. for example the tradition in the fragment targums at Gen 15:1 where the consequent reward or punishment is eschatological.)

[90]Num 18:1, 11, 19, 23.

[91]The LXX adds nothing to our knowledge of "salt" beyond what we find in the Hebrew text, except that the LXX adds καὶ ἅλα, "and salt" to the things to be offered at Lev 24:7.

146

[92] Hebrew text: ברית מלח;   in Tg. Onq. and Tg. Neof.: קים מלח.

[93] Sipre Num 118: Horovitz, Siphre, vol. 1, 142.

[94] Another use of the expression for stressing the permanence of God's agreements: God's having given the kingship to the house of David was viewed as a "covenant of salt" by the Chronicler (II Chron 13:5). In the context of statements about the covenant, salt signifies permanence according to Philo: τὴν εἰς ἅλας διαμονήν, "complete permanence"; cf. Spec. Leg. I. 53. For comments: W. J. Dumbrell, "The Logic of the Role of the Law," Novum Testamentum XXIII (1981) 12.

[95] Sipre Deut 37; Finkelstein, Siphre, vol. 2, 70.

[96] A succinct passage attributed to R. Simeon b. Gamaliel (without indication as to which tanna of the name is meant; there was one by this name in Javneh and a descendant of his by the same name at Usha). The text: "It (the earth) has four names, ארקא, אדמה, תבל, ארץ. . .(the word) תבל corresponds to the summer solstice which gives savour (מתבלת) to the crops. . . " Gen. Rab. 13:12: מדרש רבה, בראשית רבה, vol. 1, 98.
   Another attestation to the same key words is found in a collection of sayings in ᵓAbot R. Nat. 37:
   Why was it (the earth) called   למה נקרא שמה תבל
   'world'? Because it was   על שם שחיא מתובלת בכל
   be-תבל-ed above all.
Cf. Schechter, Aboth de Rabbi Nathan, 110.

[97] The pual participle, meaning "having been salted oneself," requires metaphorical understanding.

[98] For a detailed presentation of the texts and the argument leading to this conclusion, cf. Wolfgang Nauck, "Salt as a Metaphor in Instructions for Discipleship," Studia Theologica 6, 1952, 165-168.

[99] Abraham Tawrogi, ed. Der Talmudische Tractat Derech Erez Sutta, (Königsberg: E. Erlatis, 1885) 1.

[100] Also, the only occurrence of μωρολογία in Paul, at Eph 5:4.

[101] In Rom 1:18-23, Paul is speaking of those who know and suppress the truth, whom he goes so far as to think of as idolaters. Of these he says, "claiming to be wise (σοφοί) they became fools (ἐμωράνθησαν)." In the same type of context as in Deut 31:30-32:7, we have the same two roots as were used in the LXX Deut 32:6: λαὸς μωρὸς καὶ οὐχὶ σοφός.
   In I Cor 1:17-30, Paul has made "wisdom" and "foolishness" the key words of the passage: σοφία at I Cor 1:17, 19, 20, 21, 22, 24, 30; μωρός at I Cor 1:25, 27; and μωραίνω at I Cor 1:20. The citation of Isa 29:14 at I Cor 1:9 speaks of the σοφίαν τῶν σοφῶν, "the wisdom of the (worldly) wise"; it is in Isa 29:13-16 that we find the themes of the creature's self-exaltation in denying his Creator, false worship and dark deeds. Hence Isa 29:13-16 re-

flects Deut 32:5-6, in its main concepts. Perhaps we could say that there are reflections of Deut 32:5-6 and Isa 29:13-16 (with their thematic word μωρός) in I Cor 1:17-30. The same theme involving the same roots is taken up again at I Cor 3:18-20.

[102] There was a choice possible. Sirach juxtaposes μωρός and σοφός as opposites at 21:13-14, 18, 26; and μωρός and φρόνιμος at 21:16-17, 20-21. At Sir 20:13-16 there is an apparent interchangeability of μωρός and ἄφρών opposite σοφός.

There is a passage in which the meanings of the two words σοφός and φρόνιμος is brought out, Sir 19:20-24: "All wisdom is fear of the Lord, and in all wisdom there is the doing of the Law (ποίησις νόμου). But the knowledge of wickedness is not wisdom . . . Better is the God-fearing man who lacks intelligence than the highly prudent man who transgresses the Law (ἢ περισσεύων ἐν φρονήσει καὶ παραβαίνων νόμον).

[103] Matt 23:17; there is substantial manuscript evidence for μωροί at Matt 23:19 also.

[104] In the course of the chapter, the word ὑποκριτής is also clarified by the whole context.

[105] Nauck, "Salt as a Metaphor," 171.

[106] Ibid., 168.

[107] Amongst others: Nauck, "Salt as a Metaphor," 174; I. Abrahams, Studies in Pharisaism and the Gospels, vol.2 (Cambridge: University Press, 1924) 183; C. G. Montefiore, Rabbinic Literature and Gospel Teachings, 36; Strack-Billerbeck, Kommentar, vol. 1, 90; Jacques Dupont, Béatitudes, t. 1, 90; T. W. Manson, The Sayings of Jesus, 132; Matthew Black, An Aramaic Approach to the Gospels and Acts³, 166; Friedrich Hauck, "ἅλας," TDNT I, 1964, 228-229.

[108] The saying occurs in a passage reporting a discussion with R. Joshua b. Haninia (c. 90 A.D.).

[109] For this line of thought, cf. M.-E. Boismard, Synopse, t. 2 130-131.

[110] This means taking the "two-source" theory seriously, and not merely using it as a stepping stone towards veritably unattainable ipsissima verba. Of course, this is not to be simplistic; note especially the theories of Streeter and Benoit-Boismard: B. H. Streeter, The Four Gospels: A Study of Origins (London: Macmillan, 1927) 150; P. Benoit & M.-E. Boismard, Synopse, t. 2, 17.

M. Black, in the effort to see "the Aramaic" behind the key Greek words, has conflated the Gospel texts, as if there were "one original" to be found; cf. Black, An Aramaic Approach to the Gospels and Acts³, 166-167.

[111] It is well known that throughout the book of Matthew,

inclusio is often used. Cf. for example, Charles H. Lohr, "Oral Techniques in the Gospel of Matthew," CBQ 23, 1961, 403-435; Peter F. Ellis, Matthew: his Mind and his Message (Collegeville, Minn.: Liturgical Press, 1974).

[112]Felix Perles ("La parabole du sel sourd," REJ 82, 1926, 122) discussed Luke 14:35 which seemed to him an "enigmatic antithesis"; this he tried to resolve. He noted that תבל is often rendered by γῆ in the LXX, so he suggested that the Aramaic underlying Luke's clause would have been לא לתבלא ולא לזבלא כשר, "it is neither fit for spice nor for fertilizer. That "land" was read for "spice" prior to the placing of the word γῆ in Luke's text was due to both words having the consonants תבל (only the vowels differing).

[113]Perles, "La parabole du sel sourd," 123.

[114]In the extant Qumran literature, the roots שחת and תבל are associated in I QS 4:12 and in I QH passim rather loosely. Of the other roots we are considering, the Qumran literature shows no association.

[115]נבל: a word carried from the biblical Hebrew into later Hebrew, a synthetic parallel for טפש in Sipre Deut on Deut 32:5. (In the fragment targum tradition the usual word for the concept is טפש).

קבל: to obfuscate, make dark. "The Law" is its direct object in Tg. Ps.-J. Deut 32:6.

What is remarkable is that these two words (as well as חבל) are connected with Deut 32:4-6. This is precisely the passage (in the LXX) which was most significant for our understanding of the Greek word μωρός (Deut 32:6, Matt 5:13, 22, 7:26). Deut 32: 4-6 and the interpretations of it have entered into our discussions in this section (passim) more than any other Pentateuchal passage.

Matthew Black (Aramaic Approach,[3] 166) suggests תפל as the verb of the first clause, for μωρανθῇ. Joachim Jeremias (The Parables of Jesus,[3] [London: SCM, 168]) accepts תפל; but sees Mark's ἄναλος γένηται as the appropriate Greek for תפל, and μωρανθῇ as "faulty." Since we accept two sources of the saying in the Synoptics, there is no reason why one could not envision variation in the Semitic saying reflected.

CHAPTER V
THE FRUIT, THE DEEDS

The metaphor of "fruit" for deeds is well attested in the
early Church; all four Evangelists use it, also Paul in five
epistles, and James. It is occasional in the prophetic books of
the Hebrew Bible and in Sirach and Wisdom. Two facts are notable:
the proportionate increase in the NT writings, and Matthew's outright exploitation of the metaphor in 7:16-20.

We suggest that the continued and increased use of the metaphor is partially due to a particular turn of phrase in Hebrew
and Aramaic which could be taken up in the Greek language without doing violence to it. The Hebrew verb עשה signifies "do,"
but also normally figures in the idiom "bear fruit"; so that
"doing deeds" and "bearing fruit" normally utilize the same verb.
In Aramaic we find the same phenomenon, the verb being עבד;[1] and
similarly in Greek the verb being ποιέω. Of course other verbs
could also be used, as may be observed in the prophetic books
of the Hebrew Bible. For example, the formula at Ezek 17:8 and
17:23 where עשה and נשא alternate as if synonymous in this type
of context:

> . . . that it may bring forth   Ezek 17:8 לעשות ענף
> branches and bear fruit.   ולשאת פרי

> . . . that it may bear boughs   Ezek 17:23 ונשא ענף
> and bring forth fruit.   ועשה פרי

The verb נתן is also acceptable (for example, Ps 1:3). Among the
NT writers, usage is apparently according to individual preference; John uses φέρω (8 times), Mark uses δίδωμι (twice),
Luke uses ποιέω (6 times) and each of these writers is consistent
in his usage. However Matthew uses ποιέω 11 times, but also once
δίδωμι in 13:8 in obvious parallel to ποιέω in 13:23; thus the
metaphor is more prevalent in Matthew than in the other Synoptics;
and his preferred verb is ποιέω, the most versatile one. In the
book of Matthew, this verb ποιέω has as its object commandments
(5:19), My words (7:24-27), righteousness (6:1), alms (6:2), the
will of My Father (7:21, 12:50), mighty deeds (7:22, 17:58),
wondrous deeds (21:15, 21, 24, 27), a good deed (19:16), deeds
(23:3, 5), the works of mercy (25:40, 45), and lawlessness (23:
23). The use of ποιέω with the object καρπόν, "fruit," is in
every instance a transparent metaphor for "doing deeds." Given
the stylistic basis in his choice of the most versatile verb in
Greek reflecting the versatile Hebrew עשה and Aramaic עבד,
Matthew is in a very good position to use the old metaphor of
"fruit" for deeds and stand squarely in line with a traditional
theme.

The "Fruit" Metaphor in
the Hebrew Bible and Apocrypha

In the Hebrew Bible, a certain development can be observed
in the usage of the word פרי, "fruit." In the Torah it is used
literally for the fruit of plants or of the offspring of animals
and people. The figurative usages of the word פרי are found in
Isaiah, Jeremiah, Ezekiel, Hosea, Amos, Micah, Psalms and Proverbs. There seem to be two primary nuances of figurative usage,
that is, man's deeds themselves referred to as his "fruit"; and
the consequences of man's deeds referred to as the "fruit" of
those deeds, good or evil consequences dependent upon which type
of deeds were done. The phraseology of the contexts of a number
of the occurrences of the word פרי are such that it cannot always
be said precisely that one or the other connotation is intended.

In Jeremiah, we see fairly clear examples of the first of
these nuances; they recur throughout the book. Jer 11:16 contains a memory of the former faithfulness of Israel and Judah
when they were "a green olive tree fair with goodly fruit." Jer
12:2 speaks of consternation over the prosperity of the wicked,
". . . they bring forth fruit." Jer 11:19 offers words of plot-
ters against the prophet Jeremiah: "Let us destroy the tree with
its fruit." In Jer 32:19, 21:14 and 17:10 with word פרי as
regnum of the bound form acts as a simple and practically synonymous specification of the regens, hence "fruit" equals "deeds" in
these passages. In Jer 32:19, God is presented as rewarding each
person כפרי מעלליו,[2] "according to the fruit of his deeds." As
good deeds are the criterion for reward, so wicked deeds for punishment; thus Jer 21:14 presents God as speaking of his punish-
ing כפרי מעלליכם, "according to the fruit of your deeds." In a
context which could be construed as referring either to good or
evil deeds, Jer 17:10, God is said to give to each כפרי מעלליו,
"according to the fruit of his deeds." In these three instances,
whether the deeds were good or evil is not designated by an
adjectival modifier but seen in the context. The same is also
the case with the same expression at Mic 7:13.[3] also with Isa
3:10 where the second nuance could be understood.[4] Finally,
there is the metaphor in which "bearing fruit" implies doing what
is right and good, for example, in the extended metaphor in
Ezekiel 17. In Ezek 17:23 we find: ונשא ענף ועשה פרי, "and it
will bear branches and it will bear fruit." Here the verbs are
synonymous, for the same reading is found at Ezek 17:8 with the
verbs reversed. The idiom at Hos 9:16 also has the verb עשה:
פרי בלי יעשון, "they shall bear no fruit."[5]

Passages which are well known for one reason or another tend
to be influential in proliferating the metaphors they contain;
this could be said of Psalm 1, just because it is the first Psalm
of the book. The analogies and themes we are considering in our
present discussion are contained in it:

Blessed is the man who	אשרי האיש אשר
walks not in the counsel	לא הלך בעצת רשעים
of the wicked. . .	
He is like a tree planted	והיה כעץ
by streams of water, that	שתול על־פלגי מים
yields its fruit in season,	אשר פריו יתן בעתו
and its leaf does not wither.	ועלהו לא־יבול
In all that he does, he	וכל אשר־יעשה יצתיח
prospers. . .	
For the Lord knows the way	כי־יודע יהוה
of the righteous but the way	דרך צדיקים
of the wicked shall perish.	ודרך רשעים תאבד

One can suggest the influence of Psalm 1 as a contributing factor
to the continuing use of its themes.[6]

By way of examples, we shall only present a few citations
from Sirach and Wisdom which have a bearing on the topic under
discussion. In Sir 6:3, a verse occurring in a passage in the
instruction genre, the speaker warns his listener that evil
would render him ὡς ξύλον ξηρόν, "like a withered tree"; and
τούς καρπούς σου ἀπολέσεις, "you will destroy your fruit." Among
the similes listed in praise of Simeon, at Sir 50:10 we find him
compared to an "olive tree putting forth its fruit": ὡς ἐλαία
ἀναθάλλουσα καρπούς. At Sir 27:6, we have a somewhat hellenistic
exposition of the analogy:

The fruit discloses the	ηεώργιον ξύλου ἐκφεύνει
cultivation of a tree;	ὁ καρπὸς αὐτου
so the expression of a	οὕτως λόγος ἐνθυμήματος
thought discloses the	καρδίας ἀνθρώπου.
cultivation of a man's	
mind.	

In Wis 3:10-19 in which the ungodly and the righteous are contrasted, as well as their good and useless works and their res-
pective final ends, we read (v 15a): ἀγαθῶν γὰρ πόνων καρπὸς
εὐκλεής, "for the fruit of good labours is renowned."

The "Fruit" Metaphor in the Targums
and Other Early Jewish Tradition

In the targumic traditions (Tgs. Neof., Ps.-J., CTg B, MSS V,
P (N and ed. B) there is a passage added at Gen 4:8 recounting a
rather theological dispute between Cain and Abel. There are three
clauses to be noted. Citing from Tg. Ps.-J. Gen 4:8:

Cain. . . and it (the world) is not governed according to the fruits of good works.	קין . . . לא כפירי עובדין טבין הוא מידבר [7]
Abel. . . and it (the world) is governed according to the fruits of good works.	הבל . . . וכפירי עובדין טבין הוא מדבר [8]
Abel. . . because the fruits of my works were better than yours. . .	הבל . . . ועל דהוו פירי עובדיי טבין מדידך [9]

In the passage, when viewed in all the sources, it is quite clear
that "fruits" and "works" are synonymous, a usage we have already
observed above as the first figurative nuance in the prophets and
writings in the Hebrew Bible. However there is a refinement here
which was not found in the Hebrew Bible; the good deeds are
plainly designated by the attributive adjective "good" in the expression "according to the fruits of good works."

When we turn to Deut 20:20a, we find that the targumic traditions (Tgs. Ps.-J. and Neof.) have incorporated two extra words
which read well in their context. Tg. Ps.-J. reads:[10]

But the tree which you know that it is not a tree producing fruit to eat, that you may destroy and cut down. . .	לחוד אלין דתינדעון ארום לא אילן עביד פירי מיכל הוא יתיה תחבלון ותינטעון . . .

The addition of the words עביד פירי makes it possible to construe
the verse differently, that is, rather than the reference being
to trees that simply do not bear fruit (do not bear edible fruit
by nature), the reference could be to fruit trees that fail to
produce fruit. This idea is but a simple reference to a traditional thought pattern. It would be the midrashim which would
exploit the idea. Sipre Deut 203 and Sipra 92d, which make reference to Deut 20:20, both make the tree analogous to man and the

fruits to his deeds.[11]

In Genesis Rabbah the metaphor is spelled out fully:[12]

The fruit of the righteous	פרי צדיק עץ חיים
is a tree of life. What is	מה הן פרותין של צדיק
the fruit of the righteous?	צמות ומעשים טובים
Commandments and good works.	

The fruit metaphor seems to have come naturally to Philo. He
wrote that the soul must receive teaching, become ready to learn,
and learn concentration; these things are like ῥίζαι δένδρου
μέλλοντος ἡμέρους καρποὺς ἀποκυΐσκειν συνίστανται, "the roots of
the tree that will endure to bring forth mild fruit."[13] Philo
compares young people to plants which are cultivated μέχρις ἂν
στελεχωθεῖσαι καρπὸν τὸν καλοκἀγαθίας ἐνέγκωσι, "until they bear
the fruit of goodness on their stems."[14] With Philo's touch of
hellenism, he wrote, "But God sows in souls (ἐν ψυχαῖς) nothing
futile, but seeds so successful and perfect that each immediately
bears the fulness of its own fruits (ἐπιφέρεσθαι τὴν τῶν ἰδίων
καρπῶν πληθόν)."[15]

The "Fruit" Metaphor in the
Tradition of the Early Church

The use of the metaphor of καρπός, "fruit" for ἔργα would
seem to have been a commonplace in the early Christian tradition,
for it is found in one form or another in most of the books of the
NT.[16] We offer a few examples. First, in Col 1:10, Paul presents several features of the Christian life, one of them being
that such a life is ἐν παντὶ ἔργῳ ἀγαθῷ καρποφοροῦντες, "fruitful in every good work." The idea was apparently commonplace, for
Paul did not offer any comment. Second, in Galatians 5, Paul
presents his vice list and virtue list under parallel headings:
τὰ ἔργα τῆς σαρκός. . . ὁ δὲ καρπὸς τοῦ πνεύματός, "the works of
the flesh. . . but the fruit of the Spirit" - again the literary
parallel needed no explanation. In Phil 1:22 the commonplace
character of the metaphor is apparent: living in this world
amounted to καρπὸς ἔργου, "fruitful labour" for Paul. The

closing instruction to Titus was μανθανέτωσαν δὲ καὶ οἱ ἡμέτεροι
καλῶν ἔργων. . . ἵνα μὴ ὦσιν ἄκαρποι, "and let our people learn
to apply themselves to good deeds. . . and not be unfruitful."[17]

The clearest presentation of the metaphor, however, is in
the Gospels. All the instances of the word καρπός in John are
metaphorical either for works or for the effect of good works,
eternal life; the word καρπός is featured especially in chap. 15
where Jesus is presented as calling himself the vine, and his
hearers the branches which should "bear fruit," and bear "much
fruit." However it is in the Synoptics that the metaphor has a
greater variety of uses.

The word καρπός is found in the parables of the sower,[18]
and of the wicked husbandmen,[19] and in the cursing of the fig
tree;[20] all three of which are found in all three of the Synoptic Gospels. However, the use of καρπός is also very evident
in the parenetic passages in Matthew and Luke. In these, it is
very obvious that the usage is metaphorical. Such is the case in
the presentation of the preaching of John the Baptist, Matt 3:8,
10 (par. Luke 6:43-45) to which Matt 7:16-20 bears a certain parallel. It is in these last three passages that the metaphor is
extended: good tree, good fruit; bad tree, bad fruit. It is in
Matt 7:16-20 that this extended metaphor is most repeated.

In the sequence of thoughts in II Cor 11:13-15, speaking
plainly - without the metaphor, we find a certain parallel to
Matt 7:15-20. As Matt 7:15 shows concern about false prophets in
sheep's clothing, II Cor 11:13-15 shows concern about ψευδαπόσ-
τολοι, ἐργάται δόλιοι, μετασχηματιζόμενοι εἰς ἀποστόλους Χριστοῦ,
"false apostles, deceitful workers, disguising themselves as
apostles of Christ." While Matt 7:19 has "every tree that does
not bear good fruit is cut down and thrown into the fire," II Cor
11:15b flatly states, ὧν τὸ τέλος ἔσται κατὰ τὰ ἔργα αὐτῶν,
"their end will be according to their deeds." Since both Paul and
Matthew are known for thought-patterns developed in the rabbinic
milieu,[21] it is not surprising to find a parallel between these

two passages and suggest that we have one more possibility of presenting καρπός, "fruit," as a common metaphor for ἔργα, "deeds."

Conclusion: the "Fruit" Metaphor
in Matt 7:16-20

Matt 7:16-20 reads:

You will know them	ἀπὸ τῶν καρπῶν αὐτῶν
by their fruits.	ἐπιγνώσεσθε αὐτούς·
Are grapes gathered	μήτι συλλέγουσιν ἀπὸ
from thorns,	ἀκανθῶν σταφυλὰς
or figs from thistles?	ἢ ἀπὸ τριβόλων σῦκα;
So, every sound tree	οὕτως πᾶν δένδρον ἀγαθὸν
bears good fruit,	καρποὺς καλοὺς ποιεῖ,
but the bad tree	τὸ δὲ σαπρὸν δένδρον
bears evil fruit.	καρποὺς πονηροὺς ποιεῖ·
A sound tree cannot	οὐ δύναται δένδρον ἀγαθὸν
bear evil fruit,	καρποὺς πονηροὺς ποιεῖν,
nor can a bad tree	οὐδε δένδρον σαπρὸν
bear good fruit.	καρποὺς καλοὺς ποιεῖν.
Every tree that does not	πᾶν δένδρον μὴ ποιοῦν
bear good fruit is cut down	καρπὸν καλὸν ἐκκόπτεται
and thrown into the fire.	καὶ εἰς πῦρ βάλλεται.
Thus you will know	ἄρα γε ἀπὸ τῶν καρπῶν
them by their fruits.	αὐτῶν ἐπιγνώσεσθε αὐτούς.

Not only is the fruit metaphor most repeated in Matt 7:16-20, but the metaphorical dictum ἀπὸ τῶν καρπῶν αὐτῶν ἐπιγνώσεσθε αὐτούς, "by their fruits you will know them," has been used twice in such a way as to make vv 16-20 a unit within an inclusio. In Matthew 12, the dictum recurs as the concluding clause of v 33. In Luke 6, it is found again concluding vv. 43-44. Thus in Matthew 7 and 12 and in Luke 6, the metaphorical dictum,[22] which could be said to have the character of a popular proverb,[23] stands out; but especially so in Matthew 7.

Another observation we could make is this: in Matt 7:16-20 the adjectives "good" and "evil" are used attributively, modifying "fruit." It has been interesting to notice progress in the wording of the phrases under discussion. First, in the Hebrew text there was only one instance in which the word "fruit" was modified by an adjective implying good or evil. at Jer 11:16:

יפה פרי תאר, "fruit fair to look upon."[24] Second, in the Apocrypha: in Wis 3:15a we find one phrase which contributes to our
discussion: ἀγαθῶν. . . πόνων καρπός, "the fruit of good labours."
Third, the targumic traditions attached to Gen 4:8 clearly attest
the phrase "the fruit of good works"; the attributive adjective
being טב. Genesis Rabbah spells out the fullest understanding of
the metaphor: "fruit" equals "Commandments and good works."
Fourth, in Matthew and Luke the attributive adjective functions in
the metaphor for "good works"; we find the words καρποί καλοί,[25]
"good fruit" (Matt 3:10; 7:17, 18, 19; 12:33; Luke 3:9; 6:43);
and the opposite: καρποί πονηροί, "evil fruit" (Matt 7:17, 18 only)
or καρποί σαπροί, "bad fruit" (Matt 12:33, Luke 6:43).

Thus in Matthew 7:16-20, a connomplace metaphor is used; a
metaphor which had been developed in the literature of Jewish and
Christian tradition, further than in the older Hebrew Bible.
Matthew could deftly handle this metaphor and ring the changes upon
it to hold the attention of his audience. Of all the passages in
the NT which have the metaphor, Matt 7:16-20 is the foremost because it is a literary passage built upon the metaphor.

Appendix: the "Fruit" Metaphor in Further Early Christian Tradition

In early Christian literature, there are traces of the continuing popularity of the metaphor of the tree and its fruits for
man and his works.[26] In Ign. Eph. 14:2, we have a clear presentation of the words καρπός, πρᾶσσον, and ἔργον indicating the same
thing, the deeds of man; what is more, in a free manner, Ignatius
cites the proverb that a tree is known by its fruits: φανερὸν τὸ
δένδρον ἀπὸ τοῦ καρποῦ αὐτοῦ, "it is clear that a tree is known by
its fruits."[27] In Polycarp's epistle, Phil. 12:3, the metaphor of
"fruit" for deeds is joined to the theme of perfection:

. . . that your fruit may   . . . ut fructus vester
be manifest among all men,   manifestus sit in omnibus,
that you may be perfected   ut sitis in illo perfecti.
in Him.

In the Clementine Homilies, in a free rendition of the material in Matt 7:15-23, the proverb is cited exactly as it is in
Matt 7:16a.[28] Justin, in chap. 16 of his First Apology, in freely
rendering the material of Matt 7:15-23, has given us the proverb
in words which reveal his familiarity with the metaphor: ἐκ τῶν
ἔργων αὐτῶν ἐπιγνώσεσθε αὐτούς,[29] "by their works you shall know
them." In all probability, the traces of the metaphor in the
Clementine Homilies and Justin were due to the influence of the NT
writers; for as we have observed, the metaphor is well distributed
throughout the NT, and it is especially prominent in Matthew and
Luke. Furthermore, the character and context of the reference to
the proverb in the Clementine Homilies and Justin (and possibly
Ignatius) are such as to make their dependence on the Gospels,
especially Matthew, quite probable.

159

Notes

[1] Cf. for example, the phrase at Deut 11:9, ארץ זבל חלב ודבש,
"a land flowing with mild and honey"; this differs in Tgs. Onq.
and Neof. In Tg. Onq. there is a change of verb: ארע עבדא חלב
ודבש, "a land producing milk and honey." In Tg. Neof. there is a
further change: עבדה פירין טבין, ". . . producing good fruits."
We note especially the targumic preference for עבד.

[2] The substantive מעלל denotes a "deed" much more frequently
in Jeremiah than in any other book of the Hebrew Bible; the
Pentateuch has only one occurrence of this form at Deut 28:20.

[3] See also Prov 1:31, 31:16, 31:31, Hos 10:1.

[4] Similarly Amos 6:12, Hos 10:13, Prov 11:30; and possibly
Ps 58:12.

[5] Similarly, with a special verb to suit the context, Hos 14:9.

[6] This sort of suggestion is only intended to contribute to
the cumulative evidence for the specific figures of speech in
question.

[7] Tgs. Ps.-J. and Neof.

[8] Tgs. Ps.-J. and Neof.: MSS V (N and ed. B) and CTg B.
CTg B: הוא מדבר ברם־בפירי עובדין טבין. Kahle p. 6; Klein p. 7.

[9] Thus Tg. Ps.-J. and MS P. MS V (N and ed. B) and Tg. Neof.
lack the word פירי.

[10] Similarly Tg. Neof. See also Tgs. Neof. and Ps.-J.
Deut 27:3.

[11] For the established analogy of the man to the tree of life
(using the proposition כ) cf. Gen 3:24 in Tg. Neof., MSS V, P, (N
and ed. B); and Tg. Ps.-J. Gen 3:22.
Sipre Deut 20:20 shows a developed analogy in which the
producing of fruit is pivotal: ". . . if the Place cares for the
fruit of the tree, how much more Thy care for the tree which bears
the fruit. . . (Similarly with respect to) the fruit of your
strength." Cf. Finkelstein, Siphre, vol. 2, 239.
Lev 20:16 (an instance of prescription of death for sin of a
particularly heinous nature) had provoked in the mind of the
commentator in Sipra 92d a memory of the fate of the fruitless
trees of Deut 20:20. So he made the analogy of the tree's not
bearing fruit with man's not doing Torah and not doing the will of
his Father in Heaven. In both cases destruction would ensue. Cf.
J. H. Weiss, Sipra 92d.
While Sipre Deuteronomy and Sipra each make a different
point, they both presume what we have suggested as a possible
modified interpretation of the two additional words in Tgs. Neof.
and Ps.-J. at Deut 20:20.

[12] Gen. Rab. 30:6. בראשית רבה, מדרש רבה, vol. 2, 10.

[13] _Cher._ 102.

[14] _Spec. Leg._ iv. 75.

[15] _Post._ 171.

[16] In a simple word or phrase, or in a popular proverb, or in a longer treatment such as Matt 7:16-20. There is no need to see hellenistic thought such as in Sir 27:6 or Philo or in the NT books.

[17] Cf. also Jas 3:17, Jude 12.

[18] Matt 13:1-9, Luke 8:4-8. Cf. also one occurrence in the parable of the tares, Matt 13:24-30.

[19] Matt 21:33-46, Mark 12:1-12, Luke 20:9-19.

[20] Matt 21:18-19, Mark 11:12-14, Luke 13:6-9.

[21] Re Matthew, cf. for example, Peter F. Ellis, _Matthew: His Mind and His Message,_ 3-25.

[22] This metaphorical _dictum_ is not found in the NT anywhere but in Matthew 7 and 12, and Luke 6.

[23] It has been overtly dubbed a popular proverb. Cf. P. Benoit & M.-E. Boismard, _Synopse,_ t. 2, 126 and 156.

[24] Our English, in the attempt to render the basic concepts of the words involved, cannot follow the grammatical form of the Hebrew.

[25] Jas 3:17: καρποὶ ἀγαθοί - thus only here in the NT.

[26] Besides the examples we have given, note allusions in the following: A. Guillaumont, H.-Ch. Puech, G. Quispel, W. Till and Yassah 'Abd al Masiḥ, _The Gospel According to Thomas: Coptic Text Established and Translated_ (Leiden: Brill; N.Y.: Harper, 1959) 24-26. Also Ign. _Trall._ 11:1-2; _1 Clem._56:1 and 57:6; _2 Clem._1:3; _Barn._ 11:6 (quoting Ps 1:3-6); _Diogn._ 12:1 and 8.

[27] Ignatius used the adjective φανερός, "clear, visible, evident"; this word is expressive in the context, but was not the one used in this context by either Matthew or Luke.

[28] _Clementine Homilies_ 11:35; _PG_ 2:301.

[29] _PG_ 6:353.

CONCLUSION
Toward A Refinement in the Methodology of New Testament Study, with Reference to the Sermon on the Mount

Our exegetical objective has been the elucidation of several of the concepts of the Sermon on the Mount. In NT interpretation, this has involved an adjusting of focus. It has been necessary to be careful to avoid close arguments on literary dependency (among written texts), and to acknowledge a degree of fluidity in the wording of the texts. This is not surprising when we consider that the teaching and learning climate of early Christianity, in its Jewish milieu, exhibited its sense of responsibility in aural memory. The targums, tannaitic midrashim and a few other sources are what remain to us of a developing exegetical tradition. When we accept the various concepts of the Sermon on the Mount as standing within this broad tradition, then our appreciation of this content is qualitatively enhanced.

There could be some who would think there would be a difference between the ideas of the Sermon on the Mount and the materials that have come down to us from the Jewish exegetical milieu. Serious perusal of the available materials shows that there is much less difference than some writers have suggested.[1] The area of difference cannot be intrinsic to the contents presented, for according to Matt 5:17, "think not that I have come to abolish the law and the prophets. . ." Rather, we must turn to the introduction (Matt 5:1-2) and conclusion (Matt 7:28-29)

to the Sermon on the Mount and see the difference in the manner of
the presentation. In the introduction, we read, "and he sat down
and opened his mouth and taught them. . . " Here Matthew has us
envisioning the presence of Jesus to "the crowds" and their at-
tentive presence to him. In this he was acknowledged as a rabbi;
his words made rapport with what they already knew; the content
of his message was in line with the current teachings; his methodology rang true. Only the post-script to the Sermon on the Mount
tells us what was really new: "the crowds were astonished at his
teaching,[2] for he taught them as one who had authority. . . "
He brought his sense of conviction to the traditional content, a
sense of conviction so deep as to be personal - "he who hears
these my words and does them. . . " This was the kind of "authority" which could engender motivation in the audience to accept and
keep the Word of God - hearing in such a way as to result in doing
the Word. This deep sense of personal conviction with respect to
the Word of God extended from the Torah and its traditional exegesis even to the exegesis being presented in the Sermon on the
Mount: "he who hears these my words and does them. . . " Even
wider, "my words" could be taken in apposition to the whole
Gospel of Matthew, or wider still, to the full heritage of the
early Church of the words of Jesus.

The themes we have discussed, which were found together in
the Sermon on the Mount, are interrelated. In this initial study
we have selected the primary features: the title for God,
"Father" (chap. I), and the basic mandate of God, the hearing and
doing of the Word (chap. IV), and a few implications of these
features (chaps. II, III and V). In the Gospel of Matthew, it is
the Sermon on the Mount (chaps. 5-7) which carries the preponderant number of references to God as "Father" (5:16, 45, 48; 6:1,
4, 6 twice, 8, 9, 14, 15, 18 twice, 26, 32; 7:11, 21). Matthew's
imitatio Dei is imitation of the Father; his imperative of the
imitatio Dei is his conclusion of Chap. 5, "Be ye perfect, as
your Heavenly Father is perfect." Starting from Deut 32:6, the

ideas of "Father" and "Creator" were joined: "Is he not your
Father who created you, who made you and established you?" In the
beginning, the Creator's works had been completed/perfected (Gen
2:1-3: LXX: τελειόω; Tgs.: שלם). Hence there are these inter-
connected themes to be understood in Matt 5:48 which can be read:
"Be ye perfect (in good works) as your heavenly Father is perfect
(in good works)." By the emphasis given to the title "Father" in
the Sermon on the Mount, the imperative of the imitatio Dei is
reinforced. As a consequence, the exception to the imitatio Dei
cannot go unenunciated: the one thing in which the imitatio Dei
does not apply is judgement, this was a prerogative of YHWH not
to be imitated. Father, an imitatio hominis is involved: "with
the judgement ye judge, ye shall be judged." In Matt 7:1-2 in the
mandate not to judge, the title "Father" is not used, but God is
implied by the respectful use of the passive voice. The association of the concepts of "judgement" (i.e. God's judgement) and
"measure" had been strengthened in the targumic traditions.
Matthew underscores his judgement-saying with the popular "measure
for measure" saying; and thus the one thing in which the imitatio
Dei does not apply is presented carefully and unequivocally.

The concluding pericope of the Sermon on the Mount features
the basic guiding mandate: hear and do the Word. Each of these
three words is important. The Word(s) of God in Deuteronomy was
pre-eminently the Ten Words; and tradition eventually included
the whole Torah under the term Word(s), a term which was widely
used in the targums. From the targums and other early Jewish
tradition, it is clear that hearing, saying, studying, learning
the Law/Word(s) were considered as only preliminary to observing,
doing the Law. It is the same in Matt 7:24-27; what is important
is the doing. The deeds of man are important and, for literary
effect and greater appreciation, the subject of the "fruit" metaphor - "you will know them by their fruits" (Matt 7:16-20). Yet
the deeds would not be good deeds unless they proceeded from
hearing, studying Torah. Torah would have an effect upon those

who studied it as salt has an effect on its milieu. According to
the opening of Derek Erez Zuta, the disciples of the wise should
be "poor and humble of spirit, industrious and salted. . . "
(זריז וממולח). Matthew's first Beatitude (5:3) is "blessed are
the poor in spirit. . . "; Matthew's opening of the Sermon-proper
(5:13) is "you are the salt of the earth. . ." The disciples
should be "salted" with the covenant, the Law; and they should
salt the earth, bring their saltiness to effect in good works.
This dual imperative of study of the Law and good works is implicit in Matt 5:13; and it is explicit in Matt 7:24-27: "he
who hears these my words and does them will be like a wise man. ."
In 7:26, the opposite of the "wise man" is ανὴρ μωρός, "a man
devoid (of hearing and doing the Word)." In 5:13 we have the same
concept expressed in a metaphor, salt which had become devoid
(μωρανθῇ) of its savour, the implication being that the person
devoid of the Law and good works is not a disciple. The μωρ-root
is a forceful one (see Μωρέ, Matt 5:22); it is found in both
Matt 5:13 and 7:24-27, the opening and closing materials of the
Sermon on the Mount. It would not be going too far to find a real
thematic cohesion here, a suggestion of inclusio in Matt 5:13 and
7:24-27 for the entire body of the Sermon on the Mount.

So we scan the Sermon on the Mount to see what is included
in it. First and foremost, God is "Father," and the imitatio Dei
is the consequence of this. While the imitatio Dei does have its
roots in Torah, it was much developed by subsequent Jewish tradition. A primary example is the passage in the fragment targum
tradition at Gen 35:9 (and in Tg. Ps.-J. at Deut 34:6): God's
good works are to be imitated in blessing matrimony, visiting the
afflicted, and comforting those who mourn (Tg. Ps.-J. adds clothing the naked, feeding the poor and burying the dead). See also
Sirach 7:32-35 which enumerates four of the same works of mercy.
The imitatio Dei implies the works of mercy. Matthew makes the
works of mercy mandatory at the conclusion of chapters 23-25
(the literary counterpart of the Sermon on the Mount); Matthew

advocates active love of both neighbour and enemy (5:38-47) and
concludes this with the mandate to imitate the Heavenly Father
(the Creator who) is perfect (in good works). We come to the
conclusion that besides the ancient Words (Commandments, Law),
the works of mercy are also implied in μου τοὺς λόγους τούτους.
Just as the Commandments with respect to killing, adultery,
swearing falsely and talion were unfolded and carried to their
ultimate meaning in Matt 5:21-42, so too the whole Word of God is
unfolded and guarded in a practical way when the imitatio Dei
(through the active works of mercy) is encompassed within μου
τοὺς λόγους τούτους.

The Beatitudes which introduced the Sermon on the Mount
commended mercy and other good works in detail; this is commended
in the final pericope of the Sermon on the Mount as μου τοὺς
λόγους τούτους - the final commendation recapitualtes the former,
and the whole of Matt 5-7 is encompassed (logically and literarily)
within them. In Matt 5:42-47, the instruction to the "sons of the
Father in Heaven" is to wish peace (שלם is recalled) to all men,
not only the brethren - and Matt 5:48 sets the imitation of the
Father (whose work is שלם) in this context. Hence, we find the
imitatio Dei encompassed within μου τοὺς λόγους τούτους in
Matt 5-7; it is the positively oriented exegesis of the full
meaning of the Law. The imitatio Dei is the doing of the Law.

The imitatio Dei is presented as the imitation of the works
of God, but it had also been presented in a straightforward manner
in MS V Num 23:19:

. . . the sons of man say	בני אינשא אמרין
but do not. . . But God	ולא יבדין. . .
says and He does; He	ברם אלהא אמר
decrees and fulfils. . .	ועבד גזא ומקיים

Here the importance of the doing (עבד) is stressed, and the
haggadist exhorts the doing in a context of imitatio Dei. The
imitatio Dei is the doing of the Law. This holds true in the
targumic traditions and in the Sermon on the Mount.

The summary is given in Matt 5:48 where God is called

"Father," the imitatio Dei is in the imperative, and the focus is on deeds (עבד) when we read the verse as we have suggested in the light of targumic tradition and the context in Matt 5:43-48: "You shall be perfect (in good work - עבד) as your Heavenly Father is perfect (in good works)." Thus Matt 5:48 is a succinct exemplar of the thematic cohesion to be found in the Sermon on the Mount.

Certainly, within the confines of the present work we could not discuss all the inter-related themes of the Sermon on the Mount of which our understanding can be enriched by reference to the traditions preserved in the targums and other early Jewish materials. We shall give three examples of other related themes.

At Deut 6:25, צדקה, "righteousness," is equated with "to do all this Commandment." The same definition persists and is often repeated in the targumic traditions, for example, the haggadah in MS V Gen 3:24 (above p. 103). In the Sermon on the Mount, δικαιοσύνη, "righteousness," is a key concept (Matt 5:6, 10, 20; 6:1, 33; cf. also 5:45), and there is no reason to posit any shift in its basic meaning. The concept of "righteousness" entails both the hearing and the doing, otherwise stated, Commandments and good works (a thematic cohesion in Matt 5:13-20, note especially vv 16, 19, 20). This is also connected with the "fruit" metaphor in Gen. Rab. 30:6:

The fruit of the righteous	פרי צדיק עץ חיים
is a tree of life. What	מה הן פרותין של צדיק
is the fruit of the righteous?	מצוות ומעשים טובים
Commandments and good works.	

"Righteousness" also figures very strongly in the imitatio Dei theme. Hence the theme of "righteousness" is most central when we are discussing the thematic cohesion in the Sermon on the Mount.

Matt 7:13-14 is a variation on the widely attested theme of the Two Ways. It is remarkable that not only Tgs. Ps.-J. and Neof. but also Tg. Onq. have a consistent interpolation stressing the "straight (firm, right) way": it occurs at Deut 10:12, 11:22, 19:9, 26:17 and 28:9. Tg. Onq. Deut 10:12:   למהך בכל אורחן

דתקנן קדמוהי, ". . . to walk in all the ways that are straight
before Him." This, then, would be a small contribution to the
larger discussion of the development of the theme of the Two Ways.
The "straight way" is common knowledge to Philo,[3] and at one
point he equates this with the <u>doing</u> of the <u>words</u> of God:[4]

The diligent man does	οὕτως ὁ σπουδαῖος ἕκαστα
everything, blamelessly	δρᾷ τὴν ἀτραπὸν εὐθύνων
keeping the straight	ἀμέμπτως τοῦ βίου, ὥστε
path of life, so that	τὰ ἔργα τοῦ σοφοῦ λόγων
the works of the wise	ἀδιαφορεῖν θείων. . .
man are none other than	ἔφην, τοὺς τοῦ θεοῦ
godly words. . .	λόγους πράξεις εἶναι
I said that the words	τοῦ σοφοῦ.
of God were the deeds	
of the wise man.	

While Matt 7:24-28 says plainly sets <u>hearing</u> <u>and</u> <u>doing</u> the Word
in the simile of the two builders, Matt 7:13-14 uses the metaphor
of the Two Ways. <u>Tg. Ps.-J</u>. Deut 34:6 (above p. 35) contains the
long haggadah of God's example in doing the works of mercy; it is
prefaced: בריך שמיה דמריה עלמא דאליף לן ארחתיה תקניה, "Blessed be
the name of the Lord of the world who has taught us <u>his straight</u>
<u>way</u>." The themes of <u>imitatio Dei</u> and the straight way are found
equated here. We must grant a certain thematic cohesion among the
overt statements of hearing and doing the Word, the theme of the
straight way which repeats this under metaphor, and the <u>imitatio</u>
<u>Dei</u> which is the practical doing of the Word.

Treasures in heaven - Matt 6:19-21. The theme of these
verses is found in Sir 29:11-12 (c. 190 B.C.[5]): θὲς τὸν θησαυρόν
σου κατ' ἐντολὰς ὑψίστου. . . σύγκλεισον ἐλεημοσύνην ἐν τοῖς
ταμιείοις σου. . . "Lay up your treasure according to the commandments of the Most High. . . store up almsgiving in your treasury."
The theme was well known to Philo,[6] and echoed in the targums,[7]
early midrashim,[8] and Pseudepigrapha.[9] The connection of the
"treasure in heaven" with the commandments and good works is
obvious.

The words <u>perfect</u>, <u>way</u>, and <u>righteousness</u> were associated
in Psalms. These word associations developed into speech patterns

polished by usage in the Qumran documents (above pp. 48-49). In
these sources, living according to the Law (or covenant), walking
perfectly in the way, doing truth and righteousness – all these
were quite synonymous for practical purposes. This stands as another confirmation of the inter-relation of these themes in Jewish
religious interpretation just prior to the first century. Again,
it is not at all surprising to affirm that the thematic cohesion
in the Sermon in the Mount stands in harmony with the same patterns among the same themes in the Jewish exegetical milieu.

There are parallels between the Matthean materials and early
Jewish materials, including the targums. There are literary parallels and also parallel thought patterns. What McNamara wrote
with reference to the targums and the New Testament in 1965[10]
still applies: "Many parallels have already been established
but some of them await more detailed study. Much work awaits to
be done in the field, a field rich in possibilities – one whose
importance can scarcely be exaggerated."

Notes

[1] Some would immediately ask about Matt 5:21-48. Bultmann (Theology of the New Testament, vol. 1 N.Y.: Charles Scribner's Sons, 1951 13) makes his attitude toward the material in this section quite plain: "the antitheses (Mt. 5:21-48) in the Sermon on the Mount throw legalism and the will of God into sharp contrast." The acceptance of these "antitheses" as "contrast" is taken for granted by T. W. Manson in The Sayings of Jesus (London: SCM, 1950) 155-163.

G. Barth also acknowledges the "antithetic character" of the "antitheses" (Bornkamm-Barth-Held, Tradition and Interpretation in Matthew, 93). John P. Meier used the term "antitheses" in his chapter heading and in his discussion without questioning the term (Law and History in Matthew's Gospel [Rome: Biblical Institute Press, 1976] 125-161).

On the other hand, Davies was of the opinion that "the relationship between the two members of the form is not one of pure contrast"; hence they are but "so-called antitheses (which) are to be regarded more accurately as exegesis than as strict antitheses" (The Setting of the Sermon on the Mount, 102). Béda Rigaux preferred the term "fulfillment passages" for Matt 5:21-48 (The Testimony of St. Matthew [Chicago: Franciscan Herald Press, 1968] 70).

[2] A comment that the people "were astonished at his teaching" is found in various contexts: Mark 1:22 and Luke 4:32 in connection with Jesus' teaching at Capernaum; variously at Mark 11:18 and Matt 22:23; and in Acts 13:12, the converted proconsul was "astonished at the teaching of the Lord." M.-E. Boismard is of the opinion that Matt 7:28b-29 is from the hand of the final redactor of the Gospel, under Markan influence. Cf. P. Benoit & M.-E. Boismard, Synopse t. 2, 158.

[3] Note Mig. 146, 154; Gig. 64, 55; Abr. 269.

[4] Mig. 129.

[5] L. Rost, Judaism Outside the Hebrew Canon, 68.

[6] On the natural heavenly treasury of the rains (etc.): Mig. 121-122. On the analogy of the natural treasury of the elements to the metaphorical treasury of heaven: Deus 156-158. On the treasury which concerns the soul - the metaphorical treasury: Cher. 48, Mig. 161, Her. 74, 76, Praem. 103-104, Fug. 79.

[7] Cf. for example Deut 32:34 in MSS V, P (N and ed. B) and Tg. Neof.; also Tg. Ps.-J.

[8] Examples: Sipre Num 119: Horovitz, Siphre, vol. 1, 144; A crystallization of this theme probably from a late date is found in Gen. Rab. 9:9; Cf. בראשית רבה, מדרש רבה vol. 1, 63:

Thus (for whoever	כך כל מי שהוא
treasures up mitzvoth	מסגל מצוות
and good deeds,	ומעשים טובים

there is the Garden of Eden;   ‏הרי גן עדן,‏
And (for) whoever does not   ‏וכל מי שאינו מסגל‏
lay up mitzvoth and good   ‏מצוות ומעשים טבים‏
deeds, behold there is   ‏הרי גיהנם.‏
Gehenna.

[9]Cf. R. H. Charles, Apocrypha and Pseudepigrapha, vol. 2, 311, n. 5 for a list of instances.

[10]Martin McNamara, The New Testament and the Palestinian Targum to the Pentateuch, 261.

BIBLIOGRAPHY
Texts and References

Aland, Kurt - Black, Matthew - Martini, Carlo M. - Metzger, Bruce
M. - Wikgren, Allen, eds. The Greek New Testament. 2nd edn.
N.Y.-London-Edinburgh-Amsterdam-Stuttgart: United Bible
Societies. 1966. 1968.

Aland, Kurt, ed. Synopsis of the Four Gospels: Greek-English Edition of the Synopsis Quattuor Evangeliorum with the Text of
the Revised Standard Version. n.p.: United Bible Societies.
[1970.]

Arndt, William F. and Gingrich, F. Wilbur. A Greek-English Lexi-
con of the New Testament and Other Early Christian Literature.
Chicago: University of Chicago Press. London: Cambridge
University Press. 1957. 2nd edn. 1979.

Barthélemy, D. - Milik, J.T. et al. Discoveries in the Judaean
Desert. 5 vols. Oxford: Clarendon. 1955-1968.

Benoit, P. and Boismard, M.-E. Synopse des quatre évangiles en
français avec parallèles des apocryphes et des pères. 2 vols.
[Paris]: Les éditions du cerf. 1972-1973.

Biblia Rabbinica: A Reprint of the 1525 Venice Edition. Jerusalem:
Makor. 1972. 4 vols.

Blackman, Philip, ed. Mishnayoth.[2] N.Y.: Judaica. 1963.

Blass, F. and Debrunner, A. A Greek Grammar of the New Testament
and Other Early Christian Literature. Chicago: University of
Chicago Press. 1961.

Bonsirven, Joseph. Textes rabbiniques des deux premiers siècles
chrétiens pour servir à l'intelligence du nouveau testament.
Roma: Pontificio Istituto Biblico. 1955.

Brederek, Emil. Kondordanz zum Targum Onkelos. BZAW IX. 1906.

Brown, Francis - Driver, S. R. - Briggs, Charles A. A Hebrew
and English Lexicon of the Old Testament with an Appendix
Containing the Biblical Aramaic. Oxford: Clarendon. 1907-
1962.

Charles, R. H. ed. The Apocrypha and Pseudepigrapha of the Old
Testament in English. 2 Vols. Oxford: Clarendon. 1913.

Charlesworth, James H. The Pseudepigrapha and Modern Research.
Missoula, Montana: Scholars Press. 1976.

Clarke, E.G. Targum Pseudo-Jonathan of the Pentateuch: Text and Concordance. Hoboken, New Jersey: KTAV. 1984.

Cowling, G. J. Concordance to the Geniza Fragments of the Palestinian Targum. Privately mimeographed. 1969.

Díez Macho, Alejandro. ed. Neophyti I: Targum Palestinense: ms. de la Biblioteca Vaticana. Madrid-Barcelona: Consejo Superior de investigaciones científicas. t. 1. Génesis: 1968; t. 2. Éxodo: 1970; t. 3. Levítico: 1971; t. 4. Números: 1974; t. 5. Deuteronomío: 1978; t. 6. Apéndices: 1979.

Etheridge, J.W. trans. The Targums of Onkelos and Jonathan ben Uzziel on the Pentateuch with the Fragments of the Jerusalem Targum from the Chaldee. n.p.: 1862; reprint N.Y.: KTAV. 1968.

Field, Fredericus. Originis Hexaplorum. Oxonii: Clarendoniano. 1891.

Finkelstein, Louis, ed. Siphre ad Deuteronomium H. S. Horovitzii schedis usus cum variis lectionibus et adnotationibus. Berlin: Gesellschaft zur Förderung der Wissenschaft des Judentums. 1939. Republished: N.Y.: Jewish Theological Seminary of America. 1969.

Fitzmyer, Joseph A. The Dead Sea Scrolls: Major Publications and Tools for Study. Missoula, Montana: Scholars Press. 1975, 1977.

———————————————— The Genesis Apocryphon of Qumran Cave I: A Commentary.[2] Rome: Biblical Institute Press. 1971.

Freedman, H. and Simon, Maurice. Midrash Rabbah Translated into English with Notes, Glossary and Indices. London: Soncino. 1931.

Ginsburger, Moses, ed. Das Fragmententhargum (Thargum jeruschalmi zum Pentateuch). Berlin: S. Calvary & Co. 1899.

———————————————— Pseudo-Jonathan (Thargum Jonathan ben Usiël zum Pentateuch) Nach der Londoner Handschrift (Brit. Mus. add. 27031). Berlin: S. Calvary & Co. 1903.

Goldin, Judah. trans. The Fathers According to Rabbi Nathan. New Haven: Yale University Press. 1955.

Grossfeld, Bernard. A Bibliography of Targum Literature. Cincinnati: Hebrew Union College Press; N.Y.: KTAV. 1972. Supp. vol. 1977.

Hammer, Reuven. Sifre: A Tannaitic Commentary on the Book of Deuteronomy. New Haven: Yale University Press. 1986.

Hatch, Edwin and Redpath, Henry A. Concordance to the Septuagint
and the Other Greek Versions of the Old Testament (Including
the Apocryphal Books). Oxford: Clarendon. 1897.

Horovitz, H. S. ed. Siphre d'Be Rab: Fasciculus primus: Siphre ad
Numeros adjecto Siphre Zutta cum variis lectionibus et adnota-
tionibus. Lipsiae: Gustav Foch. 1917. Reprint: Jerusalem:
Wahrmann Books. 1966.

James, M. R. trans. The Biblical Antiquities of Philo now first
Translated from the Old Latin Version. London: SPCK. 1917;
Reprint: N.Y.: KTAV. 1971.

Jastrow, Marcus. A Dictionary of the Targumim, the Talmud Babli
and Yerushalmi, and the Midrashic Literature. N.Y.: Jastrow
Publishers. 1967.

Josephus, Flavius. Josephus. London: William Heinemann. 1950-63;
Cambridge, Mass.: Harvard University Press. 1969. 9 Vols.

Kahle, Paul. Masoreten des Westens II: Das Palästinische Penta-
teuch-targum, Die Palästinische Punktation, Der Bibel text
des Ben Naftali. Stuttgart: W. Kohlhammer. Reprint: Hildesheim: Georg Olms. 1967.

Kisch, Guido. ed. Pseudo-Philo's Liber Antiquitatum Biblicarum.
Notre Dame, Indiana: The University of Notre Dame. 1949.

Kittel, Rud. ed. Biblia Hebraica. Stuttgart: Württembergische
Bibelanstalt. 1937.

Klein, Michael L. The Fragment-Targums of the Pentateuch
According to their Extant Sources. Volume I: Texts, Indices
and Introductory Essays. Rome: Biblical Institute Press. 1980.

---------------- The Fragment-Targums of the Pentateuch
According to their Extant Sources. Volume II: Translation.
Rome: Biblical Institute Press. 1980.

---------------- Genizah Manuscripts of Palestinian Targum to
the Pentateuch. Volume One. Cincinnati: Hebrew Union
College Press. 1986.

Kosovsky, Binyamin. Ostar Leshon Hatannaᶜim: Concordantiae
Verborum quae in Sifra aut Torat Kohanim reperiuntur/
אוצר לשון התנאים. Vols. 1-4: ט - א. Jerusalem: Jewish Theological Seminary of America.. 1967-69.

------------------ Ostar Leshon Hatannaᶜim: Thesaurus "Sifrei"
Concordantiae Verborum quae in "Sifrei" Numeri et Deuteron-
omium reperiuntur/ אוצר לשון התנאים. Vols. 1-3: ם - א.
Jerusalem: Jewish Theological Seminary of America. 1972.

Kuhn, Karl Georg. Kondordanz zu den Qumrantexten. Göttingen: Vandenhoeck & Ruprecht. 1960.

Lake, Kirsopp. trans. The Apostolic Fathers. London: William Heinemann; Cambridge, Mass.: Harvard Universtiy Press. 1970. 1975. 2 Vols.

Lauterbach, J. Z. ed. Mekilta de Rabbi Ishmael. Philadelphia: Jewish Publication Society of America. 1933-35, 1949. 3 Vols.

Liddell, Henry George and Scott, Robert. A Greek-English Lexicon[9]. Oxford: Clarendon. 1940-1973.

Lisowsky, Gerhard. Concordantiae Veteris Testamenti Hebraicae atque Aramaicae. Stuttgart: Württembergische Bibelanstalt. 1958.

Lohse, Eduard. ed. Die Texte aus Qumran: Hebraïsch und Deutsch. München: Kösel. 1971.

Mandelkern, Solomon. Veteris Testamenti Concordantiae: Hebraicae atque Chaldaicae. Jerusalem: Schocken. 1955.

מדרש רבה, בראשית רבה Tel Aviv: Yavneh. 1958.

Moulton, W. F. and Geden, A. S. A Concordance to the Greek Testament according to the Texts of Westcott and Hort, Tischendorf and the English Revisers.[4] Edinburgh: T. & T. Clark. 1963.

Nickels, Peter. Targum and New Testament: A Bibliography together with a New Testament Index. Rome: Pontifical Biblical Institute. 1967.

Palestinian Targum to the Pentateuch: Codex Vatican (Neofiti I). Jerusalem: "MAKOR" Publishing Ltd. 1970. 2 Vols.

Philo, Judaeus. Philo. London: William Heinnemann. 1930-1962; Cambridge, Mass.: Harvard University Press. 1970-71. 12 Vols.

Rahlfs, Alfred, ed. Septuaginta: id est Vetus Testamentum graece iuxta LXX interpretes.[9] Stuttgart: Würtembergische Bibelanstalt. 1935.

Rosenthal, Franz. A Grammar of Biblical Aramaic. Wiesbaden: Harrassowitz. 1968.

Saldarini, Anthony J. The Fathers according to Rabbi Nathan (Abot de Rabbi Nathan) Version B: A Translation and Commentary. Leiden: Brill. 1975.

Schechter, Solomon. Aboth de Rabbi Nathan. Corrected edn. N.Y.: Philipp Feldheim. 1967.

Sifrei. 1st edn. Venice, 1546. Facsimile: Jerusalem: MAKOR.
[1970-1971].

Sperber, Alexander, ed. The Bible in Aramaic based on Old Manuscripts and Printed Texts. Vol. 1: The Pentateuch According
to Targum Onkelos. Leiden: Brill. 1959.

Stevenson, Wm. B. Grammar of Palestinian Jewish Aramaic.[2]
Oxford: Clarendon. 1962.

Tawrogi, Abraham, ed. Der Talmudische Tractat Derech Erez Sutta.
Königsburg: E. Erlatis. 1885.

Van der Ploeg, J. P. M. and Van der Woude, A. S. eds. & trans. Le
targum de Job de la grotte XI de Qumrân. Leiden: Brill. 1971.

Waltonis, Brianus. Biblia Sacra Polyglotta. Londini: T. Roycroft.
1655-1657. 6 Vols.

Williams, Ronald J. Hebrew Syntax: An Outline. Toronto:
University of Toronto Press. 1967.

Weiss, J. H. ed. Sifra on Leviticus. Vienna 1862. Reprint:
Vienna: J. Schlossberg. 1946.

Books

Abrahams, Israel. Studies in Pharisaism and the Gospels. Cambridge: University Press. Vol.1: 1917. Vol. 2. 1924.

Audet, J. P. The Didaché. Paris: Gabalda. 1958.

Black, Matthew, An Aramaic Approach to the Gospels and Acts.[3]
Oxford: Clarendon. 1967.

Bonnard, Pierre. L'évangile selon Saint Matthieu.[2] Geneve:
Labor et Fides. 1982.

Bonsirven, Joseph. Exégèse rabbinique et exégèse paulinienne.
Paris: Gabriel Beauchesne et ses fils. 1939.

---------------- Le Judaïsme palestinien au temps de Jésus-
Christ. Paris: Gabriel Beauchesne et ses fils. 1934. 2 Vols.

Bornkamm, Günther - Barth Gerhard - Held, Heinz Joachim. Tradition and Interpretation in Matthew. London: SCM. 1963.

Bowker, John. The Targums and Rabbinic Literature: An Introduction to Jewish Interpretations of Scripture. Cambridge: The
University Press. 1969.

Braun, Herbert. Qumran und das Neue Testament. Band I. Tübingen: J. C. B. Mohr. 1966.

Bultmann, Rudolf. The History of the Synoptic Tradition. Oxford: Blackwell. 1972.

---------------- Theology of the New Testament. N.Y.: Charles Scribner's Sons. 1951 and 1955.

Burkitt, F.C. The Gospel History and Its Transmission. Edinburgh: T. & T. Clark. 1907.

Büchler, A. Studies in Sin and Atonement in the Rabbinic Literature of the First Century. London: Oxford University Press. 1928.

Burney, C. F. The Aramaic Origin of the Fourth Gospel. Oxford: Clarendon. 1922.

Carmignac, Jean. Recherches sur le "Notre Père." Paris: Editions Letouzey & Ané. 1969.

Dalman, Gustaf. Jesus-Jeshua: Studies in the Gospels. tr. Paul T. Levertoff. London: SPCK. 1929. Reprint: N.Y.: KTAV. 1971.

------------- Die Worte Jesu. Leipzig. 1898. 2nd edn. 1930. Trans.: The Words of Jesus. Edinburgh: T. & T. Clark. 1902.

Daube, David. The New Testament and Rabbinic Judaism. University of London: Athlone Press. 1956.

Davies, W. D. The Setting of the Sermon on the Mount. Cambridge: The University Press. 1966.

------------ Torah in the Messianic Age and/or the Age to Come. JBL Monograph Series VII. 1952.

Descamps, Albert. Les Justes et la Justice dans les évangiles et le christianisme primitif hormis la doctrine proprement paulinienne. Louvain: Publications universitaires de Louvain & Gembloux: Editions J. Duculot. 1950.

Díez Macho, A. Manuscritos hebreos y arameos de la Biblia. Studia Ephemeridis Augustinianum V. Rome. 1971.

------------- El Targum: Introducción a las traducciones aramaicas de la Biblia. Barcelona: Consejo superior de investigaciones científicas. 1972.

Dodd, C. H. According to the Scriptures. London: James Nisbett.
    1952.

Doeve, J. W. Jewish Hermeneutics in the Synoptic Gospels and
    Acts. Aasen: Van Gorcum & Co. 1954

Doubles, Malcolm C. The Fragment Targum: A Critical Re-exam-
    ination of the Editio Princeps, Das Fragmententhargum by
    Moses Ginsburger, in the Light of Recent Discoveries.
    Typescript. 1962.

Drummond, James. Philo Judaeus. London: Williams and Norgate.
    1888. 2 Vols.

Dupont, Jacques. Les Béatitudes: Le problème littéraire -
    Les deux versions du Sermon sur la montagne et des
    Béatitudes. Nouvelle édition. Louvain: E. Nauwelaerts;
    Bruges: Abbaye de Saint-André. 1958.

Ellis, E. E. Paul's Use of the Old Testament. Edinburgh:
    Oliver & Boyd. 1957.

Ellis, Peter F. Matthew: His Mind and His Message. College-
    ville, Minn.: Liturgical Press. 1974.

Forestell, J. Terence. Targumic Traditions and the New Testa-
    ment: An Annotated Bibliography. Chico, Calif.: Scholars
    Press. 1979.

Foster, J. A. The Language and Text of Codex Neofiti I in the
    Light of Other Palestinian Aramaic Sources. Diss. Boston
    University Graduate School. Typescript. 1969.

Geiger, Abraham. Urschrift und Ubersetzungen der Bibel in ihrer
    Abhängigkeit von der innern Entwicklung des Judentums. 1857;
    2nd edn.: Frankfurt am Main: Verlag Madda. 1928.

Gerhardsson, Birger. Memory and Manuscript: Oral Tradition and
    Written Transmission in Rabbinic Judaism and Early Christ-
    ianity. Lund: C. W. K. Gleerup. 1964.

Grossfeld, B. A Commentary on the Text of a New Palestinian
    Targum. (Codex Neofiti I) on Gen I-XXV. Diss. Johns
    Hopkins University. 1968.

Guillaumont, H. - Puech, Ch. - Quispel, G. - Till, W. -
    'Abd al Masiḥ, Yassah. The Gospel According to Thomas:
    Coptic Text Established and Translated. Leiden: Brill;
    N.Y.: Harper. 1959.

Gundry, Robert Horton. The Use of the Old Testament in St. Matthew's Gospel. Leiden: Brill. 1967. Supp. to Novum Testamentum XVIII.

Harnack, Adolf. The Sayings of Jesus: the Second Source of St. Matthew and St. Luke. London: Withams & Norgate; N.Y.: Putman's Sons. 1908.

Harris, Birkeland. The Language of Jesus. Oslo Avhandlinger utgitt av det Norske Videnskaps-Akademi. 1954.

Harris, Rendell. Testimonies I and II. Cambridge: Cambridge University Press. 1916, 1920.

Hatch, Edwin. Essays in Biblical Greek. Oxford: Clarendon. 1889.

Hawkins, John C. Horae Synopticae. Oxford: Clarendon. 1899.

Hengel, Martin. Judaism and Hellenism: Studies in their Encounter in Palestine during the Early Hellenistic Period. Philadelphia: Fortress. 1974. 2 Vols.

Isenberg, Sheldon Robert. Studies in the Jewish Aramaic Translations of the Pentateuch. Cambridge, Mass.: Harvard University Diss. Photocopy of the typescript. 1968.

Jeremias, Joachim. Abba: Studien zur neutestamentlichen Theologie und Zeitgeschichte. Gottingen. 1966.

————————— New Testament Theology, Part One: The Proclamation of Jesus. tr. John Bowden. London: SCM. 1971.

————————— The Parables of Jesus.[3] London: SCM. 1972.

Kahle, Paul. The Cairo Geniza. London: Oxford Univerity Press. 1947. 2nd edn.: Oxford: Basil Blackwell. 1959.

Kingsbury, J. D. The Parables of Jesus in Matthew 13. London: SPCK. 1969.

Kittel, Gerhard. Theologisches Wörterbuch zum Neuen Testament. Stuttgart: W. Kohlhammer. 1933 and 1953. English: Theological Dictionary of the New Testament. Grand Rapids, Mich.: Eerdmans. Vols. I-IX. 1964-1974.

Koch, Klaus. The Growth of the Biblical Tradition. N.Y.: Charles Scribner's Sons. 1969.

Kuiper, Gérard Johannes. The Pseudo-Jonathan Targum and Its Relationship to Targum Onkelos. Studia Ephemeridis

Augustinianum. Rome: Institutum Patristicum Augustinianum. 1972.

Kümmel, Werner Georg. The Theology of the New Testament. N.Y. - Nashville: Abingdon. 1973.

Lagrange, M.-J. Évangile selon Saint Matthieu.[4] Paris: J. Gabalda et fils. 1927.

Lauterbach, Jacob Z. The Pharisees and Their Teachings. N.Y.: Bloch. 1930.

LeDéaut, Roger. Introduction à la littérature targumique. pt. 1. Rome: Inst. Bibl. Pont. 1966.

-------------- Liturgie juive et Nouveau Testament: le témoinage des versions araméennes. Rome: Scripta Pont. Inst. Biblici. 1965. English: The Message of the New Testament and the Aramaic Bible (Targum). Rome: Biblical Institute Press. 1982.

-------------- La nuit pascale: Essai sur la signification de la Pâque-juive à partir du Targum d'Exode XII 42. Rome: Institut Biblique Pontifical. 1963.

Lentzen-Deis, Leo. Die Taufe Jesu nach den Synoptikern. Frankfurt-am-Main: Joseph Knecht. 1970.

Loisy, Alfred. Les Evangiles Synoptiques I. Ceffonds. 1907.

Longenecker, Richard N. Biblical Exegesis in the Apostolic Period. Grand Rapids, Mich.: Eerdmans. 1975.

Lund, Shirley. An Introductory Study of Codex Neofiti I with Special Reference to the Marginal Readings to the Book of Deuteronomy. Diss.: University of St. Andrews. Typescript. 1966.

Malina, Bruce J. The Palestinian Manna Tradition: The Manna Tradition in the Palestinian Targums and Its Relationship to the New Testament Writings. Leiden: Brill. 1968.

Manson, T. W. The Sayings of Jesus as Recorded in the Gospels according to St. Matthew and St. Luke arranged with Introduction and Commentary. London: SCM. 1949.

Marmorstein, A. The Doctrine of Merits in Old Rabbinical Literature and The Old Rabbinic Doctrine of God. N.Y.: KTAV. 1968.

-------------- Studies in Jewish Theology. London-N.Y.-Toronto: Oxford University Press. 1950.

180

McNamara, Martin. The New Testament and the Palestinian Targum
to the Pentateuch. Rome: Pontifical Biblical Institute.
1966 (Second printing with supplement containing additions
and corrections, 1978).

---------------- Targum and Testament: Aramaic Paraphrases of
the Hebrew Bible: A Light on the New Testament. Grand
Rapids, Mich.: Eerdmans. 1968.

Meier, John P. Law and History in Matthew's Gospel. Rome:
Biblical Institute Press. 1976.

Montefiore, C. G. Rabbinic Literature and Gospel Teachings.
1930. Reprint: N.Y.: KTAV. 1970.

Moore, George Foot. Judaism in the First Centuries of the
Christian Era: The Age of the Tannaim. Cambridge, Mass.:
Harvard University Press. 1927-1930.

Neusner, Jacob. Development of a Legend: Studies on the Traditions Concerning Yoḥanan ben Zakkai. Leiden: Brill. 1970.

Oesterley, W. O. E. and Box, G. H. A Short Survey of the
Literature of Rabbinical and Mediaeval Judaism. London:
SPCK & N.Y.: Macmillan. 1920.

Patte, Daniel, The Gospel According to Matthew. Philadelphia:
Fortress. 1987.

Przybylski, Benno. Righteousness in Matthew and His World of
Thought. Cambridge: Cambridge University Press. 1980.

Rigaux, Béda. The Testimony of St. Matthew. Chicago: Franciscan
Herald Press. 1968.

Rost, Leonhard. Judaism Outside the Hebrew Canon: An Introduction
to the Documents. Nashville: Abingdon. 1976.

Sanders, E. P. The Tendencies of the Synoptic Tradition.
Cambridge: The University Press. 1969.

Schechter, Solomon. Some Aspects of Rabbinic Theology. N.Y.:
Behrman. [1936].

Schiffmann, Lawrence H. The Halakah at Qumran. Leiden: Brill.
1975.

Schürer, Emil. Geschichte des jüdischen Volkes in Zeitalter Jesu
Christi. Leipzig: Hinrich. 1898-1901. English: The History
of the Jewish People in the Age of Jesus Christ (175 B.C. -
A.D. 135). A New English Version, revised and edited by

Geza Vermes and Fergus Millar. Edinburgh: T. & T. Clark. 1973, 1979.

Sellin, Ernst & Fohrer, Georg. Introduction to the Old Testament. N.Y.: Abingdon. 1968.

Smith, Morton. Tannaitic Parallels to the Gospels. Missoula, Miss.: Scholars Press. 1951.

Stendahl, Krister. The School of St. Matthew and its Use of the Old Testament. Lund: C. W. K. Gleerup. 1954.

Strack, Hermann Lebrecht. Introduction to the Talmud and Midrash. Philadelphia: Jewish Publication Society of America. 1931.

Strack, Hermann Lebrecht and Billerbeck, Paul. Kommentar zum Neuen Testament aus Talmud und Midrasch. München: O. Beck. 1922-1928.

Streeter, B. H. The Four Gospels: A Study of Origins. London: Macmillan. 1927.

Torrey, C. Ch. Our Translated Gospels. N.Y.-London: Harper & Brothers. 1936.

Urbach, Ephraim E. The Sages: Their Concepts and Beliefs. Jerusalem: Magnes. 1975.

Vermes, Geza. Scripture and Tradition in Judaism: Haggadic Studies.[2] Leiden: Brill. 1973.

Wellhausen, J. Das Evangelium Matthaei. Berlin. 1904.

Zimmerman, Frank. The Aramaic Origin of the Four Gospels. N.Y.: KTAV. 1979.

Zunz, Leopold. Die gottesdienstlichen Vorträge der Juden historisch entwickelt.[2] Frankfurt a. Main. 1892.

Articles

Ball, C. J. "Had the Fourth Gospel an Aramaic Archetype?" Exp Tim 21. 1910. 91-93.

Bamberger, Bernard J. "Halakic Elements in the Neofiti Targum: A Preliminary Statement." JQR 66. 1975. 27-38.

Barr, James. "Which Language did Jesus Speak? - Some Remarks of a Semitist." BJRL 53. 1970-1971. 9-29.

Bartina, Sebastián B. "Aportaciones recientes de los Targumim a la interpretación neotestamentaria." Est Ecl 39. 1964. 361-76.

Baumgarten, J. M. "The Unwritten Law in the Pre-Rabbinic Period." J St. J. 4. 1973. 7-29.

Black, Matthew. "Aramaic Studies and the Language of Jesus." BZAW 103: In Memoriam Paul Kahle. 1968. 17-28.

-------------- "The Christological Use of the Old Testament in the New Testament." NTS 18. 1975. 1-14.

-------------- "Die Erforschung der Muttersprache Jesu." TLZ 82. 1957. 653-668.

-------------- "The Problem of the Aramaic Element in the Gospels." Exp Tim 59. 1947-48. 171-176.

-------------- "The Problem of the Old Testament Quotations in the Gospels." Journal of Manchester Egyptian & Oriental Society 23. 1942. 4.

-------------- "The Recovery of the Language of Jesus." NTS 3. 1957. 305-313.

Bloch, Renée. "Écriture et tradition dans le judaïsme." Cahiers Sioniens 8. 1954. 9-34.

------------ "Ezéchiel XVI: Exemple parfait du procédé mid-rashique dans la Bible." Cahiers Sioniens 3. 1955. 193-223.

------------ "'Juda engendra Pharès et Zara, de Thamar' Matth., I,3." Mélanges Bibliques rédigée en l'honneur de André Robert. Paris: Bloud & Gay. 1957. 381-389.

------------ "Midrash." Supplément au Dictionnaire de la Bible V. Paris: Letouzey et Ané. 1957. cols. 1263-1281.

------------ "Note méthodologique pour l'étude de la littérature rabbinique." RSR 43. 1955. 194-225.

------------ "Note sur l'utilisation des fragments de la Geniza du Caire pour l'étude du Targum Palestinien." REJ XIV. 1955. 5-35.

------------ "Quelques aspects de la figure de Moïse dans la tradition rabbinique." Moïse l'homme de l'alliance. Cahiers Sioniens 3. 1955. 93-167.

Bowker, J. W. "Haggadah in the Targum Onqelos." JSS 12. 1967. 51-65.

Brown, Schuyler. "From Burney to Black: The Fourth Gospel and the Aramaic Question." CBQ 26. 1964. 323-339.

Charlesworth, James H. "Christian and Jewish Self-Definition in the Light of Christian Additions to the Apocryphal Writings." Unpub. paper. 1979.

Clarke, Ernest G. "Jacob's Dream at Bethel as Interpreted in the Targums and the New Testament." SR 4. 1974-75. 367-377.

---------------- "The Neofiti I Marginal Glosses and the Fragmentary Targum Witness to Gen. VI-IX." VT 22. 1972. 259-65.

Cowling, G. J. "Targum Neofiti, Exodus 16:15." Australian Journal of Biblical Archaeology 2. 1974-75. 93-105.

Dahl, N. A. "A People for His Name." NTS 4. 1958. 319-327.

Daube, David. "Concerning the Reconstruction of the 'Aramaic Gospels.'" BJRL 29. 1945. 69-105.

------------ "The Earliest Structure of the Gospels." NTS 5. 1958-1959. 174-187.

------------ "Rabbinic Methods of Interpretation and Hellenistic Rhetoric." HUCA 22. 1949. 239-264.

Delcor, M. "La portée chronologique de quelques interprétations de targoum Néophyti contenues dans le cycle d'Abraham." J. St. J. 1. 1970. 105-119.

--------- "Le targum de Job et l'araméen du temps de Jésus." RSR 47. 1973. 232-255.

Delling, Gerhard. "τελεύος." TWNT VII. 1972. 71-77.

Derrett, J. D. M. "Midrash in the New Testament: the Origin of Luke XXII 67-68." ST 29. 1975. 147-156.

Descamps, Albert. "Du discours de Marc, IX, 33-50 aux paroles de Jésus" in La formation des Evangiles. n.l.: Desclée de Brouwer. 1957. 152-177.

---------------- "Essai d'interprétation de Mt. 5, 17-48. 'Formgeschichte' ou 'Redaktionsgeschichte'?" in Studia Evangelica: Papers presented to the International Congress on "The Four Gospels in 1957" held at Christ Church, Oxford. 1957.

De Zwaan, J. "John Wrote in Aramaic." JBL 57. 1938. 155-171.

Díez Macho, A. "Una copia de todo el Targum jerosolimitano en la Vaticana." Est. Bibl. 1956. 446-447.

------------ "Deraš y exegesis del nuevo testamento." Sefarad 35. 1975. 37-89.

------------ "En torno a la datación del Targum 'Palestinense.'" Sefarad 20. 1960. 3-16.

------------ "La lengua hablada por Jesucristo." Oriens Antiquus 2. 1963. 95-132.

------------ "El Logos y el Espíritu Santo." Atlantida 1. 1963. 381-396.

------------ "Magister-Minister, P. E. Kahle Through Twelve Years of Correspondence." Recent Progress in Biblical Scholarship. Ed. M. P. Hornik, Oxford: Lincombe Lodge Research Library. 1965. 13-67.

------------ "Un nuevo fragmento del Targum palestinense a Génesis (Ms. T.-S. N.S. 76 de la Biblioteca Universitaria de Cambridge)." Augustinianum 9. 1969. 120-124.

------------ "Nuevos Fragmentos de Tosefta Targumica." Sefarad 15. 1955. 313-324.

------------ "Nuevos Fragmentos del Targum Palestinense." Sefarad 15. 1955. 31-39.

------------ "The Recently Discovered Palestinian Targum: Its Antiquity and Relationship with the other Targums." Supp. VT 7. 1959. 222-245.

------------ "Le targum palestinien." RSR 47. 1973. 169-231.

------------ "Targum y Nuevo Testamento." Mélanges Eugène Tisserant. Studi e Testi 231. Vol. 1. Rome. 1964. 153-185.

Diez Merino, Luis. "El Decalogo en el Targum Palestinense: Origen, Estilo y Motivaciones." Est. Bibl. 34. 1975. 24-48.

Doubles, Malcolm. "Indications of Antiquity in the Orthography and Morphology of the Fragment Targum." BZAW 103. In Memoriam Paul Kahle. 1968. 79-89.

----------------- "Towards the Publication of the Extant Texts of the Palestinian Targum(s)." VT 15. 1965. 16-26.

Dumbrell, W. J. "The Logic of the Role of the Law." NovT 23. 1981. 1-21.

Dupont, Jacques. "'Soyez parfaits' (Mt., V.48) 'Soyez misericor-
dieux' (Lc., VI,36)." Sacra Pagina II. Paris: Librarie
Lecoffre; Gembloux: Duculot. 1959. 150-162.

Edgar, S. L. "New Testament and Rabbinic Messianic Interpretation."
NTS 5. 1958. 47-54.

Ellis, E. E. "Midrash, Targum and New Testament Quotations."
Neotestamentica et Semitica: Studies in Honour of Matthew
Black. Ed. E. Earle Ellis and Max Wilcox. Edinburgh: T. &
T. Clark. 1964. 256-263.

Emerton, J. A. "The Problem of Vernacular Hebrew in the First
Century A.D. and the Language of Jesus." JTS 24. 1973. 1-23.

Epstein, A. "Tosefta du Targoum Yerouschalmi." REJ 30. 1895.
44-51.

Faur, J. "The Targumim and Halakha." JQR N.S. 66. 1975. 19-26.

Feigin, S. E. "The Original Language of the Gospels." JNES 2. 1943.
187-197.

Fensham, F. Charles. "The Legal·Background of Mt. vi 12." NT 4.
1960-61. 1-2.

Finkelstein, Louis. "The Development of the Amidah" in Pharisaism
in the Making: Selected Essays. N.Y.: KTAV. 1972. 245-331.

Fitzmyer, Joseph A. "The Aramaic Language and the Study of the New
Testament." JBL 99. 1980. 5-21.

------------------ "The Contribution of Qumran Aramaic to the
Study of the New Testament." NTS 20. 1974. 382-407.

------------------ "'4Q Testimonia' and the New Testament." TS 18.
1957. 513-537.

------------------ "The Languages of Palestine in the First
Century A.D." CBQ 32. 1970. 501-531.

------------------ "Methodology in the Study of the Aramaic
Substratum of Jesus' Sayings in the New Testament." Jésus
aux origines de la Christologie. Ed. J. Dupont. Gembloux:
Leuven University Press. 1975. 73-102.

------------------ "The Use of Explicit Old Testament Quotations
in Qumran Literature and in the New Testament." NTS 7. 1961.
297-333.

Flusser, D. "Blessed are the Poor in Spirit. . ." IEJ 10. 1960.
1-13.

Gertner, M. "Midrashim in the New Testament." JSS 7. 1962.
267-292.

Ginsburger, Moses. "Zum Fragmententhargum." Monatsschrift für
Geschichte und Wissenschaft des Judentums 41. 1897. 289-296
and 340-349.

Ginzburg, Louis. "The Religion of the Jews at the Time of Jesus."
HUCA 1. 1924. 307-321.

Goldenberg, David. "The Halakha in Josephus and in Tannaitic
Literature." JQR 67. 1976. 30-43.

Goldin, Judah. "The Youngest Son or Where Does Genesis 38 Belong?"
JBL 96. 1977. 27-44.

Goodblatt, David. "The Beruriah Traditions." JJS 26. 1975. 68-85.

Gooding, D. W. "On the Use of the LXX for Dating Midrashic
Elements in the Targums." JTS 24. 1974. 1-11.

Goodspeed, Edgar J. "The Possible Aramaic Gospel." JNES 1. 1942.
315-340.

Grech, P. "The 'Testimonia' and Modern Hermeneutics." NTS 19.
1973. 318-324.

Grelot, Pierre. "Etudes néotestamentaires et sources haggadiques."
Biblica 42. 1961. 455-459.

-------------- "Les Targums du Pentateuque: Etude comparative
d'après Genèse, IV, 3-16." Semitica 9. 1959. 59-88.

-------------- "Tradition as source and environment of Scripture."
Concilium 20. 1966. 7-28.

Grossfeld, Bernard. "Targum Neofiti I to Deut 31:7." JBL 91. 1972.
533-534.

------------------ "Targum Neofiti I to Dt 31:7 - the Problem
Re-analyzed." AusBR 24. 1976. 30-34.

Grintz, J. M. "Hebrew as the Spoken and Written Language in the
Last Days of the Second Temple." JBL 79. 1960. 32-47.

Guelich, Robert A. "Mt 5:22: Its Meaning and Integrity." ZNW 64.
1973. 39-52.

Guillaume, Alfred. "The Midrash in the Gospels.." Exp Tim 37.
1926. 392-398.

Gundry, R. H. "The Language Milieu of First-Century Palestine:
Its Bearing on the Authenticity of the Gospel Tradition."
JBL 83, 1964. 404-408.

Hamerton-Kelly, R. G. "Attitudes to the Law in Matthew's Gospel:
a discussion on Matthew 5:18." BR 17. 1972. 19-32.

Harris, J. Rendel. "The Diatessaron and the Testimony Book." The
Expositor 2. 9th series. 1924. 453-463.

Havazelet, M. "Parallel References to the Haggadah in the Targum
Jonathan Ben 'Uziel and Neofiti: Genesis, Exodus and
Leviticus." JJS 27. 1976. 47-53.

Heinemann, Joseph. "Early Halakhah in the Palestinian Targum."
JJS 25. 1974. 115-122.

Howard, George. "The Textual Nature of Shem-Tob's Hebrew Matthew."
JBL 108. 1989. 239-257.

Isenberg, Sheldon Robert, "An Anti-Sadducee Polemic in the
Palestinian Targum Tradition." HTR 63. 1970. 433-444.

------------------------ "On the Jewish-Palestinian Origins of
the Pentateuch." JBL 90. 1971. 69-81.

Johnson, Sherman. "The Biblical Quotations in Matthew." HTR 36.
1943. 135-153.

Jeremias, Joachim. "Matthäus 7,6a." Abraham Unser Vater: Juden
und Christen im Gespräch über die Bibel: Festschrift fur
Otto Michel. Leiden: Brill. 1963. 271-275.

Kahle, Paul. "Erwiderung." ZNW 51. 1960. 55.

----------- "Das palastinische Pentateuchtargum und das zur Zeit
Jesu gesprochene Aramaisch." ZNW 49. 1958. 100-116.

Klein, Michael. "Deut 31:7, תבוא or תביא?" JBL 92. 1973. 584-585.

-------------- "Elias Levita and Ms. Neofiti I." Bib 56. 1975.
242-246.

-------------- "The Extant Sources of the Fragmentary Targum
to the Pentateuch." HUCA 46. 1975. 115-137.

-------------- "A New Edition of Pseudo-Jonathan." JBL 94. 1975.
277-279.

188

Klein, Michael. "The Notation of Paraŝot in Ms Neofiti I." Textus 8. 1973. 175-177.

-------------- "Notes on the Printed Edition of Ms Neofiti I." JSS 19. 1974. 216-230.

-------------- "The Targumic Tosefta to Exodus 15:2." JJS 26. 1975. 61-67.

-------------- "Text and Vorlage in Neofiti I." VT 22. 1972. 490-491.

Kohler, Kaufmann. "Abinu Malkenu." The Jewish Encyclopedia. Vol. 1. N.Y.-London: Funk & Wagnalls. 1901. 85.

Komsala, Hans. "Matthew xxvi 52 - A Quotation from the Targum." NT 4. 1960-61. 3-5.

Kuiper, G. J. "A Study of the Relationship between A Genesis Apocryphon and the Pentateuchal Targumim in Genesis 14 1-12." BZAW 103. In Memoriam Paul Kahle. 1968. 149-161.

------------ "Targum Pseudo-Jonathan: A Study of Genesis 4:7-10:16." Augustinianum 10. 1970. 533-570.

Kutscher, Eduard Y. "Das zur Zeit Jesu gesprochene Aramaïsch." ZNW 51. 1960. 46-54.

Lauterbach, Jacob Z. "Midrash and Mishnah: A Study in the Early History of the Halakah." JQR 5. 1915. 503-527; JQR 6. 1915. 23-96; JQR 6. 1916. 303-323.

LeDéaut, Roger. "A propos d'une définition du midrash." Bib 50. 1968. 395-413.

-------------- "A propos d'une leçon du codex Neophiti I (Lev. V 21)." VT 17. 1967. 362-363.

-------------- "Actes 7,48 et Matthieu 7,14(par) à la lumière du targum palestinien." RSR 52. 1964. 85-90.

-------------- "Aspects de l'intercession dans le Judaïsme ancien." J. St. J. 1. 1970. 35-57.

-------------- "The Current State of Targumic Studies." BTB 4. 1974. 3-32.

-------------- "De nocte Paschatis: la Nuit Pascale: Essai sur la signification de la Päque juive à partir du Targum d'Exode 12,42." VD 41. 1963. 189-195.

LeDéaut, Roger. "Les études targumiques: état de la recherche et perspectives pour l'exégèse de l'ancien testament." ETL 44. 1968. 5-34.

———————— "Goûter le calice de la more." Bib 43. 1962. 83-86.

———————— "Jalons pour une histoire d'un manuscrit du Targum palestinien (Neophiti I)." Bib 48. 1967. 509-533.

———————— "Lévitique XXII 26 - XXIII 44 dans le targum palestinien: de l'importance des gloses du codex Neofiti I." VT 18. 1968. 458-471.

———————— "Miryam, soeur de Moïse, et Marie, mère du Messie." Bib 45. 1964. 198-219.

———————— "Un phénomène spontané de l'herméneutique juive ancienne: le 'targumisme.'" Bib 52. 1971. 505-525.

———————— "La présentation targumique du sacrifice d'Isaac et la soteriologie paulinienne." Studium paulinorum congressus internationalis catholicus. 1961. 563-574.

———————— "Le targum de Gen. 22,8 et I Pt. 1,20." RSR 49. 1961. 103-106.

———————— "Le titre de Summus Sacerdos donné à Melchisédech est-il d'origine juive?" RSR 50. 1962. 222-229.

———————— "La tradition juive ancienne et l'exégèse chrétienne primitive." Rev. d'hist. et de phil. rel. 1971. 31-50.

———————— "Traditions targumiques dans le corpus paulinien? (Hebr. 11,4 et 12,24; Gal 4, 29-30; II Cor 3, 16)." Bib 42. 1961. 28-48.

Levine, Etan. "British Museum Aramaic Additional Ms 27031." Manuscripta 16. 1972. 3-13.

—————— "Internal Contradictions in Targum Jonathan ben Uzziel to Genesis." Augustinianum 9. 1969. 118-119.

—————— "Neofiti I: A Study of Exodus 15." Bib 54. 1973. 301-330.

—————— "A Paleographic Note on the Colophon of Ms. Neofiti I." VT 21. 1971. 494-497.

Levine, Etan. "Some Characteristics of Pseudo-Jonathan to Exodus." Augustinianum 11. 1971. 89-103.

.------------ "A Study of Targum Pseudo-Jonathan to Exodus." Sefarad 31. 1971. 27-48.

------------ "The Syriac Version of Genesis IV 1-16." VT 26. 1976. 70-78.

Lindars, Barnabas. "The Place of the Old Testament in the Formation of New Testament Theology." NTS 23. 1977. 59-66.

Lohr, Charles H. "Oral Techniques in the Gospel of Matthew." CBQ 23. 1961. 403-435.

Lund, Shirley. "An Argument for Further Study of the Paleography of Codex Neofiti I." VT 20. 1970. 56-64.

------------ "The Sources of the Variant Readings to Deuteronomy 1.1 - 29.17 of Codex Neophiti I." BZAW 103. In Memoriam Paul Kahle. 1968. 167-173.

Luzarraga, J. "Principios hermenéuticos de exégesis bíblica en el rabinismo primitivo." Est Bib 30. 1971. 177-193.

Malfroy, Jean. "L'utilisation du vocabulaire sapientiel du Deutéronome dans le targum palestinien (Codex Neophiti I)." Semitica 17. 81-96.

Malina, B. J. "The Literary Structure and Form of Matthew XXVIII 16-20." NTS 17. 1970. 87-103.

Mann, Jacob. "Rabbinic Studies in the Synoptic Gospels." HUCA 1. 1924. 323-255.

Martin, M. Fitzmaurice. "The Paleographical Character of Codex Neophiti I." Textus 3. 1963. 1-35.

McNamara, Martin. "The Aramaic Translations: A Newly Recognized Aid for NT Study." Scripture 18. 1966. 47-56.

---------------- "The Ascension and the Exaltation of Christ in the Fourth Gospel." Scripture 19. 1967. 65-73.

---------------- "Jewish Liturgy and the New Testament." BiTod 33. 1967. 2324-2332.

---------------- "Logos of the Fourth Gospel and Memra of the Palestinian Targum (ex. 12,42)." Exp Tim 79. 1967. 115-117.

McNamara, Martin. "Novum Testamentum et Targum Palaestinense ad Pentateuchum." VD 43. 1965. 288-300.

---------------- "Some Early Rabbinic Citations and the Palestinian Targum to the Pentateuch." AnBib 27. 1966. 1-15.

---------------- "Targumic Studies." CBQ 28. 1966. 1-19.

McCown, C. G. "Aramaic and Greek Gospels." Ang Theol Rev 25. 1943. 281-294.

Metzger, Bruce M. "The Formulas Introducing Quotations of Scripture in the NT and the Mishnah." JBL 70. 1951. 297-307.

Miller, Merrill P. "Targum, Midrash and the Use of the Old Testament in the New Testament." J St. J. 2. 1971. 29-82.

Murphy, Frederick J. "Retelling the Bible: Idolatry in Pseudo-Philo." JBL 107. 1988. 275-287.

Nauck, Wolfgang. "Salt as a Metaphor in Instructions for Discipleship." ST 6. 1952. 165-178.

Neusner, Jacob. "The History of Earlier Rabbinic Judaism: Some New Approaches." HR 16. 1977. 216-236.

Ohana, Moïse. "Agneau Pascal et Cironcision: le problème de la Halakha premishnaique dans le Targum Palestinien." VT 23. 1973. 317-332.

------------ "Prosélytisme et Targum palestinien: données nouvelles pour la datation de Néofiti I." Bib 55. 1974. 317-332.

Okamoto, Abraham O. H. "A Geonic Phrase in Ms. Targum Yerushalmi, Codex Neofiti I." JQR 66. 1976. 160-167.

Olmstead, Albert T. "Could an Aramaic Gospel be Written?" JNES 1. 1942. 41-75.

Orchard, Bernard. "The Meaning of Ton Epiousion (Mt 6:11 = Lk 11:3)." BTB 3. 1971. 274-282.

O'Rourke, John J. "The Fulfillment Texts in Matthew." CBQ 24. 1962. 394-403.

Ott, H. "Um die Muttersprache Jesu, Forschungen seit Gustaf Dalman." NT 9. 1967. 1-25.

Patte, D. "Scripture at the Synagogue: Targum and Liturgy."

Early Jewish Hermeneutic in Palestine. Missoula, Montana: Scholars Press. 1975. 49-86.

Perles, Felix. "La parabole du sel sourd." REJ 82. 1926. 122-123.

Rabinowitz, J. J. "The Sermon on the Mount and the School of Shammai." HTR 49. 1956. 79.

Ramón Díaz, José. "Dos notas sobre el targum palestinense." Sefarad 19. 1959. 133-136.

---------------- "Ediciones del Targum samaritano." Est Bib 15. 1956. 105-108.

---------------- "Palestinian Targum and New Testament." NT 6. 1963. 75-80.

---------------- "Targum palestinense y Nuevo Testamento." Est Bib 21. 1962. 337-342.

Reider, D. "On the Targum Yerushalmi MS Neofiti I." Tarbiz 38. 1968. 81-86.

Rigaux, B. "Révélation des mystères et perfection à Qumran et dans le Nouveau Testament." NTS 4. 1958. 237-262.

Rüger, Hans Peter. "Mit welchem Mass ihr messt, wird euch gemessen werden." ZAW 60. 1969. 174-182.

Sabourin, L. "The MEMRA of God in the Targums." BTB 6. 1976. 81-85.

Saldarini, Anthony J. "The End of the Rabbinic Chain of Tradition." JBL 93. 1974. 97-106.

Sandmel, S. "The Haggada within Scripture." JBL 80. 1961. 105-22.

Selwyn, E. G. "The Authority of Christ in the New Testament." NTS 3. 1956. 83-92.

Siegel, Seymour. "Imitation of God (Imitatio Dei)." EncJud 8. 1971. 1291-1292.

Simian, H. "La Biblia: Su mundo y problemas." Stromata 23. 1967. 405-412.

Smith, M. "The Jewish Element in the Gospels." JBR 24. 1956. 90-96.

Stephenson, T. "The Old Testament Quotations Peculiar to Matthew." JTS 20. 1918-19. 227-229.

Teicher, J. L. "A Sixth Century Fragment of the Palestinian Targum." VT 1. 1951. 125-129.

Turner, N. "Jewish and Christian Influence on New Testament Vocabulary." NT 16. 1974. 149-160.

Vermes, G. "Baptism and Jewish Exegesis: New Light from Ancient Sources." NTS 4. 1958. 308-319.

--------- "Bible and Midrash: Early Old Testament Exegesis." Cambridge History of the Bible I. Ed. P. R. Ackroyd and E. F. Evans. Cambridge. 1970. 199-231.

--------- "The Decalogue and the Minim." BZAW 103. In Memoriam Paul Kahle. 232-240.

--------- "Deux traditions sur Balaam. Nombres XXII 2-21 et ses interpretations midrashiques." Cahiers Sioniens 9. 1955. 289-302.

--------- "La figure de Moïse au tournant des deux testaments." Moise l'homme de l'alliance. Cahiers Sioniens. 1955. 63-92.

--------- "Haggadah in the Onkelos Targum." JSS 8. 1963. 159-69.

---------- "He is the Bread." Neotestamentica et Semitica: Studies in Honour of Matthew Black. ed. E. Earle Ellis and Max Wilcox. Edinburgh: T. & T. Clark. 1964. 256-263.

---------- "The Impact of the Dead Sea Scrolls on the Study of the New Testament." JJS 27. 1976. 107-116.

---------- "The Qumran Interpretation of Scripture in its Historical Setting." ALUOS 6. 1966-1968. 85-97.

---------- "The Targumic Versions of Genesis IV 3-16." ALUOS 3. 1961-1962. 81-114.

Venard, L. "Citations de l'AT dans le NT." DBSup II. 23-51.

Weil, Gérard E. "Le Codex Neophiti I: A propos de l'article de M. Fitzmaurice Martin." Textus 4. 1964. 225-229.

Wernberg-Møller, Preben. "An Inquiry into the Validity of the Text-Critical Argument for an Early Dating of the Recently Discovered Palestinian Targum." VT 12. 1962. 312-330.

---------------------- "Prolegomena to a re-examination of the Palestinian Targum Fragments of the Book of Genesis published by P. Kahle, and their relationship to the Peshitta." JSS 7. 1962. 253-266.

Wernberg-Møller, Preben. "Some Observations on the Relationship of the Peshitta Version of the Book of Genesis to the Palestinian Targum Fragments Published by Professor Kahle, and to Targum Onkelos." ST 15. 1961. 128-180.

Wieder, N. "The Habakkuk Scroll and the Targum." JJS 4. 1953. 14-18.

Wiesenberg, E. "Observations on Method in Talmudic Studies." JSS 11. 1966. 16-36.

Wikgren, Allen. "The Targums and the New Testament." JR 24. 1944. 89-95.

Wright, Addison G. "The Literary Genre Midrash." CBQ 28. 1966. 105-138 and 417-457.

York, Anthony D. "The Dating of Targumic Literature." J St. J 5. 1974. 47-62.

INDEX

198

Targum Citations

Rabbinic Sources

Qumran Writings

Philo

Early Christian Writings

Barnabas		Didache		Ign. Smyrn.	
11:6	160	8:2	84	4:2	72
				10:2	72
1 Clement		Diognetus			
9:2	58	10:1	72	Ign. Trall.	
13:1-2	83, 84, 86	10:4	72	1:2	58
28:1	89	12:1	160	11:1-2	160
33:1	57	12:8	160		
33:2-6	57			Pol. Phil.	
33:2-8	57, 72	Ign. Eph.		2:3	83, 84, 86
50:3	72	1:1	58	12:3	58, 157
53:5	72	14:2	157		
56:1	160			Clementine Homilies	
57:6	160	Ign. Phld.			158, 160
		7:2	58	Justin, apologist	
2 Clement		12:3	58, 157		158
1:3	160				

Josephus

Antiquities				Bellum Judaicum	
I 20, 155	31				
I 230	31	IV 262	31	III. 375	31, 72
II 152	31	V 93, 112	31	Contra Apionem	
III 375	31	VII 380	31	II. 166-167	20, 31
IV 201	31	VIII 350	31	II. 193	20, 31

Rabbis

Aqiba	16, 17, 88, 105	Juda	87
Elazar b. Azariah	108, 119	Me'ir	88
Eleazar b. Arakh	29	Nathan	15, 29
Eleazar of Modi'im	15, 107	Nathan b. Joseph	88
Elisha b.Abuyah	108, 119 136	Saul	39 62
Gamaliel II	15, 28, 107	Simai	30
Hezekiah	xix	Simeon b. Gamaliel	146
Jose	xix	Simeon b. Yohai	107, 126, 142
Joshua	15	Yoḥanan b. Zakkai	15, 16, 29
Joshua b. Hananiah	16, 147	Yuda b. Tema	30

Authors and Editors

STUDIES IN THE BIBLE AND EARLY CHRISTIANITY